DAILY LIFE OF

THE AZTECS

Recent Titles in
The Greenwood Press Daily Life Through History Series

DAILY LIFE OF

THE AZTECS

Second Edition

DAVÍD CARRASCO AND
SCOTT SESSIONS

The Greenwood Press Daily Life Through History Series

 GREENWOOD

AN IMPRINT OF ABC-CLIO, LLC
Santa Barbara, California • Denver, Colorado • Oxford, England

Library of Congress Cataloging-in-Publication Data

Carrasco, Davíd.
    Daily life of the Aztecs / Davíd Carrasco and Scott Sessions. — 2nd ed.
            p. cm. — (The Greenwood Press daily life through history series)
    Includes index.
    ISBN 978-0-313-37744-0 (hardback) — ISBN 978-0-313-37745-7 (ebook)   1. Aztecs.   I. Sessions, Scott.   II. Title.
    F1219.73.C355   2011
    972'.018—dc22   2011007649

ISBN: 978-0-313-37744-0
EISBN: 978-0-313-37745-7

15   14   13   12   2   3   4   5

This book is also available on the World Wide Web as an eBook. Visit www.abc-clio.com for details.

Greenwood
An Imprint of ABC-CLIO, LLC

ABC-CLIO, LLC
130 Cremona Drive, P.O. Box 1911
Santa Barbara, California 93116-1911

This book is printed on acid-free paper ∞

Manufactured in the United States of America

Copyright Acknowledgment

The authors and publisher gratefully acknowledge permission for use of the following material:

Text from Bernardino de Sahagún, *Florentine Codex: General History of the Things of New Spain*, ed. and trans. Arthur J. O. Anderson and Charles E. Dibble, introductory vol. and 12 books (Santa Fe, NM: School of American Research and University of Utah, 1950–82) was used by permission of the University of Utah Press.

CONTENTS

PREFACE

Where is your heart?
If you give your heart to each and every thing
You lead it nowhere; you destroy your heart.
Can anything be found on earth?[1]

Let us have friends here!
It is time to know our faces.[2]

Each day when the sun arose...they greeted it saying, "The
sun has emerged...but how will he go on his way? How will
he spend the day? Perhaps something evil will befall his common people."...And also it was said that those who died in
war went to the home of the sun; they dwelt with the sun.[3]

When the Spaniards, led by Hernán Cortés, first encountered the
majestic Aztec capital of Tenochtitlan, they compared it to the great
cities of Europe, including Venice, Constantinople, and Salamanca.
But when the Aztecs first encountered the invading Spaniards, they
weren't sure whether to compare them with gods or beasts. In fact,
the Aztecs considered themselves to be the "people of the sun and
earth" and had managed to organize, through political persuasion,
intimidation, warfare, and trade, an empire of more than 400 towns
and communities that paid rich tributes to the royal families and
markets of the capital.

This book is about the daily life of the Aztecs, especially as they dwelled in and around the island city of Tenochtitlan. It is concerned with presenting a human face of the Aztec peoples, who as poets asked about the destiny of their hearts, as citizens strove to build lasting friendships, as parents thought of their children as "precious necklaces," and as the faithful ritually greeted the sunrise and died in war believing that while they were buried in the earth or had their ashes spread across it, they also went to live in the house of the solar god. The book attempts a new interpretation of the complex relationships between cultural practices, material conditions, social order, and religious myths and symbols. As the above quotations show, these peoples felt intimately connected with the natural world around them and they also believed the earth, sky, and sun to be more than just natural forces; these physical elements were also filled with sacred powers.

This revised edition extends the new interpretive developments of the earlier version with the most recent archaeological discoveries in and around the Basin of Mexico, including ongoing excavations of the Great Aztec Temple in downtown Mexico City and at the site of Teotihuacan, the City of the Gods, where startling new finds at the Pyramid of the Moon have been taking place. This edition also utilizes a number of the pictorial manuscripts drawn and painted by native scribes prior to and after the conquest, including the beautiful and complex *Mapa de Cuauhtinchan No. 2,* which recently resurfaced into public knowledge. This revision of *Daily Life of the Aztecs: People of the Sun and Earth* will enhance public knowledge about the interactions between the geographical world, sacred spaces, ritual practices, and educational processes that provided children and adolescents with a sense of profound loyalty to the Aztec earth, sun, gods, ancestors, and each other. As this new version appears there is a worldwide, growing fascination with the idea that the Aztecs and their predecessors, the Classic Maya, prophesied a cataclysmic end of the world in the year 2012. Films, books, academic conferences, television specials, and newspaper articles have picked up this story, exaggerated the facts and stimulated confusion and fear. We will explore and explain this mistaken idea that Mesoamerican peoples prophesied the end of the universe during our lifetimes.

The book is organized as a journey through Aztec geography, cosmology, and society that organized the life of the city in which children, teenagers, warriors, merchants, priests, rulers, and artists worked together to create a life of balance and devotion to the gods.

The first chapter orients the reader by providing an overall image of the geography, material conditions, and geographical imagination of the Aztec people. It uses the images of the blue-green bowl and the pyramid to help the reader see and think about the natural context in which the Aztecs dwelled. Chapter 2 discusses the cosmology of the Aztecs, symbolized by the cosmic tree and the pivot of the four quarters. Chapter 3 continues with rich imagery as it explores the city of Tenochtitlan as a Mountain of Water, the Nahuatl term for community or city. Chapter 4 focuses on the human life cycle, especially the educational processes that Aztec children underwent to become useful and effective citizens. Chapter 5 examines the social pyramid, class structures, and status designations of Aztec society, showing its strong commitment to maintaining the social constraints ordained by elders, tradition, and labor demands. Chapter 6 explores the artistic genius, color, and designs of Aztec society, in which the notion of "flowers and songs" was the chief metaphor for what Western society calls "the muse." The difficult topic of human sacrifice is discussed in chapter 7 and is related to its principal companion—warfare. But human sacrifice is also discussed as a religious practice expressed in the notion of paying debts, through sacrifice, to the gods. The world-shaking event of the Aztec encounter with Europeans is the focus of chapter 8, which explores the meetings, translations, mistranslations, and wars leading up to the destruction of the Aztec capital. The final chapter looks at the "long event"—how Aztec ideas, practices, beliefs, and images have persisted and continue to be meaningful to the present day, in and beyond Mexico. Also included are a chronology, a helpful glossary with a pronunciation guide, and a selected bibliography to assist the reader in placing these people of the sun and earth in a linguistic, historical, and scholarly setting.

This book is the result of a long-term collaboration by a team of scholars working in the Mesoamerican Archive and Research Project. The ideas and design of the chapters were influenced by the writings and teachings of Pedro Armillas, Eduardo Matos Moctezuma, Paul Wheatley, Charles Long, and Mircea Eliade, as well as Philip Arnold, Anthony Aveni, Elizabeth Boone, Johanna Broda, Robert Bye, Edward Calnek, José Cuellar, Doris Heyden, Lindsay Jones, Edelmira Linares, Alfredo López Austin, Leonardo López Luján, and H. B. Nicholson. Several other individuals read specific chapters and offered critical and supportive suggestions, including Octavio and Laanna Carrasco, who as teenage children at the time of the first edition cautioned the authors not to bore students and made helpful suggestions about language, photographs, and the writing. We also have benefited from the critical comments of several teachers from the El Paso (Texas) School District who participated in a summer institute organized by the National Faculty of the Humanities. One teacher in particular, Cheryl Diane DeLacretaz, made special efforts to help us write in ways that would give students access to the Aztec story. We were also fortunate to have 90 students from West Windsor-Plainsboro Middle School (New Jersey) read specific chapters, under the tutelage of Joan Ruddiman, and provide critical suggestions that helped make this a better book. Others who assisted were Samantha Alducín (a Princeton University student) and Gail Eshleman (secretary of Mathey College, Princeton University).

This book attempts to provide an overview of Aztec life and does address the disturbing practice of ritual human sacrifice by providing descriptions and interpretations. It is easier to condemn ritual sacrifice than to understand it. Understanding the different practices of ritual killing is a daunting challenge, but one we must attempt. In an ironic way, the Western philosophic claim that "nothing human is foreign to me" takes on new meaning when we study, understand, and criticize Aztec religion. Perhaps in working to understand it all—their sacrifices, poetry, schools, clothes, warfare, and art—we will also realize that we come to "know our faces." Our hope is that this book serves to bring the Aztec peoples into a human focus that allows the reader to appreciate, understand, and make critical reflections on their creativity, destructiveness, problems, limitations, and extraordinary abilities and gifts.

NOTES

1. Miguel León-Portilla, ed. and trans., *Native Mesoamerican Spirituality: Ancient Myths, Discourses, Stories, Doctrines, Hymns, Poems from the Aztec, Yucatec, Quiche-Maya and Other Sacred Traditions* (New York: Paulist Press, 1980), 184.

2. Ibid., 185.

3. Bernardino de Sahagún, *Florentine Codex: General History of the Things of New Spain*, ed. and trans. Arthur J. O. Anderson and Charles E. Dibble, introductory vol. and 12 books (Santa Fe, NM: School of American Research, and University of Utah, 1950–82), 2: 216–17.

CHRONOLOGY OF CENTRAL MEXICO

5000 B.C.E.–2000 B.C.E.	Domestication of agricultural plants such as corn, squash, and beans.
1800 B.C.E.–200 C.E.	Formative Period.
200 C.E.–900 C.E.	Classic Period.
900 C.E.–1519 C.E.	Postclassic Period.
1800 B.C.E.–300 B.C.E.	Olmec civilization flourished on the Gulf Coast and extended its influence into Central and Southern Mexico.
1 C.E.–550 C.E.	Teotihuacan flourished in Central Mexico.
950 C.E.–1150 C.E.	Toltecs flourished in Central Mexico.
1300	Mexica groups migrated into the Basin of Mexico from the north.
1325	Island settlement of Tenochtitlan founded in Lake Tezcoco; by mid-century, the Mexica had become vassals and mercenaries of the Tepanecs.
1375–96	Acamapichtli reigns as first *tlatoani* of Tenochtitlan.
1396–1417	Huitzilihuitl reigns as second *tlatoani*.
1417–27	Chimalpopoca reigns as third *tlatoani*.

1427–40	Itzcoatl reigns as fourth *tlatoani*.
1428	Mexica of Tenochtitlan ally themselves with Tezcoco and Tacuba to defeat Azcapotzalco and the Tepanecs and form the Triple Alliance, which will later become the Aztec empire.
1440–69	Motecuhzoma Ilhuicamina reigns as fifth *tlatoani*.
1469–81	Axayacatl reigns as sixth *tlatoani*.
1473	Mexica of Tenochtitlan conquer Tlatelolco.
1474	Nezahualcoyotl, poet-philosopher-ruler of Tezcoco, dies.
1481–86	Tizoc reigns as seventh *tlatoani* of Tenochtitlan.
1486–1502	Ahuitzotl reigns as eighth *tlatoani*.
1502–20	Motecuhzoma Xocoyotzin reigns as ninth *tlatoani*.
1519	Hernán Cortés and Spaniards arrive on the Gulf Coast near modern-day Veracruz, make alliances with the Cempoalans and Tlaxcalans, conquer Cholula, proceed into the Basin of Mexico, and enter the city of Tenochtitlan as guests of Motecuhzoma Xocoyotzin.
1520	Cortés goes back to the coast to intercept a Spanish contingent from Cuba coming to arrest him; Pedro de Alvarado attacks and kills Aztec nobles during an important ceremony at the Great Temple; Motecuhzoma dies; Cuitlahuac rules Tenochtitlan for a short time, leading an attack that drives the Spaniards and Tlaxcalans out of the city, before dying from smallpox.
1521	Spaniards and Tlaxcalans lay siege to Tenochtitlan and conquer the city; Aztecs make last stand in the marketplace of Tlatelolco; Cuauhtemoc, the last *tlatoani*, surrenders Tlatelolco to Cortés on August 13.
1531	The Virgin of Guadalupe appears to Juan Diego at Tepeyac.

1

CEMANAHUAC: THE LAND SURROUNDED BY WATER

Mountains form the massive backbone of this land, and these mountains set off the three precincts of the Middle American citadel: a central highland in south-central Mexico, a southern highland in southern Mexico, and a southeastern highland in southeasternmost Mexico and Guatemala. Economically and politically, the most important of these precincts has always been the central highland.... In shape, *this mountain mass resembles one of the pyramids built by its early inhabitants:* massive walls, an eastern and a western escarpment, thrust upward from narrow coasts into a great tableland where the snow-capped mountains with the forbidding names—Citlaltepetl, Iztaccihuatl, and Popocatepetl—maintain their ice-bound vigil.... This central pyramid contains a number of chambers, each set off from its neighbors by mountainous partitions. *The central chamber is the Valley of Mexico, the heartland of Middle America.*
—Eric Wolf[1]

On the night of 11 Death, during the late summer of the year 13 Flint Knife, Nezahualpilli (Fasting Prince), the *tlatoani* (chief speaker, or ruler) of the Aztec city of Tezcoco, ascended to the roof of his palace with his royal astronomers to stargaze. After the afternoon rains had drenched the cities and towns around the five lakes in the middle of the Great Basin, the sky had grown clear, and the royal entourage knew it would be a good night for watching the heavens.

Like his famous father, Nezahualcoyotl (Fasting Coyote), the poet-philosopher-king who had died in 1474, Nezahualpilli drew knowledge and inspiration from the movements and relationships of certain celestial bodies. In fact, he based his most important governmental decisions and programs, in part, on the messages and patterns he and his astronomers discerned from the positions of stars, the lunar cycle, comets, and the movements of the sun and Venus along the horizon and across the sky. Like all Aztec rulers, he had a cosmological conviction, a deep belief that the nature and destiny of his own life and the lives of his people were intertwined with their many *teteo,* the gods who inhabited the lush natural forces, both near and far away. One historical account tells us that the Tezcocoan ruler was a great astrologer who understood the patterns of celestial bodies and invited other skygazers to his palace to exchange knowledge about the heavens. Together they would watch the stars and debate various questions that arose. On this particular night, Nezahualpilli could have been watching the movements of the moon or the planet Venus or tracking the progress of a star cluster called Tianquiztli (Marketplace), known to us as the Pleiades, as it made its way toward the zenith (its most vertical position in the sky). These observations were done in relation to the Aztec calendar, which was used to keep cosmos and society in synchronicity.

On the same night, September 17, 1492, in the European calendar, more than 2,000 miles away, three lonely ships sailing in the general direction of the lakes and land of Nezhualpilli's palace floundered anxiously in a vast ocean, lost at sea. The captain, one Cristóbal Colón (Christopher Columbus), and his mates often watched the stars, some of the same stars at which the Tezcocoan ruler gazed. The Spaniards were also seeking another kind of guidance from the stars through the practice of celestial navigation. They had set out from Palos, Spain, on August 3 in search of a western passage to the Indies, where new discoveries and trading opportunities would extend Spain's power and authority around the globe. The three ships, the *Niña,* the *Pinta,* and the *Santa María,* had stopped briefly in the Canary Islands; on August 9, they set off, latitude sailing westward, which meant that they sailed along a constant latitude using the North Star as a guide. Something strange happened that night. The pilots, while practicing their celestial navigation, were bothered that the compass did not line up on the North Star as expected. Not unlike Nezahualpilli debating with his astronomers in Tezcoco, Columbus debated with his pilots about the meaning of this deviation. They were anxious, but Columbus had them make

An Aztec ruler watches a passing comet from the roof of his palace. (Diego Durán, *Códice Durán*. Mexico City: Arrendadora Internacional 1990 facsimile edition)

their measurements again in the early morning. When the alignment of the compass and the North Star was true, he realized and announced to his crew that "the North Star moves," and the crew was calmed.

Within 30 years the successors of these two celestial navigators would meet each other in one of the most momentous transformations in the history of the world—the exchanges of gifts, tongues, lust, greed, information, and battle leading to the collapse of the Aztec capital, Tenochtitlan, and the destabilization of the Aztec empire. Their meeting would take place on the edges and in the center of the Aztec empire, a world containing more than 5 million inhabitants living in or near 400 towns and cities spread over an area as large as Spain, France, and England. The drama of their meeting, which we will review near the end of this book, took place primarily in and around the grand city of Tenochtitlan, the home of Motecuhzoma and his predecessors.

Almost all narratives about the peoples and cultures of the Americas begin with the arrival of Europeans in the New World in either 1492, 1519, or 1534. This way of beginning with Columbus's landfall, or Cortés's encounter with the Maya in Yucatán, or Pizarro's arrival in Peru, gives exaggerated credit and prestige to the Europeans' initiatives, discoveries, and colonial projects. But native American peoples were also active on and long before those dates— farming, loving, giving birth, painting, watching the stars, fighting, singing, working, and making prized works of ritual art—and this book strives to outline, describe, and illuminate the world and daily lives of one of these groups of native peoples, the Aztecs. In fact, the Aztecs created one of the two most powerful empires in the Americas prior to the coming of the Europeans in the 16th century. They considered their capital the queen of all settlements, and the Spaniards described it as a place belonging to legend. It is to the great natural basin that surrounded that capital city, where the Aztec nobleman watched the stars in the year 13 Flint Knife, that we now turn.

THE PYRAMID AND THE BLUE-GREEN BOWL

> What is a little blue-green bowl filled with popcorn? Someone
> is sure to guess our riddle; it is the sky.
>
> —Aztec riddle

The Aztec capital was located in the center of a large ecological basin situated at the top of an immense geographical pyramid whose sides sloped gradually toward the lowlands of Mesoamerica and the oceans. The Aztec peoples who migrated into this part of Mesoamerica during the 13th and 14th centuries came to call their world Cemanahuac (Land Surrounded by Water). Not only was their city located on an island in the midst of a sprawling lake system, but the Mexica, as they called themselves, knew that great bodies of water—the Pacific Ocean, the Gulf of Mexico, and the Caribbean Sea—surrounded the empire they eventually dominated.

This chapter uses the images of a pyramid and a blue-green bowl as a way of organizing information about the geographical and historical setting of the Aztecs.[2] Visualize the shape of a Mesoamerican pyramid and think of it in the following terms: *geographical, social,* and *ceremonial.* The Aztecs lived at the top of a *geographical* pyramid, and this natural fact influenced their history, lifestyles, successes, and defeats. Also, their peoples were organized into a *social* pyramid, with masses of agricultural workers and commoner families forming the economic base of the society. This widely distributed group supported a smaller number of merchants, warriors, and priests who formed the narrower middle section of society. Merchants and warriors often traveled beyond the confines of the capital, interacting through intimidation, violence, and exchange with nearby and distant communities, thereby spreading out Aztec values, policies, and goods, as well as bringing in important information and materials that were utilized on the island capital. At the apex of this society was a still smaller but nevertheless sizable group of nobles, high-level warriors, artists, priests, and especially the ruler and his elaborate entourage. This pyramidal image also helps us understand the *ceremonial* character of society, for the larger Aztec communities were organized around impressive ceremonial centers dominated by a sizable pyramid temple. This ritual structure was the architectural and religious point of authority from which priests and ruler-priests communicated with gods and directed the political and cultural events in the lives of the people who lived below them within the social pyramid.

Several surviving riddles and poems tell us that the Aztecs and their neighbors thought of the sky above them and the high plateau they lived on, which was surrounded on all sides by hills and mountains, as blue-green bowls—vessels containing life-giving waters and sun. The mountains around them were sometimes compared with jugs of water, and the valleys into which the mountain waters flowed were life-giving bowls. In Aztec times the higher slopes were covered with green forests of pine, spruce, cedar, and ash trees.

The story of the Aztec migration into the high plateau with its many interconnected valleys is fascinating. According to their sacred history, the Mexica originally lived in Aztlan (Place of the White Heron), an island surrounded by water, after emerging from Chicomoztoc (Place of Seven Caves). As they told and painted their origin myth, their patron god, Huitzilopochtli (Hummingbird on the Left), appeared in dreams to their leader and spoke to him of a faraway place where he wanted them to travel to find their place of destiny. Inspired by this god's message, they organized themselves for an extended journey, crossed the lake, and undertook a long, arduous migration that lasted more than a century and was filled with hardships, wonders, and surprises. Eventually they climbed through the forested hills and mountains surrounding the Great Basin of Mexico and descended into the valleys, where they encountered many towns and cultures that had been in existence for more than 1,500 years. As promised, their god appeared to them in the form of a huge eagle perched on a blooming cactus in the

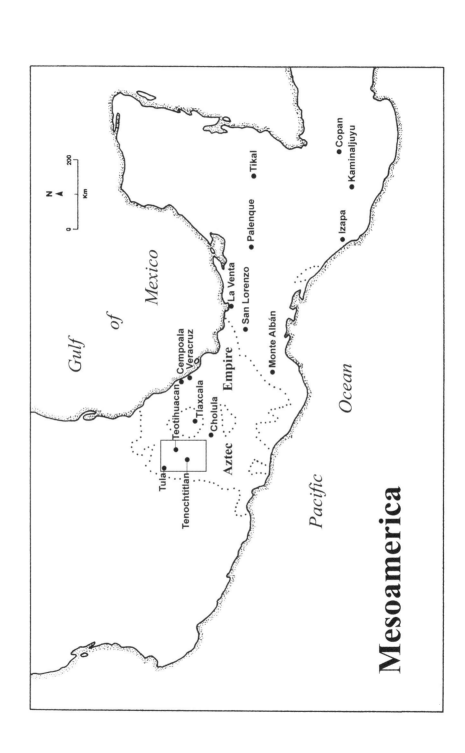

Mesoamerica

middle of a lake, and they knew they had arrived at their promised land. They had migrated into one of the most dynamic, complex, and tense ecological systems in the Americas. In spite of the common notion that the Aztec world consisted of five lakes occupying the central area of the Basin of Mexico, its ecology included mountainous areas, flat plains, and extensive valley regions that spread out in various directions.

The geographical term for the central Aztec area is the Basin of Mexico, which is a central high plateau bounded on all sides by mountain ranges and hills. This great plateau is 2,236 meters above sea level and spreads 120 kilometers from north to south and 80 kilometers from east to west. The basin is framed on the east by two of the most spectacular mountains in all of the Americas, the snow-capped volcanoes Iztaccihuatl and Popocatepetl, whose peaks rise more than 6,000 meters above sea level. To the north, the basin is framed by the less imposing mountains near Zacatecas and Guanajuato; to the west, by the Western Sierra Madre; and to the south, by the nonvolcanic Sierra Ajusco. In Aztec times, this basin was a huge self-contained ecological system in which mountain springs, continually melting water from the high snowfields, and summer rains, at times torrential, drained into five interconnected lakes that sometimes formed a great, single sheet of water at slightly different levels. These shallow lakes, which influenced the political, religious, social, and commercial aspects of daily life, were one to three meters in depth and afforded the citizenry an extensive transportation and communication system. In years of drought, however, the lakes would shrink during the dry seasons, creating transportation and communication problems because the people living in the lake region depended on canoes and barges for engaging in commerce and transmitting information.

The slightly higher northern lakes of Xaltocan and Xumpango were freshwater lakes, while the central and larger lake of Tezcoco into which they drained was saline. Also, two southern lakes, Xochimilco and Chalco, were fed by freshwater springs and runoff. Xochimilco, in particular, was covered with vegetation in pre-Hispanic times. Over the years these lakes were drained and filled in, though a few remnants still exist today, affording students and tourists who visit Xochimilco the chance to travel in Aztec-style boats through the *chinampa* fields, or what the Spaniards mistakenly called "floating gardens." Beyond the focus of the lakes, the high plateau is interrupted by an irregular series of valleys, enclosed smaller basins, and tablelands.

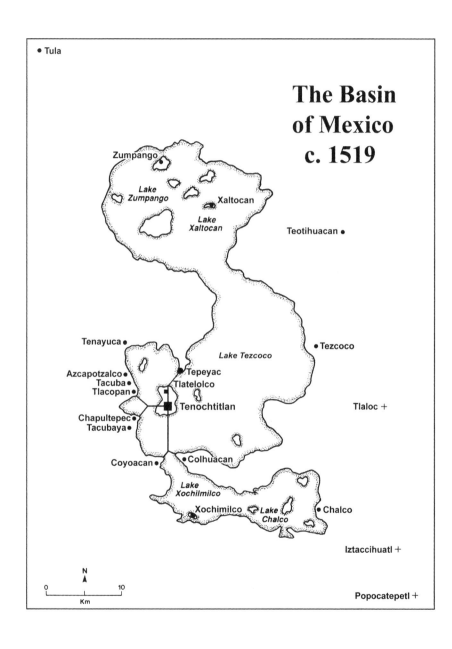

The Basin
of Mexico
c. 1519

- Tula

Zumpango

Lake
Zumpango

Xaltocan

Lake
Xaltocan

Teotihuacan •

Tenayuca •

Lake Tezcoco

• Tezcoco

Azcapotzalco •
Tacuba •
Tlacopan •

• Tepeyac
Tlatelolco
Tenochtitlan

Chapultepec •
Tacubaya •

Tlaloc +

Coyoacan •

• Colhuacan

Lake
Xochilmilco

Xochimilco

Lake
Chalco

• Chalco

Iztaccihuatl +

N

0   10
Km

Popocatepetl +

In spite of this appearance of a secure relationship between mountains and lakes, the Aztecs lived in an unstable, irregular ecological cycle. Instead of having four seasons—spring, summer, autumn, and winter—during the year, the Basin of Mexico, along with the rest of Mesoamerica, has only two—the wet season and the dry season. This fact is fundamental to understanding the labor pressures, social attitudes, and religious practices of the Aztecs. They lived in a world that fluctuated between periods of abundance and periods of limited resources, between an irregular rainy season and unforgiving and sometimes catastrophic droughts. Nevertheless, they were able to develop an agricultural system that sustained one of the largest capital cities in the world, especially between 1470 and 1521 c.e. These people developed significant food surpluses that supported more than 1.5 million people (in the basin area), including armies, temple communities, government officials, and a rich nobility. The importance of rain is reflected in recent excavations in the center of Mexico City, where archaeologists have uncovered the main temple precinct of the Aztecs, called the Templo Mayor, or Great Temple. Beneath the floors of the temple, Mexican archaeologists discovered statues and offerings to the rain god, Tlaloc (He Who Makes the Plants Spring Up). The abundance of objects, along with the painted record of the many ritual sacrifices in honor of Tlaloc, shows how deeply the people were committed to the forces of rain, agriculture, and water.

We can begin to understand the challenges the inhabitants faced when we learn that 80 percent of their annual rainfall came between the months of June and October, followed by threatening frosts from November through February. Killing frosts could come as early as September and as late as May, creating planting and harvesting problems of immense proportions. Rains fell in monsoon patterns, often inundating parts of the central valley in May, but sometimes were delayed until mid-June. Today, the annual rainfall is 450 millimeters (18 inches) in the northern part of the basin and 800 millimeters (32 inches) in the southern part. The major problem facing the farmers was timing the growing season to avoid the killing frosts. The ideal conditions were showers in April and May so that early germination could lead to mature ears of corn by September, before the October frosts did their damage. As we shall see, the Aztecs expended enormous human energy to get the timing down, but they also evoked and depended on a large and sometimes fantastic pantheon of divine forces to help them.

Agriculture and food production in the Basin of Mexico. The men on the right plant and harvest the maize plants, while the women on the left grind and roll the product into tortillas. Behind them is a deity impersonator dressed as a corn goddess. Rows of *chinampa* plots stretch across the lake as far as the eye can see. Two great volcanoes—Popocatepetl (Smoking Mountain) and Iztaccihuatl (White Woman)—can be seen at the top. From a Diego Rivera mural at the National Palace in Mexico City. (Courtesy of Scott Sessions)

CORN AND CREATION

> What is it that bends over us all over the world? The maize tassel.
>
> —Aztec riddle

Crucial to their agricultural success were the soils of the Great Basin, which fortunately were fertile, in some areas exceptionally so. The earth was also considered a divine entity, a great sprawling god, sometimes many different gods (or many different vessels), who provided food for humans and also consumed humans after they died. The people not only grew crops, but, as we shall see, believed that they were created by the spirits of the crops, especially the maize god. A general view of this human/agricultural relationship appears in this passage from the Maya creation story in the *Popol Vuh*, where human ancestors, "our first mother and father," were created: "Only yellow corn and white corn were their bodies. Only food were the legs and arms of man."

The point is that one of the most significant and creative cultural events in the development of pre-Aztec life, and one that was essential to the daily existence of Mexica families, was the control of food energy contained in plants. The domestication of several agricultural plants began before 6500 B.C.E. and was flourishing by 2000 B.C.E. in numerous areas within and beyond the Basin of Mexico. During this period, ancient Mesoamericans came to rely upon three important crops: corn, squash, and beans. This important group of vegetables, when consumed together, provided native Mesoamericans with the proper combination of proteins necessary for a complete diet. But for several millennia prior to the emergence of the Aztecs, the central crop of Mesoamerica was (as it continues to be) corn—white, black, red, and yellow maize. The most productive strands take six months to mature, though some types can take as little as four months. These different varieties of corn provided protein and calories and were transformed into the widely useful corn tortillas as well as tamales filled with beans, chilies, and sometimes meats. Corn was also turned into *atole*, a kind of soup drink.

The problem facing the Aztecs was that maize, originally developed at altitudes lower than the basin, had little resistance to frost. This meant that a late rainy season or early frosts could disrupt the growing season and cause havoc with the economic well-being of the Aztecs. The Aztecs also inherited the growing of beans, tomatoes, squash, and avocados, as well as the cultivation of nopal and maguey plants, the latter of which could be used as rope, nets, foot-wear, sewing needles, and even paper. While the Aztecs were highly successful at cultivating all these plants, the surviving records tell us of devastating droughts and famines in the 1450s during the reign of the first Motecuhzoma (Motecuhzoma Ilhuicamina). In one report, some Aztecs sold themselves to the Totonacs for 400 cobs of maize for a young woman and 500 for a working male. During these periods some families had to sell their children into servi-tude or periods of slavery, later to buy them back when abundance returned. In times of regular harvests, the agricultural system was a model of order and productivity. As one scholar notes:

Irrigation was fairly widespread in the Valley and the neighboring upland regions. Canals and ditches led from the fresh-water streams and the lake to the fields on the valley floor, and one of the farmer's regular tasks was to keep the channels clear. In Motecuhzoma's garden at Huaxtepec, irri-gation methods were so well developed that the inhabitants grew tropi-cal plants like vanilla and cocoa under the supervision of forty gardeners who, with their families, had been brought by the ruler from the Hot Lands where these crops were native. In other regions, especially in the arid lands around the Rio Balsas in western Mexico, it was impossible to raise a harvest at all without irrigation, and the inhabitants were obliged to dig canals or to sow their maize on land which flooded each year.[3]

In addition to the *chinampas,* which consisted of channels water-ing highly productive rows of mixed crops, rainfall agriculture included intensive terracing of hillsides so that nearby inhabitants could cultivate plants. Raised fields, local canals, aqueducts, and even household gardening were all widely used, as recent archae-ological research has taught us. Along with agricultural produce, the Aztec diet included dogs, turkey, deer, fish, rats, iguanas, and numerous types of snakes for which they were well known.

FINDING OUT: THE SOURCES OF
OUR KNOWLEDGE

Some years ago, *Life* magazine published an issue about the 25 most important events in the history of mankind. One of them was the conquest of Mexico City/Tenochtitlan by the Spaniards in 1519. The magazine noted that one Spanish writer, Francisco López de Gómara, considered the discovery of the New World the second most important event in the history of mankind, after the appearance of Jesus. He stated, "The greatest event since the creation of the world, with the exception of the incarnation and death of He who created

it, is the discovery of the Indies, as the New World is called." Still
another writer, Cornelious DePauw, called the discovery of the New
World "the most calamitous event in human history." Of course, followers of the Buddha, Confucius, and other great religious and cultural leaders would rank world events quite differently, but the point
is that the daily life of the Aztecs stands on the edge of some of the
most important expansions of human knowledge in world history.
We know that the discovery of the New World and the encounters
with Caribbean and Central American peoples, especially the great
Maya, Inca, and Aztec civilizations, shocked European scientists,
scholars, rulers, and citizens, who were forced to realize that their
maps of the world, theological teachings, geographical knowledge,
and political powers were limited instruments of understanding and
domination. When the news of the Aztecs and their neighbors came
rolling into Europe through the ports where ships brought people,
goods, and ideas from the Americas, Europeans were forced to ask
such questions as, "Are these beings humans?" "Did they descend
from Adam and Eve?" "Can they become Christians?" "Can we
launch just wars against them?"

Finding out about the Aztecs was very difficult in the 16th century, and we still have to organize an effective strategy to approach
and use the available information and resources. As eyewitnesses
from Europe first reported, there were many human-made pyramids and monumental stone and stuccoed ceremonial centers on
top of and along the sides of the Mesoamerican geographical pyramid. Every Aztec community had a ceremonial center made up of
a sacred shrine, a governmental house, and a *tianquiztli,* or marketplace. This ceremonial center oriented daily life and allowed
the people to come in contact with each other and the ideas and
policies of their leaders, and to communicate through rituals with
their gods and goddesses. Unfortunately, all of these ceremonial
centers, especially the most important pyramids and temples, were
attacked and at least partially torn down by the invading Spaniards. In fact, many sections of the capital city, which covered 10
square miles, were smashed to bits and used as the base for the
building of the new Spanish capital during the 16th century. Given
this record of destruction and partial recovery, how do we find out
about the daily life of Aztec families, individuals, towns, and cities?
Students must begin by asking, "What cultural materials are available upon which to reconstruct the Aztec worldview, daily activities, education, warfare, sacrifice, child rearing, games, fashions,
music, and rules of law? Where do we begin, and how did these

materials become available given the conquest, disease, and social catastrophes of the 16th century?"

Fortunately for students, in spite of the material destruction of the city and its buildings, there exists a rich variety of archaeological, written, pictorial, and living evidence that reveals aspects of the daily life and worldview of the Aztecs. This range of evidence forms an ensemble or collection of different types of evidence. We have an ensemble of surviving painted books, countless ruins yielding rich ritual offerings, sculpture, and written accounts by Aztecs, Spaniards, and mestizos, or people of mixed Indian and European ancestry, who described the myths, histories, calendars, medicines, wars, gods, and trading patterns of daily life. Let us turn to four major types of evidence—archaeological, pictorial, written, and ethnohistorical—and see how they are available to us.

ARCHAEOLOGY: DIGGING THE AZTEC GODDESS

In the early morning hours of February 21, 1978, electrical workers who were laying down lines behind the National Cathedral in Mexico City uncovered the edges of a huge circular stone with unusual carvings on it. Thinking that their discovery would interrupt their work and perhaps suspend their pay, they decided to keep the stone a secret. But an anonymous phone call to the National Institute of Anthropology and History reported the discovery, and archaeologists rushed to the site. They were amazed to find themselves gazing at the largest and most significant single piece of sculpture uncovered in the Americas since the Aztec Calendar Stone was excavated in 1790! Scientists who knew Aztec mythology well soon realized that the stone, 11 feet in diameter, depicted the carved image of the moon goddess, who had been dismembered by the sun god in a celestial war during the creation of the Aztec world. She wore an elaborate headdress of eagle and turkey feathers, had two-headed serpents on each of her dismembered arms and legs, and bled jeweled or precious blood. This discovery led to the excavation of the entire area, and the Great Temple of the Aztec capital of Tenochtitlan came to light during the next 15 years. More than 135 buried offerings to the gods, often in walled containers, were excavated, yielding more than 8,000 ritual objects.

Mexican archaeology is considered one of the most productive scientific research traditions in the world today. Throughout the 20th century, Mexican archaeologists and some foreign teams have steadily dug into the foundations of Mexico City and other important sites in and beyond the Basin of Mexico, uncovering ceremonial centers, pyramids, temples, pieces of sculpture, ritual burials, and human and animal remains. These discoveries have taken place in the center and on the edges of the great capital, and in the valleys and mountain areas of the basin, and they have continually revised our view of Aztec life. For instance, some equally important archaeological work on earlier cultures that were important to the Aztecs has taken place at sites such as Teotihuacan, a city to the northeast of Mexico City that flourished from 1 to 550 c.e., and Tula, a ceremonial center in the modern state of Hidalgo, north of Mexico City, that flourished from 950 to 1150 c.e. Tula was the center of the Great Tollan, the imperial kingdom of the Toltecs, to whom the Aztecs traced their heritage and right to rulership. These and other archaeological excavations ultimately cast some light on the Aztecs because the rulers, from Acamapichtli, who reigned from 1376 to 1396, through Motecuhzoma Xocoyotzin, whose reign started in 1502 and who was in power when the Spaniards arrived, constantly looked to their ancestral cultures for legitimacy and inspiration. In fact, the excavations in downtown Mexico City show that the Aztecs were archaeologists themselves! They walked more than 30 miles to the great pyramids of Teotihuacan centuries after the great city had fallen into disrepair, dug up sacred objects, and transported them to their capital, where they reburied the objects as offerings to their gods in their own sacred precincts at the Great Temple of Tenochtitlan. Later in this book we will see images and discuss the meaning of effigy vessels, ritual masks, sacrificial knives, jade beads, marine animals and seashells, human sacrifices, and sculptures of underworld gods found in these offertory caches. The study of this temple and other archaeological finds will serve in part as a focusing lens for our understanding of the daily life of the Aztecs. We shall see how the Great Temple was the site of mythic events, human sacrifices, architectural innovations, and political decisions, and the place where the Aztecs made part of their last stand against the Spaniards before the city fell.

SURVIVING THE ASHES: WISDOM OF THE RED AND BLACK

In 1535 the first Spanish bishop (and later, archbishop) of Mexico, Juan de Zumárraga, ordered the confiscation and collection of the pictorial manuscripts belonging to the Nahua cultural capital, Tezcoco. Zumárraga and other churchmen had long known that these painted histories, cosmologies, and calendars on deerskin, bark, or *maguey* paper contained the vital indigenous worldviews and ritual formulas for the daily life of the native peoples. These manuscripts had become the target of intense suspicion, and Zumárraga, according to some reports, had hundreds of them collected in the marketplace of the town and, in a ceremony legitimated by Christian ritual and teachings, burned them to ashes.

It is sad to know that, of the hundreds of pictorial manuscripts extant in Mexico in 1521 carrying knowledge and symbols of traditions reaching back more than 2,000 years, only 16 remain today. These pictorials, or storybooks, used a picture-writing system that served to communicate literal and metaphoric messages about all aspects of life. When these books were destroyed, the time-honored legacies of education and knowledge concerning medicine, astronomy, history, nature, and the cosmos were seriously damaged. One surviving passage describes the wisdom and educational importance of these manuscripts: "The wise man: a light, a torch, a stout torch that does not smoke. A perforated mirror, a mirror pierced on both sides. His are the red and black ink, his are the illustrated manuscripts, he studies the illustrated manuscripts." The phrase "the red and black ink" refers to the images painted on the illustrated books of bark or *maguey* paper, or on deerskin, which we call *screenfolds* because they were often folded like an accordion. Some images of, for example, animals, plants, mountains, dances, battles, or sacrifices, were pictographs because they represented those persons, places, and things themselves. Other images were ideographs, or symbols of objects that stood for ideas associated with the image. For instance, in the first case, an image of a flower represented a flower, but as an ideograph, a flower could mean a poem or sacrificial blood, depending on the context. The image of a bundle of reeds likely signified a bundle of reeds as a pictograph, but a tied bundle of reeds appearing as an ideograph could refer to a 52-year cycle of ritual completion in the Aztec calendar. We will come across and examine a number of these images in our study.

While only a few of the surviving pictorial storybooks come from Aztec communities, many of the other manuscripts share the same symbol system with the Aztecs and can be used to study domestic life, the education of teenagers, courtship rules, time reckoning, the gods, genealogies, and other crucial aspects of life. And we are very fortunate that native peoples *continued* to produce these manuscripts after the conquest. Among the most relevant pictorials for

Ruler examines a pictorial screenfold manuscript while two individuals paint other manuscripts below him. From a Diego Rivera mural at the National Palace in Mexico City. (Courtesy of Scott Sessions)

the study of Aztec life are the *Codex Fejérváry-Mayer* (painted some-time before the Spaniards arrived), the *Codex Borbonicus* (painted about the same time as the Spaniards arrived), and the *Codex Mendoza* (painted a few years after the Spaniards arrived). The first two are remarkable for their calendrical and ritual information, while the *Mendoza* gives us rich historical information about Mexica warfare, kingship, economics, parenting, and the life cycle of the people. Also, picture writing in the native style appears on many surviving archaeological objects and structures, so that comparisons and contrasts can be made between the images carved in stone and those painted on the screenfolds.

Even today we can be astonished by the sudden reappearance of a colonial painting in the Aztec style that contains important symbols and other information about the ritual life and worldview of pre-Hispanic peoples. Recently the beautiful *Mapa de Cuauhtinchan No. 2* came back into public knowledge and it shows the epic story of Aztec neighbors who emerge from their caves of origin, go on a hazardous pilgrimage to the religious capital of Cholula, fight a great battle, and are rewarded with the prize of a new homeland and community they will call Cuauhtinchan, or Place of the Eagle's Nest. We will see parts of this story and imagery later in the book.

Research into American Indian cultures can be an invigorating and enlarging experience. The history of knowledge as presented by and about the native peoples of Mexico needs to be told in scholarly books, novels, films, poems, and plays in order to approach the profundity, drama, and various kinds of wisdom developed by the Aztecs and their neighbors. Throughout the 16th century, the descendants of the Aztecs, as well as Europeans and mestizos, produced accounts written in Nahuatl (the native language spoken by many of the Indians of Central Mexico), Spanish, and even French about the cosmovision and ceremonial centers of the various Aztec communities. Among these important documents are the *Leyenda de los Soles* (Legend of the Suns), the *Anales de Cuauhtitlan* (Annals of Cuauhtitlan), and the *Histoyre du Mechique* (History of the Mexica). One of the greatest surprises and tools for learning is the 12-book *Florentine Codex*, produced during the middle of the 16th century by a Spanish missionary named Bernardino de Sahagún and his Aztec students. This document was modeled on time-honored European encyclopedias that organized knowledge in terms of (1) the gods and theology, (2) humans and society, and (3) the natural world.

Sahagún was a Franciscan friar who came to Mexico City in 1529 to participate in the great Spanish Catholic project of the evangelization and spiritual conquest of the natives. He was a very learned man with special abilities in language, and he planned to (1) learn as much as possible about the Indian religions, (2) create a Nahuatl vocabulary to assist in the effective preaching of the Holy Gospel, and (3) create a documentary record of native culture so that it could be understood and transformed. How did he go about his work?

In 1536 the Spanish Crown, through the office, in part, of the book-burning Juan de Zumárraga, set up the Colegio Imperial de Santa Cruz de Tlatelolco (Imperial College of the Holy Cross of Tlatelolco), to be directed by a select group of Franciscan friars. This college, like the earlier *calmecac* (the most rigorous of the various pre-Hispanic Aztec schools), was designed to train native boys in the new educational traditions brought from Spain. Sahagún was one of the teachers and described some of its characteristics:

After we came to this land to implant the Faith, we assembled the boys in our houses, as is said. And we began to teach them to read, write, and sing. And, as they did well in all this, we then endeavored to put them to the study of grammar. For this training a college was formed in the city of Mexico, in the Santiago Tlatelolco section, in which were selected from all the neighboring villages and from all the provinces the most capable boys, best able to read and write. They slept and ate at the same college.[4]

When the school first opened, other Spaniards derided the Franciscans at Tlatelolco, claiming that the Indians would not be able to learn grammar and Latin and the other subjects taught at the school. But those who mocked them were soon proved wrong, as Sahagún reported that after a few years the Aztec teenagers "came to understand all the subjects of the grammar book and to speak Latin…and to write Latin, and even to compose hexametric verses."[5] In spite of continued controversy, for some Spaniards now objected that the Indians were learning too well and would discover in the Bible that the patriarchs had many wives (like some of the Aztecs) and would also discover in other books that the Spaniards had been conquered in the past, the school remained open and began to attract native *tlacuiloque*, or painters and scribes, who became important to the encyclopedia that was eventually produced.

Sahagún's teachings, along with those of the other missionaries, focused the native students on the *trivium* (grammar, rhetoric, and logic) and the *quadrivium* (arithmetic, geometry, astronomy, and music), along with Christian moral principles and the study of the Holy Scriptures. Painting and medical matters were also included, and the result was a select group of students whom Sahagún called trilingual because they spoke and read Nahuatl, Castilian (Spanish), and Latin. These students and others who came to work with him helped Sahagún do important research on many aspects of Aztec life prior to and after the conquest. Sahagún organized a questionnaire and set up long-term interview sessions with groups of elders to learn about their gods, mythology, history, kings, medicine, astronomy, plants and animals, rhetoric, and omens, and even their experience of the conquest. It is important to emphasize that these elders, talking with Sahagún 20, 30, or even 40 years after the arrival of the Spaniards, often used the surviving pictorial books we discussed earlier. Sahagún wrote about the elders: "They gave me all the matters we discussed in pictures, for that was the writing they employed in ancient times. And the grammarians [his trilingual students who listened to the elders' 'readings' of the painted books] explained them in their language, writing the explanation at the bottom of the painting."[6]

Sahagún must have learned that this oral recitation was exactly the way the Aztecs had taught their own children prior to the coming of Europeans. We know from surviving traditions that native youth were instructed by preceptors who used large and beautiful books with pictures and symbols in them. The key method of transmitting knowledge during the pre-Hispanic period, however, was the *oral* description or recitation of the knowledge on the pages.

Sahagún used this method—interviewing elders who recited or interpreted pictorial manuscripts to the trilingual students, who then wrote down their explanations—to develop the chapters that finally went into the *Florentine Codex*, which provides us with extraordinary insights into the daily life of Tenochtitlan and its citizens. One of the most extensive sections of the 12 books is Book 6, entitled "Rhetoric and Moral Philosophy." We find page after page of eloquent speeches for different events and transitions in the life cycle of the community. Of particular importance are passages about the correct education of children and teenagers. Another priest noted, for instance, that "no people loved their children more" than the Aztecs. Consider this passage from one of the *huehuetlatolli* (ancient sayings) collected by Sahagún in which a ruler is speaking to his daughter when she reaches puberty: "Here you are, my little girl, my necklace of precious stones, my plumage, my human creation, born of me. You are my blood, my color, my image.... Listen, much do I want you to understand that you are noble. See that you are very precious, even while you are still only a little lady. You are a precious stone, you are a turquoise."[7] A number of other important books produced under the guidance of or by Catholic missionaries, in spite of their goal of stamping out Aztec beliefs and ideas, can teach us a good deal about the ways these people thought and acted toward one another, nature, and their gods.

AZTECS TODAY: HEALING PLANTS

Contrary to popular belief, there are many communities in and around the Basin of Mexico where some of the ideas and practices from pre-Hispanic times are still carried on. There are more than a million Nahuatl-speaking people living in Mexico today and many are knowledgeable about native ways of cooking, healing, praying, planting, growing, speaking, weaving, drawing, and telling stories. Some of these people have migrated into the United States, bringing their knowledge of native languages and cultural practices. It is true that the Spanish culture and the many innovations made by Mexicans in the areas of culture and technology influence the lives and thoughts of these people, but important patterns of pre-Hispanic life continue and are mixed in with contemporary Mexican life. A number of anthropologists and other kinds of contemporary field-workers are in touch with some of these ongoing traditions. One example is the husband-and-wife team of Robert Bye and Edelmira Linares, who have dedicated their lives to studying the cultivation and usage of a broad range of plants, fruits, and flowers by contemporary indigenous and mestizo peoples. This research has involved intensive fieldwork conducted in and around the Basin of Mexico with shamans, healers, growers, and their families in an attempt to discover some of the continuities and changes in their medicinal practices from Aztec times to the present. We will make reference to some of these studies throughout the book.

Besides the work of ethnobotanists like Bye and Linares, there are new studies of archaeological sites, calendars, mythology, dream life, clothes, market systems, and public ceremonies that help us reflect back on the daily routines, beliefs, and ritual actions that animated the many native communities in and around the lake cultures of Central Mexico.

MYSTERIOUS ORIGINS VERSUS RESEARCH

Where did the peoples and cultures who engendered the Aztecs originate? We know that the Mexica groups who became known as the Aztecs migrated into the Basin of Mexico in the 13th and

14th centuries from the north, but where did their ancestors originally come from? This question has challenged scholars and laypersons alike from the earliest contacts with indigenous American peoples up until today. One historian noted how problematic the origins of the Aztecs were to the Spaniards in the 16th century: "Even before the first decade had passed, these plumed and painted peoples—so erroneously called Indians—had become the principal mystery which perplexed the Spanish nation, conquistadors, ecclesiastics, crown, and common citizens alike. Who were they? Whence came they?"[8] Over the years some remarkable theories have emerged.

One line of thought has emphasized the similarities between Aztec and Maya architecture and the temples and buildings in Egypt. It was once argued that Egypt was the original homeland of American Indian civilizations because of the similarities in pyramid structures, calendars, forms of writings, and some of the symbolism attributed to the gods. Closer inspection reveals striking differences between the uses and meanings of Egyptian pyramids and the pyramid temples of Mesoamerica. The Egyptian pyramids were basically tombs for the pharaohs and their families. While they are magnificent to look at and are monumental in the extreme, they were ritually important as *interior* architecture and not basically stages for ongoing public rituals, though rituals were held at their bases. In the Aztec world of temples and pyramids, the emphasis was on ongoing *exterior* performances of myths, rituals, calendrical cycles, and imperial displays in a continuing cycle of ceremonies. As recent archaeological work over the last 30 years has shown, however, it is true that the Aztecs also buried precious ritual objects, animals, and the remains of very important people within some of their pyramid-temples, but the differences in architectural form and ritual usage suggest independent invention, and not cultural diffusion from Egypt.

Another view, expressed as early as 1804 by the German explorer Alexander von Humboldt, was that Asian peoples had migrated to the New World in ancient times, disseminating ideas, symbols, and ritual practices to the ancestors of the Aztecs and Toltecs. In the 20th century, the idea of trans-Pacific contacts was explored by the anthropologist-adventurer Thor Heyerdahl, who constructed a huge raft called the *Kon-Tiki* and sailed across a large section of the Pacific Ocean to the Americas. He hoped to prove that it was possible for ancient seafarers to have made the journey and to have stimulated the development of civilization in the Americas. Later,

Great Pyramid and Sphinx of Cheops at Giza, Egypt. (Francis Frith, © 1870s. From Alfred Grimm, *Ägypten: De photographische Entdeckung im 19.* Jahrhundert. Munich: Laterna magica, 1980)

Great Pyramid of the Sun at Teotihuacan. (Courtesy of Scott Sessions)

Heyerdahl attempted to show that Mediterranean peoples could have made the journey to the Americas by sailing across the Atlantic, although his Egyptian-style reed boat, named the *Ra*, was actually designed and constructed by natives from the Lake Titicaca area of South America. Still others have suggested that members of ancient Chinese and South Asian communities migrated down the west coast of the Americas, bringing elements of civilization that served as the basis for the ceremonial centers, calendars, and rituals of the Aztecs and the Maya. Some scholars have argued that Asian cultures strongly influenced the Costa Rican area of Mesoamerica, bringing the Buddhist artistic and theological tradition to the New World 3,000 years ago. Taking a *cultural diffusionist* approach, these interpretations argue that the great cultural centers of the Americas were developed by migrating peoples who left centers of culture in the Old World and transplanted the roots of civilization (monumental architecture, writing, calendars, and extensive market systems) on American soil. The problem with this notion is that not a single object from Asia or the Mediterranean has ever been found in any archaeological site in the New World!

Sometimes, the problem of the origins of the Aztecs and their precursors has produced fantastic ideas. In the 19th century, American and European anthropologists debated whether the lost continent of Atlantis in the Atlantic or Mu in the Pacific could have been the original home of ancient American civilizations. Using Plato's description of the sinking of the legendary Atlantis, proponents of the submerged continent theory argued that the aboriginal Americans saved themselves in the nick of time and brought their great civilization to America. Again, the problem with this explanation is simple. Where is the material evidence?

Lack of evidence occasionally leads to invention of evidence. The best example, and the one most fun to think about, is the idea found in Erich von Däniken's *Chariots of the Gods* that the great pyramidal and other monumental structures in Mexico, Guatemala, and Peru were left on earth by ancient cosmonauts whose extraterrestrial visits stimulated the development of, if not actually populated, the American continents. And von Däniken went so far as to suggest that these great architectural structures were markers for the return of people from outer space at some future time.

It can often be fascinating to make comparisons, and in fact it appears that humans do it naturally without even intending to look for similarities and differences. The 16th-century Dominican friar Diego Durán, who lived in Central Mexico for most of his life, hoped to find evidence in the surviving pictorial manuscripts that the "Holy Gospel in Hebrew" had made it to the New World centuries before the Spaniards. When Durán heard the many stories about the religious leader Quetzalcoatl (Feathered Serpent), he speculated that one of the apostles of Jesus Christ, the wandering St. Thomas, had visited the New World centuries before, spreading a now-distorted version of the Gospel among the ancestors of the Aztecs.

While these different types of comparisons and speculations are fun to make and should be left open for future researchers, we must be very cautious about notions of cultural diffusion. The implication of some diffusionist interpretations is that native Americans were not capable of achieving extraordinary levels of cultural creativity on their own, but needed the stimulus and cultural remnants of superior foreigners to reach impressive levels of civilization. The idea here is sometimes, but not always, that Old World cultures were superior, more highly civilized, and more deserving of our attention and admiration. This is an utterly false and ethnocentric view of history and culture.

It has been clearly proved that New World cultures, including the Mesoamerican civilizations that gave rise to the Aztecs and the Maya, developed primarily as a result of cultural creativity indigenous to the Americas. This is not to deny that impressive similarities between the Old and the New Worlds exist. But such similarities are no more impressive than the remarkable differences, innovations, and diversities among the cultural productions of Asia, the Mediterranean, Africa, and the Americas, and *within* the Americas as well. Although it appears that very limited contact between Asian cultures and the peoples of the Americas may have taken place, the Olmec, Huastec, Tlaxcalan, Toltec, Ñuu Dzaui (Mixtec), Nähñu (Otomí), Maya, Aztec, and all other indigenous cultures in the Western Hemisphere developed their own cultural processes independent of contributions from outside civilizations. And if such contact did in fact take place, it may just as well have traveled in the opposite direction, that is, from the Americas to the rest of the world. Why not consider the kinds of reciprocal stimulations moving in all directions? Regardless of these very slim possibilities of cultural diffusion, what is clear is that the indigenous peoples of Mesoamerica were more than capable of developing their own cultural traditions based on their work, imaginations, and interactions with their social and natural environment. These cultural processes were concentrated and crystallized in the numerous ceremonial centers, city-states, and day-to-day patterns of human beings. As we shall see, this creativity was particularly evident in the Aztec world.

A DIVERSITY OF PEOPLES

One of the most important points to make about the ecological and social background of Aztec life is that Mesoamerica was a diverse space and time. We should know something of this diversity. Just as we know that there were 13 colonies and a number of languages spoken within them prior to the eventual rise of English as the chief language of discourse and the formation of the United States, it is important to know that there were several hundred ethnic groups among the natives of Mesoamerica who spoke many different languages. As we shall see, in Aztec times, their Nahuatl language became the most important to know in central Mesoamerica, but many other languages were spoken and sung by millions of people. Even though this book focuses specifically on the Mexica, or Aztecs of the 14th through 16th centuries, they were not the only—or even the most powerful or impressive—cultural group in Mesoamerican history. But they did inherit and integrate many cultural elements from their precursors, and it is important for us to review the diversity of cultural history before turning to the lives of the Aztecs. Remembering our pyramid image, we can say that the Aztecs, who were latecomers to the Basin of Mexico, lived at the top of the historical pyramid and claimed to be supported by great civilizations of the past.

Archaeological evidence makes clear that human populations from northeast Asia (groups of Mongoloid peoples) entered the New World as early as 25,000 b.c.e. and as late as 13,000 b.c.e. over and along the Bering Strait land bridge that connected Siberia and Alaska. They were hunters and gatherers who slowly migrated southward and eastward into the areas of present-day Canada and the United States. It appears that these peoples reached the Basin of Mexico by 20,000 b.c.e. and developed diverse languages, ritual expressions, and myths during this long period of human migration. They carried an elaborate hunting culture into the Americas, which included shamanism, artistic expressions, and ritual relationships with animals and their spirits. Surprisingly, various human physical types speaking more than 250 languages migrated into North America and Mesoamerica, and on into South America.

As these peoples struggled to find stable places in the environment, they encountered a marvelous geography of contrasts and wonders, highlands and lowlands, and a wide variety of ecosystems. After crossing the deserts and canyons of northern Mexico, these human groups found various mountain ranges, periodically volcanic, and high valleys and plateaus where major cultural centers developed at different periods in history. Names of important cultural groups include the Olmec, Zapotec, Ñuu Dzaui (Mixtec), Ñähñu (Otomí), P'urehpecha (Tarascan), Huichol, K'iche', Tz'utujil, Huastec, Toltec, and scores of others. Archaeologists have identified three major stages of historical development for Mesoamerican peoples, called the Formative Period (1800 B.C.E.–200 C.E.), the Classic Period (200–900 C.E.), and the Postclassic Period (900–1519 C.E.). Each of these stages was organized, in part, by complex settlements that had major and minor civic-ceremonial centers consisting of ritual spaces, elite compounds, and eventually sizable marketplaces where the shared worldview, religion, and mythology were expressed in architecture, sculpture, painting, and ritual performances. Even in the Formative Period, certain ceremonial centers, especially among the Olmec peoples of the Gulf Coast, reached monumental proportions. The Aztecs appeared in the last stages of the Postclassic Period, but it is important to know something of their precursors.

SACRED PLANTS

The most creative cultural event that slowly brought about major changes in the social and imaginative world was the control of food energy contained in plants. The development of agriculture was the fundamental change that led to the rise of village cultures, ceremonial centers, and social differentiation. We know from the art of this period and the poetry of later peoples that plants and the lush cycle of plant life gave human beings a new attitude toward the idea of creativity—both the creativity of their gods and human creativity. These changes took place between 5000 B.C.E. and 2000 B.C.E. as peoples learned to plant and harvest corn, beans, squash, avocados, chilies, tomatoes, cacao (from which chocolate is made), and a host of other crops. As we shall see when discussing Aztec religion and the cults of the rain and corn gods and goddesses, all these plants and their seeds were believed to contain sacred powers and came to play crucial roles in the myths, rituals, calendars, costumes, and performances in Aztec life. Consider for a moment how young females ritually cared for seeds during the festival dedicated to the maize deities: "And all the girls bore upon their backs ears of maize [grown] the year before. They went in procession, to present them to the goddess Chicomecoatl, and they returned them once more to their house[s] as blessed thing[s] and from there they took the seed to plant next year. And also they put it [away] as the heart of the grain bins, because it was blessed."[9]

GIANT HEADS AND THE HEAVENS

Another important marker in the Aztec background was the rise of the Olmec world, whose scattered ceremonial centers took shape around 1800 B.C.E. and collapsed by 300 B.C.E. The name *Olmec* means *people from the land of the rubber trees* and was used by an indigenous group living in this area at the time of the conquest. It is not known what the ancient peoples of this area called themselves. The Olmecs are outstanding because of their style of art and architecture. Called the Mother Culture of Mesoamerican civilizations because their images of gods and religious forces were spread throughout an extensive geographical area and elaborated by many later peoples, the Olmecs reshaped the earth and natural objects as ways to communicate with their gods and their own people. They especially used jade, basalt, clay, and the earth itself in the forms of caves and hills. Artificial mountains were created at the site of La Venta to represent an earth pyramid. Caves and cliffs were the settings for elaborate paintings and carvings of human-animal-spirit relations. The Olmecs had ritual calendars and ritual burials, and their ceremonial centers were decorated with fantastic mixtures of animal and human forms, including human-jaguar, jaguar-bird, bird-jaguar-crocodile, and crocodile-human combinations. These expressions represent a profound belief in the spirit world.

One of the most fascinating elements of the Olmec peoples appeared in the excavation of San Lorenzo. Colossal stone heads carved with human faces, each wearing helmet-like headgear, were found at different parts of the site. These heads, some nine feet in height and weighing up to 40 tons, were carved on huge rocks quarried from the Tuxtla Mountains, more than 45 miles from the site. Their transportation to San Lorenzo over land and water, as well as their artistic sophistication, shows a complex level of social order and a deep commitment to religious symbols. Perhaps these heads represent dead warriors or portraits of rulers who were believed to

One of many giant stone heads carved by Olmec sculptors at ceremonial centers on the Gulf Coast. (Courtesy of Salvador Guil'liem Arroyo, INAH)

have become gods, gigantic beings protecting the community from their enemies.

Another development during the Formative and Classic Periods in sites such as the Zapotec site of Monte Albán (near modern-day Oaxaca City) and the Maya site of Izapa (in southwestern Guatemala) was an elaborate interest in and understanding of astronomy. Anthony Aveni, an archaeoastronomer from Colgate University, has written several excellent books on the ancient sky-watchers of Mexico showing the long and complex tradition of stargazing, astronomical calculation, and ceremonial buildings oriented toward celestial passages of the sun, Venus, and the Pleiades. For instance, at the magnificent site of Teotihuacan and others in the Basin of Mexico, Aveni and his colleagues have shown conclusively that a number of the buildings were constructed to face specific astronomical events occurring along the horizon, probably as a means of calculating the passage of the year from the dry to the wet season. Teotihuacan is particularly important because the Aztecs believed that it was the site of the creation of the Fifth Sun, or the universe in which they dwelled. The Aztec myth of creation tells how this Fifth Sun emerged out of the sacrifices of gods at Teotihuacan, thereby providing humans with an ordered and reliable universe. The great stairway of the Pyramid of the Sun at Teotihuacan faces a westerly point on the horizon where the Pleiades, called Tianquiztli, or Marketplace, by the Aztecs, set directly in front of it at an important time of the year. In Aztec times, events such as solstices, equinoxes, and Venus cycles played a very important role in daily life.

THE ENIGMATIC MAYA

One culture in Mesoamerica's diverse history that competes in the popular imagination with the Aztecs' is the Classic Maya civilization, which flourished between 200 and 900 c.e. The Maya achieved real advances in their mathematically ingenious calendar, lavishly decorated ceremonial centers, and cult of rulers, and especially in their writing system, which told of their complex mythology, the underworld, and cosmic rebirth. Called the Mysterious Maya for generations, they were once believed to have been a peace-loving civilization of stargazing rulers and priests

Artist's reconstruction of the Maya ceremonial center of Copán in present-day Honduras. (From *An Album of Maya Architecture* by Tatiana Proskouriakoff, new edition copyright © 1963 by the University of Oklahoma Press)

whose balanced lifestyle should be emulated by people today. Recent studies in the ceremonial centers of Tikal, Palenque, Copán, and Kaminaljuyú, among many others, show that the Maya were a rather typical civilization, motivated by warfare, the desire to control riches, royal family quarrels, elite devotions to the gods, and cults of blood sacrifice. One of the most challenging mysteries for students to consider seriously is the collapse of large parts of Maya culture (and in the Zapotec culture in Oaxaca) during the short period from 830 to 930 C.E. It appears that an escalation of monumental building programs that put undue labor and resource demands on the populace plus a pervasive series of crises, including hurricanes, rebellions, famines, and warfare, coincided during this period and brought the great achievements of the Classic Maya centers to a standstill, although new Postclassic Maya sites would subsequently emerge.

Well before the florescence of the Classic centers, the Maya developed, among other things, the fabulous Long Count calendar. Having understood the concept of zero, they combined a number of calendars, including the *tzolkin* (a 260-day count possibly related to the period of human gestation), the *haab* (a 365-day count related to the solar cycle), and the Calendar Round (a 52-year cycle in which the *tzolkin* and *haab* counts came together), within the Long Count (a linear calendar associated with ancestor worship, dynastic lineages, and long-term prophesies) to map out and relate to the prodigious natural and cultural rhythms of their world. Each day in the Long Count, which measured the passage of time from the present cosmic era's beginning in 3114 B.C.E. to its prophesied end in December of 2012 C.E., was expressed in a series of five numbers made up of bars and dots. This calendrical system enabled Maya priests to compute dates in colossal cycles going back to at least nine million years B.C.E., as marked on inscriptions in several ceremonial centers.

At the present time there is worldwide interest in what might happen on December 21, 2012, as shown by films, books, television specials, and magazines that speak of some kind of universal or cosmic shift in our lives at that time. In fact, that date does mark the completion of a 5,125-year Great Cycle in the Maya Long Count. But anyone who knows the shape and meaning of Mesoamerican timekeeping understands why the Maya believed that this date will be followed by a new cosmic cycle that will both repeat the meaningful patterns of the past and reveal new mysteries in the heavens and on earth. Rather than a worldwide catastrophe, the Maya cal-

COSMIC COLLAPSE IN 2012?

Mesoamerican calendars were cyclical and included periods of darkness, danger, and liminality, always followed by the regeneration of time and the cosmos. The Maya believed, not in a catastrophic end of the universe in 2012, but in cosmic renewal and the rebirth of time.

endar speaks of periodic days of confusion and tension followed by an orderly rebirth of the cosmos.

TEOTIHUACAN: CITY OF THE GODS

When the excavators of the Great Aztec Temple in present-day Mexico City penetrated the interior of an adjacent building, which they called the Eagle Warrior Precinct, they were thrilled to find materials and artistic styles dating back to the Toltec empire (950–1150 C.E.) and even to earlier Mesoamerican cultures. For instance, they found several fine vases that had been excavated by the Aztecs themselves from the ruins of Teotihuacan, the City of the Gods, which had fallen into decline during the seventh and eighth centuries. Seven or eight centuries later, the Aztecs looked back to Teotihuacan as the place of origin of the era or universe in which they lived.

Teotihuacan, popularly known today as the Pyramids, is located 30 miles northeast of Mexico City, and the name means the Place Where One Becomes Deified. Teotihuacan is the most visited archaeological site in the Americas. Visitors today can see not only that it contained monumental architecture, including the so-called Pyramids of the Sun and of the Moon and the great Street of the Dead, but that the entire city was designed as a gigantic image of the cosmos. It was an architectural and ritual microcosm, a small (but by human standards, colossal) image of the great cosmos created by the gods. At its peak, around 450 C.E., Teotihuacan was populated by more than 200,000 people who shared in the prestige of a capital that influenced many cities and towns within and beyond the central plateau of Mexico, including the Zapotecs in Oaxaca and the Maya in Copán. Its influence also extended through time, reaching into the minds of the Aztecs and other communities of the 16th century. Thus, they went to the ruins, dug up valuable and beautiful objects, and deposited them in the sacred burials at their greatest sacred shrine, which they called Coatepec (Serpent Mountain).

Teotihuacan had its beginnings in a cave. Excavations have shown that directly beneath the largest building in the site, the Pyramid of the Sun, lie the remains of an ancient tunnel and shrine area that served as one of the earliest sacred centers for rituals and offerings to the gods of the underworld. Throughout Mesoamerican history, caves were valued as the place of origin of ancestral peoples (remember, the Aztecs claimed that they came from Chicomoztoc, the Place of Seven Caves). Caves were also considered passageways to the underworld, and rituals performed in caves could symbolically transport human beings into the realms of the world below. The cave beneath the Pyramid of the Sun was decorated and artificially reshaped into the form of a four-petaled flower.

The entire inhabited space of the city was laid out by its planners and architects as a four-part metropolis imitating the structure of the cosmos. The city's hundreds of residential, ritual, and commercial buildings were organized into an intricate grid pattern

Photograph of Teotihuacan. This view of the Street of the Dead and the Pyramid of the Sun in the distance is taken from the monumental Pyramid of the Moon. Note the elegant order of the ceremonial buildings. (© Angelo Hornak / CORBIS)

emanating from the north-south Street of the Dead and the east-west avenue, which crossed at right angles in the center of the city, dividing it into four great sections.

The art of the city shows that during its rise and florescence (150 B.C.E.–750 C.E.), there were many religious cults dedicated to agriculture, warfare, the ballgame, deities, dynastic families, and sacrificial burials. It is important to remember that we must rely mainly on the archaeological (art and architecture) part of the ensemble in our studies of Teotihuacan. Very limited oral and written traditions directly related to Teotihuacan exist, yet we can see that the people were mighty warriors with profound religious convictions devoted to gods and goddesses of rain, corn, knowledge, celestial bodies, and rulers. It is clear that the Aztecs looked to Teotihuacan as their place of origin. Their Fifth Sun, the Aztec era in which the great city of Tenochtitlan was founded and flourished, was created in a sacrificial fire at the beginning of time. Here is how one version of the creation of the Fifth Age of the cosmos begins: "It is told that when all was in darkness, when yet no sun had shown and no dawn had broken—it is said—the gods gathered themselves there at Teotihuacan. They spoke… 'Who will take it upon himself to be the sun, to bring the dawn?'"[10] Then, in a gesture that was very important to the Aztecs when thinking about the great ancestors of Teotihuacan, the gods sacrificed themselves in the fire and under the sacrificial knife to give life and energy to the sun. The sun was born on the eastern horizon and, after wobbling in the sky for a period of time prior to more sacrifices, it ascended the sky and began its long pattern of passages through the heavens and the underworld.

An intensive excavation recently carried out at the Pyramid of the Moon, which is located at the northern end of the Street of the Dead, has revealed a series of mortuary chambers containing the remains of more than a dozen sacrificial victims accompanied by a large variety of offerings and the remains of various animals of symbolic importance as well as highly controversial Maya-style greenstone objects. The humans had their hands bound behind their backs and many were decapitated. In some cases the bodies were richly ornamented with greenstone ear spools and beads, a necklace made of imitation human jaws, and other items indicating high political rank.

Among the animals found were numerous canine (wolf or coyote) and feline (puma or jaguar) skeletons, 13 complete bird remains (probably eagles), and several rattlesnakes, as well as 18 decapitated animal heads. Archaeologists believe these animals to be symbols of warriors and it is remarkable that a number of the animals were also bound, like the humans, when they were ritually killed. Other objects found included obsidian sculptures of humans, knives, projectile points, shell pendants, beads, and ceramic containers. What is also significant about this recent excavation in the Pyramid of the Moon is a group of ritual jades that come from Maya city-states far to the south of Teotihuacan. This city was a great political and symbolic center for many of its contemporary cultures in Mesoamerica.

TOLLAN: THE PLACE OF REEDS AND THE CITY OF THE FEATHERED SERPENT

The site that captured the Aztec imagination most strongly was the Toltec ceremonial center and city-state of Tollan (Place of Reeds). When the Aztecs migrated into the Basin of Mexico under the inspiration of their patron god Huitzilopochtli, they found a Lake Culture where many towns and city-states were constantly trading, fighting, and negotiating with one another. There were a number of competing ethnic groups, including the Acolhua, who occupied the eastern region of the Basin; the Tepanecs, who controlled the western region; the Culhua, who resided in the Iztapalapa peninsula; the Xochimilca and Chalca, who controlled the extreme southern area; and the Otomies, who lived in the northern sections. But the older tradition (9th to 11th centuries) from which all of these groups claimed descent and legitimacy was that of the Toltecs, who had been great artists and political leaders of the honored past and, according to legend (though not supported by the archaeological or historical record), the inventors of astronomy, the calendar, legal systems, featherwork, and all other important arts.

At the center of the legends and myths about Tollan lived the great priest-king, Topiltzin Quetzalcoatl (Our Young Prince, the Feathered Serpent), who was the devotee and representative of the god Quetzalcoatl. During Topiltzin's reign, Tollan (the main city was located 50 miles to the north of Tenochtitlan) achieved political stability, agricultural abundance, and a reputation of having achieved a kind of golden (or in Toltec terms, turquoise) age. Once the Aztecs learned the traditions of the Lake Culture, they too came to sing the Toltec songs, imitate Toltec art styles, and claim to be direct descendants of the wise and mighty artists and politicians who had easy access to the gods. Among the important discoveries at the Aztec Eagle Warrior Precinct in Tenochtitlan were benches decorated with colorful friezes of warrior processions that imitated very closely the warrior friezes of the Toltec ruins of Tollan. In a sense the Toltecs marched on into the minds and art of the Aztecs centuries after they had disappeared. We get a sense of this feeling of descent among the Aztecs from the phrases they chanted in the 15th and 16th centuries about the Toltec priest-king: "Truly with him it began, truly from him it flowed out, from Quetzalcoatl—all art and knowledge."

The art and knowledge that flowed out of Tollan into the cities, farmlands, mountains, and other places beneath the blue-green bowl of Quetzalcoatl's heaven stopped abruptly in the 12th century when the Toltec kingdom collapsed. The priest-ruler, Topiltzin Quetzalcoatl, was driven from his throne; new, more aggressive factions took control; and migrations and invasions of northern warrior-farmers swept into Tollan to stimulate massive changes. The general order of society achieved by the Toltecs for a century and a half collapsed, and the center of authority and culture shifted southward into the center of the Basin of Mexico. There, remnants of the Toltec culture and descendants of the Toltec aristocracy set up new ceremonial centers and established small, struggling city-states.

It was in this shifting political and cultural setting that the ancestors of the Aztecs migrated into this basin during the 12th and 13th centuries. These migrants settled into small interdependent communities, most of which had been forming for centuries. The typical organization had a ruler who claimed legitimacy, in part, on the basis of descent from the Toltec kingdom and Topiltzin Quetzalcoatl during a golden age of abundance and order. The typical governmental apparatus in these communities included the ruler and his family and other noble groups, warriors, and priests as well as tribute collectors, judges, and bureaucrats dedicated to farming and the temple schedule. As described elsewhere in this book, each settlement, many predating the Aztec migration, was centered on a small complex of ceremonial buildings that often included a royal palace area, pyramid-temples, and a plaza for public gatherings, the size of which depended on the prestige, wealth, and power of the particular community.

By 1300 c.e. a handful of settlements such as Tezcoco, Azcapotzalco, Cuauhnahuac, and Calixtlahuaca had risen to the level of regional capitals that controlled small tributary (tax-gathering) empires that used intimidation and torture, ceremonial performances and sacrifices, and marriage and political alliances to insure the steady income of goods in the forms of foodstuffs, animal skins, luxury items, and human beings. The most powerful kingdom was centered in Azcapotzalco in the Basin of Mexico and ruled by a great ruler named Tezozomoc from 1374 to 1427. Toward the end of his reign, the Aztecs, centered in Tenochtitlan on a modest but growing island in one of the lakes, formed a Triple Alliance with Tezcoco to the east and Tlacopan to the west and attacked Tezozomoc's settlements. Victorious, the Aztecs turned this military alliance into a governmental one that agreed to split the tribute payments each capital would extract from its weaker neighbors. The arrangement was that Tenochtitlan would receive two-fifths, Tezcoco two-fifths, and Tlacopan one-fifth of all the tribute gathered through alliances, intimidation, and warfare. The wealth and stability of the Triple Alliance came to depend on a closely regulated schedule of agricultural production and successful military prowess.

It is important to emphasize, however, that the Aztec social and economic world was not confined to the island capital of Tenochtitlan and Tlatelolco or the settlements of Tlacopan and Tezcoco. Archaeologists working in Aztec sites beyond Tenochtitlan in recent years have uncovered evidence of an intensive urbanization process at the local level during the centuries leading up to and including the Aztec florescence that resulted in a number of city-states within and beyond the Basin of Mexico. In particular, Elizabeth Brumfiel working in the center of Huexotla, Michael Smith at the site of Yautepec, and Thomas and Cynthia Charlton along with Deborah Nichols in the area of Otumba, all have illuminated important aspects of the material life and culture of several diverse Aztec communities. These city-states were typically organized around a small local capital centered by a palace and temple complex where administrative and ritual activities managed the daily lives of people. The majority of the people worked as peasants who farmed on landed estates where they managed small irrigation systems and worked the terraced foothills. Each city-state had local and regional markets where important exchanges took place. Craft specialists produced artistically and technologically significant items that enhanced labor and ceremonial life. During this period of intensive urbanization it appears that luxury goods such as featherwork and greenstone jewelry, previously restricted to elite households, were now made accessible to other levels of society through marketplace exchanges. These marketplaces were also where people could trade for cacao, salt, and elaborately decorated pottery and textiles. Of particular importance was the devel-

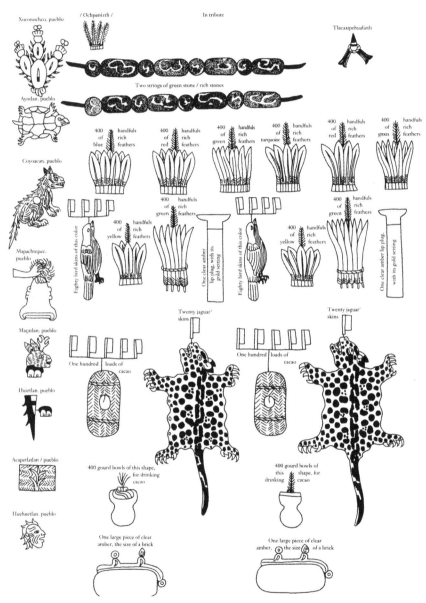

A 16th-century manuscript illustrates some of the tribute paid to Tenochtitlan by various communities. (*Codex Mendoza,* courtesy of Frances F. Berdan and Patricia Reiff Anawalt)

opment of obsidian industries in various locations that resulted in the widespread and daily use of these kinds of tools, decorative images, and ritual implements. Mainly black but also red and green obsidian was particularly useful for cutting tools such as knives and razors that were also used as weapons, with numerous types of the latter described by Spanish conquistadores in their memoirs.

In time, the Aztec capital of Tenochtitlan, with its abundant *chinampa* agriculture and aggressive warfare practices, became the dominant force in the world of the Triple Alliance and local city-states, and by the time the Spaniards arrived in Yucatan in 1517 it was the centerpiece of a pulsating empire. It was in this fertile, dramatic, blue-green bowl that those Mexica ancestors first arrived and found their new identities and built a capital that was the pivot of a four-quartered empire to which we now turn.

NOTES

1. Eric R. Wolf, *Sons of the Shaking Earth* (Chicago: University of Chicago Press, 1959), 3. Emphasis added.

2. We would like to acknowledge and thank María Elena Bernal-García for her idea of the "blue-green bowl," presented in her excellent PhD dissertation entitled "Carving Mountains in a Blue-Green Bowl: Mythological Urban Planning in Mesoamerica" (University of Texas at Austin, 1993).

3. Warwick Bray, *Everyday Life of the Aztecs* (London: B. T. Batsford, 1968), 114.

4. Bernardino de Sahagún, *Florentine Codex: General History of the Things of New Spain*, ed. and trans. Arthur J. O. Anderson and Charles E. Dibble, introductory vol. and 12 books (Santa Fe, NM: School of American Research and University of Utah, 1950–82), *Introductory Volume:* 82.

5. Ibid.

6. Ibid., 54.

7. Ibid., 3: 93–94.

8. Lewis Hanke, *Aristotle and the American Indians: A Study in Race Prejudice in the Modern World* (Chicago: Henry Regnery, 1959), 6.

9. Sahagún, *Florentine Codex*, 2: 7.

10. Ibid., 7: 4.

2

THE WORLDVIEW OF BALANCE: THE COSMIC TREE AND THE FOUR QUARTERS

Carry me to your tree of the dead
carry me to your tree of water
carry me to your blazing tree
carry me to your tree of the sun.[1]

On an early morning around the year 1300, a Chichimec warrior named Xolotl (Divine Dog) ascended a mountain on the edge of the Basin of Mexico and carried out two rituals that signified that his people were establishing their new community in Cemanahuac. Xolotl stood at a point where he had a full view of the valleys below and shot four arrows, one each toward the four directions of the world. The flight and landing site of these four arrows marked the organized territory that Xolotl's people would now occupy. Then, along with his helpers, he collected some dried grasses and had them woven into the shape of a large ring. A prayer was sung, the grass ring was set on fire, and the ashes were scattered to the four directions of the world. It was understood that the symbols and actions carried out by the warrior-leader meant that the people had arrived in the new territory they could call home. He had ritually mapped out their new living space.

This seemingly simple event is a good way to begin a study of the general picture of the world, or *worldview,* of the Aztec peoples, which affected *every aspect of their lives.* Aztec peoples lived their daily lives and interacted with one another, especially through their ceremonial practices, according to the worldview outlined in this chapter. As we shall see, the Aztec world was understood to be a grand horizontal disk intersected by an immense vertical shaft. The horizontal disk was believed to be surrounded by sea waters and raised up on its outer edges to form the walls that held up the sky. This disk (sometimes pictured as a rectangle) was organized into five major sections, with four quarters of the world and the *axis mundi,* or navel of the world, in the center. The center is depicted in one manuscript as a precious green stone that unites the four petals of a gigantic flower. The vertical shaft was conceived of as a series of layers of heaven, earth, and the underworld joined together by the *axis mundi*—the central sacred shrine of the Great Temple in the heart of the capital, Tenochtitlan. Each of these layers was divided into two opposing pairs, which represented the crucial idea of duality that permeated all elements of the Aztec world. In Xolotl's rituals we see the confluence of all of these ideas—the horizontal, the vertical, the four quarters, the center, and duality—with Xolotl's arrows defining the four directions; the grasses of the earth transformed by fire into ashes scattered among the four directions and into smoke that ascended into heaven; and all this taking place on a mountain, a place linking the sky, the earth, and the underworld. This chapter will explore the Aztec worldview by focusing on five major questions:

1. How was the world created?
2. How was the world organized?
3. Who were the major gods, and what were their powers?
4. What was the general purpose and meaning of sacrifice?
5. What was the shape of time and the calendar?

By answering these questions, we, like Xolotl, may be able to perceive the organization of the Aztec cosmos and come to appreciate its importance in their daily lives.

HOW WAS THE WORLD CREATED?

One Latin American writer said, "There are only two stories really worth writing about: someone leaves home or a stranger comes to town." The Aztecs, like all peoples, told and retold the story of their ancestors, the Chichimecs, who left a primordial home, traveled across an expansive terrain filled with hardships and losses, and finally arrived in a fertile valley where they could build a new community. We will examine this migration story in some detail. But there is an even earlier story of how the world in which they were born and traveled was created and given a basic order. Let us first review that cosmic adventure.

CALENDAR STONE

The Calendar Stone, or Sun Stone, was discovered beneath the street of the Zócalo or main square in Mexico City in 1790 when surface repairs were underway. It is about 4 feet thick and 12 feet in diameter and weighs over 22 tons. It depicts the five cosmic eras or suns of Aztec theology.

Fortunately, an image on the famous Aztec Calendar Stone refers to the Aztec view of the creation of the cosmos. In the center of the stone is carved the image of the five ages or suns through which the universe passed prior to the great migration of the Chichimecs. It is interesting that this stone image of the myth of the five ages conforms to the earlier story of Xolotl dividing the new territory into five sections. At least one Nahuatl text about the five ages of

Close-up of the center of the Aztec Calendar Stone depicting the four previous ages of creation and destruction around the central image of Tonatiuh, the sun deity presiding over the Fifth Age in which the Aztecs lived. (Courtesy of Salvador Guil'liem Arroyo, INAH)

the world begins by stating, "Here is the oral account of what is known of how the earth was founded long ago." The First Age, or First Sun, had its beginning more than 3,000 years ago and was called 4 Jaguar. That age lasted 676 years, during which the different gods did battle to gain ascendancy, and then ocelots descended on the people and devoured them in a ravenous battle. The First Sun was destroyed and the cosmos was in darkness. Then the Second Sun, called 4 Wind, was created, and it lasted 364 years. The gods battled again before huge winds came and destroyed the homes, trees—everything—and the sun was also carried away by the storm. Then the Third Sun was created and called 4 Rain, which really meant rain of fire. Again there was a dramatic confrontation among the gods, and the people were destroyed again, this time by fire, which rained for a whole day. The sun was also burned up and the cosmos was in darkness once again. Then the Fourth Sun, called 4 Water, was created; it lasted for 52 years before the heavens collapsed and the waters swallowed up everything, including the mountains. Finally, the Fifth Sun, the age in which the Aztecs dwelled, was created. It was called 4 Movement, which meant two things. On the one hand, it meant that the sun would move in an orderly fashion across the heavens. On the other hand, it meant that the age would end when the earth moved violently. It was feared in Aztec times that their age would be destroyed by colossal earthquakes. We can feel the tension of Aztec worry when we look at the details of the following story of how their age, the Fifth Sun, was created.

The world was dark and without movement at the end of the Fourth Sun when the gods gathered in a place called Teotihuacan, the Abode of the Gods. The gods gathered around a fire that gave them warmth, and they contemplated how to re-create the sun, the world, and life. It was decided that one of the gods must sacrifice himself by hurling himself into the fire, out of which the sun would be born. The gods debated among themselves about who would make the ultimate sacrifice.

Then the gods spoke: they said to Tecuciztecatl, "Now, Tecuciztecatl, enter the fire!" Then he prepared to throw himself into the enormous fire. He felt the great heat and he was afraid. Being afraid, he dared not hurl himself in, but turned back instead.... Four times he tried, four times he failed. After these failures, the gods then spoke to Nanahuatzin, and they said to him: "You Nanahuatzin, you try!" And as the gods had spoken, he braced himself, closed his eyes, stepped forward, and hurled himself into the fire.

The sound of roasting was heard, his body crackled noisily. Seeing him burn thus in the blazing fire, Tecuciztecatl also leaped into the fire.[2]

Then the "gods sat waiting to see where Nanahuatzin would come to rise—he who fell first into the fire—in order that he might shine as the sun. In order that dawn might break." The gods sat for a long time looking in all directions, and a reddening of dawn appeared in all directions. But there was confusion because the gods did not know from which direction the sun would rise. "They expected that he might rise in all directions, because the light was everywhere." This confusion about the direction of the sunrise was solved by one of the gods, Quetzalcoatl (Feathered Serpent), who faced east and was imitated by other gods, including the Red Tezcatlipoca. And the sun rose in the east. "When it appeared, it was flaming red...no one was able to look at it: its light was brilliant and blinding, its rays were magnificently diffused in all directions."[3]

But there was a problem. The sun did not move across the sky but rather "kept swaying from side to side." Faced with this partial sunrise and the crisis of no heavenly movement, the gods decided to sacrifice themselves. "Let this be, that through us the sun may be revived. Let all of us die." They cast themselves into the fire, but still the sun did not move, and the age or sun named 4 Movement did not begin. Only Ehecatl, the wind god, was left, so he "exerted himself fiercely and violently as he blew" the sun into motion across the sky. The dawn had truly come, and the orderly universe was created!

What do you make of this amazing story? First, it is important that, as with the other four ages of the world, it is very hard to get *stability and order* in the universe. The orderly flow of the sun is achieved only after extreme efforts. Second, this long struggle to bring the world into order and motion depends on sacrifices, real sacrifices of the gods, who give their lives so that the sun will move across the heavens. This involves violence, which, paradoxically, according to the believers in these myths, results in creation. The sun is created out of death, and even that is not quite enough. The last god, Ehecatl, must exert himself to the fullest. Finally, and this is a key point to understanding the expectations that Aztec peoples carried around during their days and nights, the universe was filled with a pessimistic tone. The myth of the four suns ends, "And as the elders continue to say, under this sun there will be earthquakes and hunger, and then our end shall come." The worldview was

This 16th-century image, depicting the founding of
Tenochtitlan, is very similar to the one found today in
the center of the Mexican national flag. (Diego Durán,
Códice Durán. Mexico City: Arrendadora Internacional
1990 facsimile edition)

of a universe that was dynamic, unstable, and one day doomed
to collapse. As one of the great poets sang in the festivals of the
capital city:

It is not true, it is not true
that we came to live here.
We came only to sleep, only to dream.

In fact, it was in a dream that the Chichimec ancestors of the
Aztecs received their marching orders to migrate in search of a new
home.

THE MIGRATION STORY

The image on the national flag of Mexico shows a huge eagle
fighting and eating a serpent while perched on a blooming cactus
growing from a rock. This powerful image refers to the other great
story of origins that was told and retold to Aztec children, teenagers,

and adults about their ancestors. More than a dozen accounts of the Mexica migration story have come down to us from the 15th and 16th centuries. And just as the story of the creation of the Fifth Sun in Teotihuacan emphasizes one of the powerful places in Aztec memory, the Abode of the Gods, so the story of the Aztecs leaving their homes in Aztlan and traveling to their new city of Tenochtitlan emphasizes the importance of certain sacred places located at the beginning and the ending of their story of origin.

When the Spaniards began to listen to the native survivors talk about their own sacred history, they heard many versions of the Aztec migration story. This story told that the Mexica left their primordial homeland of Aztlan (Place of the White Heron) and Chicomoztoc (Place of Seven Caves) and took a long journey in search of a new home. The people were led by a shaman-priest who had a dream in which he was ordered by the tribal god to leave Aztlan and travel with his people until they witnessed the god's sign of their new home. The sign would be the giant eagle on the cactus. Following the great dream, the Chichimec leader spoke

Mexica ancestors emerge from Chicomoztoc (Place of Seven Caves). (Diego Durán, *Códice Durán.* Mexico City: Arrendadora Internacional 1990 facsimile edition)

to the community and told them that they needed to leave the Place of Seven Caves and travel until they saw that a

prickly pear cactus standing upon a rock…has grown…so tall and luxuriant that a fine eagle has made his nest there. When we discover it we shall be fortunate, for there we shall find our rest, our comfort, our grandeur. There our name will be praised and our Aztec nation made great. The might of our arms will be known and the courage of our brave hearts…. We shall become lords of gold and silver, of jewels and precious stones, of splendid feathers and of the insignia [that distinguish lords and chieftains]…. Our god orders us to call this place Tenochtitlan. There will be built the city that is to be queen, that is to rule over all others in the country. There we shall receive other kings and nobles, who will recognize Tenochtitlan as the supreme capital.[4]

In this speech we see some of the major social themes of the Aztec worldview: (1) the human world is ruled by gods who communicate their wishes to priest-shamans, (2) the Aztecs were destined to leave home and travel to find the greatest city in the known world, (3) they were to be great warriors, and (4) they were to find abundant riches.

The story goes on to tell that Huitzilopochtli was a fierce god who drove the Mexica on a long march for several years to many places where they built shrines in his honor. The Mexica, the story tells us, were only one of at least eight Nahuatl-speaking groups who left their homeland in the arid north to seek fertile lands in the Great Basin of Mexico. At some places on the march, the people settled for many years and had many adventures, conflicts, battles, and religious experiences. When the Aztecs finally found their prickly pear cactus in the middle of Lake Tezcoco and saw Huitzilopochtli in the form of an eagle, "with his wings stretched outward like the rays of the sun," they humbled themselves, and the god "humbled himself, bowing his head low in their direction." Some versions tell that the great eagle held a bird in his mouth, whereas others say it was a snake. The Mexica marked the site and then rejoiced and rested before their first community action—the construction of a shrine to the god Huitzilopochtli, which, as we shall see, became the greatest temple in the entire empire.

Another version of the arrival in the lake region of the Basin of Mexico says that one of the priests who saw the eagle dove into the lake and disappeared. When he failed to surface, his companions thought that he had drowned, and they returned to their camp. Later, the priest returned and announced that he had descended into the underworld, where he met the rain god Tlaloc, spoke with him, and was granted permission for the Mexica to settle in this sacred place. Thus we have both the forces of the sky (the eagle, Huitzilopochtli) and of the earth (the lake god, Tlaloc) granting permission to build the new center of the world.

Fortunately for our study, a beautiful pictorial map of another community's migration story has recently come back into public knowledge and it contains a vivid image of ancestors emerging from Chicomoztoc, the Place of Seven Caves. On the rediscovered *Mapa de Cuauhtinchan No. 2*, as the accompanying image shows, the place of origin is a semicircular hill with seven distinct niches or caves out of which are flying 12 male ancestors led by a larger,

Chichimec ancestors led by the warrior goddess Itzpapalotl (Obsidian Butterfly) emerge from Chicomoztoc in the newly rediscovered *Mapa de Cuauhtinchan No. 2* (1540s). (Photo by Jorge Pérez de Lara. Courtesy of the Mesoamerican Archive and the David Rockefeller Center for Latin American Studies, Harvard University)

powerful female warrior named Itzpapalotl, or Obsidian Butterfly. Notice that all of the males are carrying bows and arrows and that six of them have sacred bundles attached to their backs. The body of the woman leader is pierced by four arrows, indicating that she has survived a difficult battle, and she also is carrying a solar disk on her back, indicating that she is bringing new light into the world as she leads the others out of the caves. Strangely, she is holding in her right hand a trophy leg from a defeated enemy warrior, signaling her powers to triumph over her adversaries. The original image is painted in bright colors and appears at the beginning of a long, arduous journey depicted in fascinating detail as the pilgrims pass through a series of ordeals (tornadoes, floods, earthquakes, omens) on their way to the great pilgrimage city of Cholula and then beyond to their new sacred lands in Cuauhtinchan (Place of the Eagle's Nest). We mention this vivid example of the migration story to emphasize the widespread tradition in central Mesoamerica of communities believing their ancestors had emerged from the earth, survived grueling odysseys, and eventually founded and built a new town or city.

HOW WAS THE WORLD ORGANIZED?

The Aztec universe, like most Mesoamerican peoples' worldviews, had a geometry consisting of three general levels: an overworld, or celestial space; the middleworld, or earthly level; and the underworld, sometimes known as Mictlan (Place of the Dead). In some cases, a World Tree joined these three levels; its roots were in the underworld, its trunk was in the middleworld, and its highest branches reached up into the celestial world. In the celestial realm above the earth there were 13 levels (some sources say nine), each inhabited by diverse gods and supernatural beings, often depicted as conjugal pairs. Each level had a certain color, power, and name. Here is a list of celestial levels and gods:

Omeyocan, Place of Duality [Levels 12 and 13]
The God Who Is Red
The God Who Is Yellow
The God Who Is White
The Place that Has Corners of Obsidian Slabs
The Sky that Is Blue-Green
The Sky that Is Blackish

The Sky Where Gyrating Occurs
The Sky-Place of Salt
The Sky of the Sun
The Sky of the Skirt of Stars
The Sky of Tlalocan and the Moon

Each of these 13 levels was inhabited by powerful gods and minor supernatural beings. The gods usually came in pairs, reflecting the other major pattern of the Aztec universe: cosmic duality. There was a pervasive dual opposition of contrary elements working in all things. As Alfredo López Austin, the brilliant Mexican anthropologist, notes, "Sky and earth, heat and cold, light and darkness, man and woman, strength and weakness, above and below, rain and drought are conceived at the same time to be polar and complementary pairs, their elements interrelated by their opposition as contraries in one of the great divisions and by their arrangement in an alternating sequence of dominance."[5] As will become apparent when we discuss the character of the human body, this duality was a key concept in Aztec notions of illness, medicine, and healing.

Below this celestial column of gods, forces, colors, and dualities floated the four-quartered earth in the sacred waters. And below the earth were the nine levels of the underworld:

The Place for Crossing the Water
The Place Where the Hills Are Found
The Obsidian Mountain
The Place of the Obsidian Wind
The Place Where the Banners Are Raised
The Place Where People Are Pierced with Arrows
The Place Where People's Hearts Are Devoured
The Obsidian Place of the Dead
The Place Where Smoke Has No Outlet

These nine levels served as way stations for the souls of the dead as they passed slowly toward the bottom rung. As with the celestial world, the terrestrial levels were occupied by gods and minor supernatural forces who were capable of escaping into the earthly level and influencing daily life.

In some versions of this universe there were four other trees, giant *ceiba* trees that held up the sky at the four quarters of the world.

In the natural world, these *ceiba* trees reached up above other plants and trees and had extensive root patterns that spread along the surface of the earth before plunging below the ground. They came to be considered an *axis mundi* or main axis of the natural world through which the gods and their influences from the upper and lower worlds entered onto the surface of the earth and into the world of humans. These influences and forces radiated along lines of communication between the four quarters and the central section, where the old god, the lord of fire, transformed all things. In a cosmic image from a manuscript painted by native peoples before the Europeans arrived, the universe is divided into five major sections, with four trapezoidal sections, each representing one of the four quarters of the universe, arranged around a center space. In the central square is a warrior armed with his weapons while streams of blood flow into the four quarters of the universe. Each of the four

This image from the *Codex Fejérváry-Mayer* is both a divinatory calendar and a map of the cosmos. (From the Eduard Seler edition: Berlin, 1901)

quarters has a blooming tree emerging out of a different symbol; on top of each tree is a different bird, perched but alert. This combination of symbol, tree, and bird is reproduced in the image of the founding of the Aztec city, where the giant eagle sits atop a blooming cactus that is growing out of a rock in the water.

On each side of these celestial trees two gods face one another in different kinds of ritual poses. This pattern reflects the Aztec notion of duality, mentioned earlier, repeated in each of the four quarters of the universe. In addition to a celestial tree, each of the four quarters also has two gods who are responsible for their quadrant's well-being and balance.

Besides the great trees, which served as conduits for sacred energy—the sacred forces erupted from the trees every moment of the day—and flowing across the landscape, there were fountains, forests, and caves, all of which were considered openings by which the supernatural forces entered and escaped the social world of humans. Also, sunlight, fire, stones, and animals were considered openings for the powers of gods to enter the world. These openings were sometimes referred to as *malinalli,* or two pairs of intertwined bands flowing in constant motion that helped the forces of the underworld rise to the surface and the forces of the celestial world descend to the earth.

THE MAJOR GODS AND THEIR POWERS

We have seen that gods played a major role in the Aztec creation story and the stories of migration. But who were these gods, and what powers did they have for these Mesoamerican peoples? Another question to consider is, how do *you* think about God or gods, what are they, and what powers do they have? This is important because we now know that one of the biggest conflicts that European peoples had with native Americans was over their different views and practices concerning gods.

The Aztecs had what can be called a pantheon—a world with many gods. There was a supreme creator deity, Ometeotl, or the Giver of Life, who was a dual god consisting of the pair Ometecuhtli and Omecihuatl. This god was celestial and androgynous (both male and female) and was the primordial creator of the universe. Like the God of certain Western traditions, this god was omnipotent, omniscient, and omnipresent—all-powerful, all-knowing, and present everywhere. The male aspect was especially found in fire, in the sun, and in all the corn gods, who ensured the growth of corn. The female aspect was in the plants, the water, and the earth and ensured regeneration. A song that reflects the multipresences and powers of this dual god goes like this:

He is the Lord and Lady of Duality
He is Lord and Lady of our maintenance
He is mother and father of the gods, the old god
He is at the same time the god of fire, who dwells in the navel of fire
He is the mirror of day and night
He is the star which illumines all things, and he is the Lady of the shining
   skirt of stars
He is our mother, our father
Above all, he is Ometeotl who dwells in the place of duality, Omeyocan.[6]

Before we get deeper into the pantheon, it is important to realize that there were scores of gods associated with all aspects of existence. This was because all of life was considered inherently sacred and literally filled with the potency of divine beings. These gods were expressions of the sacred powers that permeated the world. References to these numinous forces were expressed in the Nahuatl term *teotl*, which the Spaniards translated as *god, saint,* or *demon.* But to the Aztecs, *teotl* signified a sacred power manifested in natural forms (such as a tree, a mountain, or a rainstorm), in persons of high distinction (such as a king, an ancestor, or a warrior), or in mysterious and chaotic places (such as caves, whirlpools, or storms). What the Spanish translated as *god* really referred to a broader spectrum of sacred powers and forces that animated the world.

Fortunately, the deities were represented in story, pictorially, and in sculpture as anthropomorphic beings. Even when gods took an animal form, as in the case of Xolotl, the divine dog, or the form of a ritual object, as in the case of Iztli, the knife god, they often had human features like arms, legs, a torso, a face, and so on. Many of these gods dwelt in the different levels of the 13-layered celestial sphere or the 9-layered underworld. Remember what we said about the four-quartered cosmos? That pattern also organized the pantheon. In many cases there were quadruple or quintuple groups of gods. For instance, in one of the remaining storybooks, the *Codex Borgia,* Tlaloc (the rain god) inhabits the central region of heaven, while four other Tlaloque inhabit the four regions of the sky, each dispensing a different kind of rain.

To understand how these gods, especially the creator gods, acted, consider this story of Quetzalcoatl traveling through the different

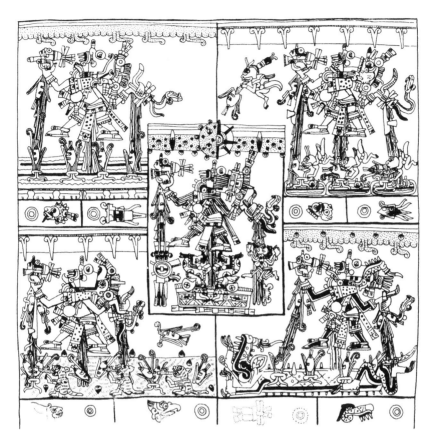

Tlaloc and four Tlaloque making rain. (*Codex Borgia,* from the Eduard Seler edition: Berlin, 1904)

sacred regions of the universe in order to re-create human life. It shows one of the major powers of Aztec gods—the power to create or destroy life.

At the end of the Fourth Sun, when no humans were alive and the process of re-creating the world was under way, one of the gods, Quetzalcoatl, dove into the underworld in search of the bones of the ancestors. He traveled through the eight layers of the under-world and arrived at the ninth—Mictlan—where he announced that "the gods are anxious that someone should inhabit the earth." He was confronted with Mictlantecuhtli and Mictecacihuatl, the Lord and Lady of the Region of the Dead. Quetzalcoatl told them, "I have come in search of the precious bones in your possession," and they put him to several tests. First, the Lord of Mictlan replied, "Very well, sound my shell horn and go around my circular realm four times." But the shell horn had no holes, so Quetzalcoatl called the worms, who made holes. Then the bees flew through the horn and it sounded. Mictlantecuhtli informed him that he could take the bones of the ancestors away, but told his assistants not to let Quetzalcoatl escape with them. Quetzalcoatl searched for the bones and found them. He gathered them up in his pouch and began to slip out of Mictlan. As he walked along a trail, a flock of quail suddenly emerged from the grasses and startled him. He fell into a pit and dropped the bones, which broke into many pieces upon which the quail began to gnaw. Because of this, the new humans would be created in many different sizes. Although Quetzalcoatl was killed in the fall, he had the power to regenerate his life. He managed to escape with the bones and traveled to one of the Aztec paradises, Tamoanchan, where he gave them to Cihuacoatl (Serpent Woman). She ground them up into a paste and put them into her sacred jar. Blood was poured on them and human life was recreated. And the two of them said, "People have been born, o gods, the *macehualtin* (those given life or deserved into life through penance)."[7]

We see some of the special powers of the gods in this story. First, they cross and inhabit the different regions of the world—Quetzalcoatl starts on the earthly level, descends into the underworld, and ascends to the celestial world. Second, as a messenger of re-creation, Quetzalcoatl must undergo a trial in the underworld. We know that in Maya cosmology, the underworld, Xibalba, is filled with a series of houses in which the travelers undergo magical trials that can freeze, burn, or dismember them. Third, the gods come in pairs. There is a pair of gods in the underworld, and there is a pair of creator gods in the paradise of Tamoanchan who must cooperate in order for human life to be restarted. Also, we are introduced to three of the major themes of the pantheon. There are creator gods, fertility gods, and gods who sacrifice. Let us discuss all three and show some of the characteristics of each god who contributed to the daily life of the Aztecs.

CREATOR GODS

Besides Ometeotl, the Lord of Duality, who was the Supreme Creator God, there were a series of creator gods who did the work of organizing the universe. Each was revered by the general populace, from ruler to commoner. The four main creator gods, Quetzalcoatl, Tezcatlipoca, Xiuhtecuhtli, and Tlaloc, received widespread representations carved in wood and stone or painted in murals and manuscripts. These were the gods who struggled for ascendancy during the four suns that preceded the Fifth Sun. There are widespread images of these deities as well as myths about their powers, adventures, and influences.

One of the most powerful creator gods was Tezcatlipoca, the Lord of the Smoking Mirror. He was lavishly decorated with feathers and mirrors. On the social level of the local community, he was the great sorcerer whose smoking obsidian mirror revealed the powers of darkness, night, jaguars, and shamanic magic. He was active, involved, intimidating, and overbearing. Consider this list of alternative names for this god: he was also called Yohualli Ehecatl (Night Wind), Moyocoyatzin (Capricious One), Monenequi (Tyrannical One), Yaotl (Enemy), and Necoc Yaotl (Enemy on Both Sides).[8] In other words, he was awesome. In fact, he was capable of being everywhere. One prayer to Tezcatlipoca went like this: "O master, O our lord…O night, O wind; thou seest, thou knowest the things within the trees, the rocks. And behold now, it is true that thou knowest of things within us; thou hearest us from within, what we say, what we think; our minds, our hearts. It is as if smoke, mist arose before thee."[9]

Another creative power was Xiuhtecuhtli, the ancient fire god who influenced every level of society and the cosmos. Xiuhtecuhtli was the fire of existence that was kept lighted in certain temples at all times. He was also the fire in each family's home, providing warmth, light, and power for cooking. Xiuhtecuhtli was especially present in the various new fire ceremonies that accompanied the inauguration of new temples, ballcourts, and palaces, and he was especially important during the great New Fire Ceremony that took place once every 52 years at the end of the Aztec calendar round. When we discuss the general meaning and purpose of human sacrifice, we shall see both the popularity and power of this creator god.

GODS OF FERTILITY

Daily life in the Aztec world revolved in large part around farming and the powers of fertility and agricultural regeneration. Every family depended on various forms of intensive agriculture that required organized labor schedules of planting, nurturing, and harvesting. The gods of agriculture were all around and part of everyday existence. People carried out rituals for burning fields, preparing the ground for seed, planting, observing the stages of growth, sowing the maize, storing the food, and eating it. Like young children, the fields needed constant attention, care, and nurturance. While many female deities inspired worship and the regeneration of plants, the most ancient and honored fertility-rain god was the male god Tlaloc, who lived on mountain peaks where clouds were thought to emerge from caves to fertilize the land with rain. One mountain in particular, Mt. Tlaloc, was worshiped as the original source of the waters and vegetation. As you would expect, Tlaloc was accompanied by a female counterpart, sometimes known as Chalchiuhtlicue, the goddess of the lake and running water; she was represented in various forms, including precious greenstone effigies.

One of the most fascinating aspects of Tlaloc was his paradise, Tlalocan. It was one of the desired places of afterlife, a kind of earth paradise setting. The Aztecs who spoke to Bernardino de Sahagún about their worldview told him that in Tlalocan "there was great wealth. Never did one suffer. Never did the ears of green maize, the gourds, the squash blossoms, the heads of amaranth, the green chilis, the tomatoes, the green beans, the *cempoalxochitl*, fail. And there dwelt the Tlalocs, who were like the offering priests."[10] People struck by lightning and those who drowned were assured of a place in Tlalocan. Dying in these ways meant that Tlaloc had chosen them as a reward or as a way of demonstrating his power. Most of all, Tlalocan was conceived of as a great storehouse of water and fertilizing energy. The Tlalocs, or Tlaloque, gave and took the treasured forces of new life.

There was an ensemble of mother goddesses, and some were thought of as earth-mother figures who represented the abundant powers of the earth, women, and fertility. These were the deities of earth, water, the moon, drunkenness, sex, the birth of life, fertilization, illness, and healing of cold diseases. The underlying concept was of the mother who could provide comfort or harm, love or terror, and life or death. One of the most important mother goddesses was Tonantzin (Our Venerable Mother), who was revered far and wide in Aztec times. Shortly after the Spaniards arrived, the Virgin of Guadalupe appeared on the same hill that was dedicated to the worship of Tonantzin. Perhaps the most powerful earth-mother goddess was Coatlicue (Serpent Skirt), whose astonishing sculptural image will be examined in chapter 6. Other earth goddesses who present the opposing, life-giving elements of the earth include Xochiquetzal (Precious Flowery Feather), who was the goddess of romance, love, and sexual desire and was associated with flowers, feasting, and pleasure. There was also Tlazolteotl (Goddess of Filth), who was associated with sexual sin, and Mayahuel (Circle of Arms), who was the goddess of drinking. Following the pattern of duality seen earlier, these goddesses could also appear in masculine forms.

It is difficult on paper to grasp the immense powers these deities held in the Aztec imagination; but a recent discovery unearthed from beneath the streets of Mexico City may help us enlarge our awareness of the Aztec commitments to their gods and goddesses. As we discuss elsewhere in the present book, Mexican archaeologists have been excavating the elaborate complex of the Templo Mayor or Great Aztec Temple of Tenochtitlan since 1978, when the giant monolith of the goddess Coyolxauhqui was found. In the fall of 2007, another startling discovery was made just 30 yards away from the Coyolxauhqui Stone. Archaeologists digging in front of a stairway found the largest single Aztec sculpture ever excavated in Mexico City. After painstaking excavation, photography, cleaning, and study, we understand that this sculpture is a giant image of the goddess Tlaltecuhtli depicted in a pose of receiving the dead into the underworld. She is carved to appear on her back with her clawed hands and feet in gestures ready to grip the dead as they enter the earth. She has an elaborate, curly hairstyle and blood is flowing from her large gaping mouth. Excavators have discovered the color pattern that covered her body as well as some calendar dates associated with the death of one of the Aztec kings, Ahuitzotl, who ruled from 1486 to 1502. The accompanying image of this 4×3.57 meter sculpture will clue us into the depth of the Aztec commitment to the cults of their gods and the care they took in depicting them for people to see and worship.

THE HUMAN BODY AS A COSMOS

Before turning to the sacrificial gods, it will be helpful to discuss the most pervasive type of sacred space in the Aztec world—the human body. The human body was considered a potent receptacle of cosmological forces, a living, moving center of the world. As in the elaborate image of the cosmos from the *Codex Fejérváry-Mayer,* at the heart of the universe stands the body of Xiuhtecuhtli, the Fire God. From his body flow four streams of blood into the four quarters of the universe, giving them energy and life. In Aztec cosmology, the human body was the recipient of divine forces that were internalized and lodged within different body parts, giving them sacred potency. Another way of saying this is that the human body was believed to contain three souls, or animistic entities, which could be strengthened or weakened during a person's lifetime. These souls were called the *tonalli,* the *teyolia,* and the *ihiyotl.*

The *tonalli* (from *tona,* to irradiate or make warm with sun) was collected and nurtured in the human skull. The original source of *tonalli* was Ometeotl, the supreme Dual God residing at the top of the 13 celestial layers. But the divine *tonalli* reached the human through the action of celestial beings inhabiting other levels of the sky. It was believed that at the moment of the conception of a human being, Ometeotl intervened on one of the celestial levels and sent vital energy into the uterus of the female. This energy was deposited into the head of the embryo, resulting in the original shape of one's temperament and destiny. After being born containing this initial amount of *tonalli,* the child was ritually placed near a fire and eventually exposed to the sun in order to increase his or her *tonalli.* Although the sun was believed to be the most powerful visible source of *tonalli,* people could acquire *tonalli* from members of their family or other people with whom they had intimate contact.

The term *tonalli* has a rich range of meanings referring to vigor, warmth, solar heat, summertime, and soul. *Tonalli* infiltrated animals, gods, plants, humans, and objects used in rituals. The hair that covered the head, especially the fontanel area, was a major receptacle of *tonalli.* The hair prevented the *tonalli* from leaving the body and was therefore a major prize in warfare. It was believed that the fortitude and valor of a warrior resided, in part, in the hair, and there are many pictorial scenes showing Aztec warriors grabbing the hair of enemies. The hair of warriors captured in battle was kept by the captors in order to increase their own *tonalli.* The decapitated head of an enemy warrior was a supreme prize for the city, which gained more *tonalli* through ceremonies.

The *teyolia,* which resided in the human heart, was another divine force animating the human body. *Teyolia* was thought of as divine fire, and it animated the human being and gave shape to a person's sensibilities and thinking patterns. It was the rational force in human life. Every human heart contained this divine fire, but an extraordinary amount resided in the hearts of priests, artists, and the men and women who impersonated deities during festivals. Each of these human types was considered a living channel of *teyolia* into the social world, a kind of gift of good energy for the community. When one did something extraordinary in art, government, war, or other social expressions, one's *teyolia* increased.

When a person died, his or her *teyolia* traveled to the celestial world of the dead, known as the "sky of the sun," where it was transformed into birds. This pattern of spiritual transformation was a crucial idea in Aztec thought, because the extraction of enemy hearts (after the enemy warrior had been transformed into a god) resulted in a larger supply of divine energy for the sun god. One text states: "Therefore, the ancients said that when they died, men did not perish, but began to live again almost as if awakened from a dream and that they became spirits or gods. They said to them, 'Lord, lady, awaken, now it is beginning to dawn, now it is day break; the yellow, plumed birds are beginning to sing, and now the multicolored butterflies are flying.'"[11]

Teyolia resided in mountains, lakes, towns, temples, plants, people, and powerful objects. All important landscapes, such as the lakes of Mexico and the mountains, had *teyolia*, or heart. Each community had an *altepeyollotl*, or heart of the town, a living divine force sometimes represented in a sculpture or decorated image. During the recent excavation of the Great Aztec Temple a number of statues were discovered representing the *teyolia* or heart of the sacred pyramid.

The third human soul or animistic entity was the *ihiyotl*, which resided in the liver. The *ihiyotl* was believed to be a luminous gas that could attract and cast spells over other human beings. It could be used to charm and bring health to another person or be used magically to cause damage to human life, plants, animals, and events. The *ihiyotl* was expelled through a person's breath or the breeze caused by the wave of a hand.

These three souls gave the human body extraordinary value, vulnerability, and power; and showed how human beings were little images of the cosmos, filled with divine power.

SACRIFICIAL GODS AND WORLDVIEW

One of the most challenging parts of Aztec life was the sacrifice of humans, animals, plants, and various substances, which will be discussed in more detail in a later chapter. As with all acts of life, sacred forces were present, and there were a number of gods associated with sacrificial ceremonies. In fact, it may be that all the gods were part of the sacrificial cult. One way for gods to become a central part of the sacrifice was through the intermediary of the *teotl ixiptla,* the deity impersonator. The deity impersonator, or better, the *image* of the god, could be an animal, plant, object, or, most significantly, a human being. The human being was transformed magically through complicated ritual techniques into a *living image of the god.* This *teotl ixiptla,* or god image, was then sacrificed, resulting in the rebirth of the god as a potent new being. The ceremony known as Toxcatl illustrates this conception. It consisted of transforming a warrior with ideal attributes into the god Tezcatlipoca. The warrior was carefully chosen, dressed, taught, worshiped, and finally sacrificed in a public setting. The individual needed to possess a perfect physique. This perfect individual would be adorned as the god; he was taught to play flutes, to speak eloquently, and to parade around the city. At the end of one year, he was given four women *ixiptla* for companionship, and then he was sacrificed and decapitated. His head was displayed in the central marketplace, and Tezcatlipoca was regenerated.

The practice of sacrifice should come as no surprise given our earlier study of the myths of the creation of the Fifth Sun, when the gods sacrificed themselves in the fires of Teotihuacan to bring forth the sun. The sun, Tonatiuh (whose visage appears in the center of the so-called Aztec Calendar Stone), depended on continued nourishment from human hearts. His tongue is a sacrificial knife extended as if parched with thirst.

To develop a general understanding of the way sacrifice reflected and influenced the overall worldview of the Aztecs, it helps to focus on one sacrifice in particular. The New Fire Ceremony, held once every 52 years in order to re-create the world in which the Aztecs dwelled, helps us see the strange relationship between *creativity* and *sacrifice.* Notice how different sacred places and the calendar are interwoven in this ritual.

On the morning of the New Fire Ceremony, a procession of fire priests with a captive warrior, "arranged in order and wearing the garb of the gods," passed out of the capital city toward a sacred shrine on the Hill of the Star.[12] During the weeks prior to the decisive night on which the ceremony took place, the populace all over the Aztec world extinguished their fires, cast statues of gods into the water, and swept clean their homes, patios, and walkways. Pregnant women put on masks of *maguey* leaves, children were punched and nudged away to avoid being turned magically into mice, and some women were closed up in granaries to prevent them from being turned into beasts who would devour men.

For on this night in the calendar round of 18,980 nights, the Aztec fire priests regenerated the entire cosmos through the heart sacrifice of a captive warrior specifically chosen by the king. We are told that when the procession arrived "in the deep night" at the Hill of the Star, the populace climbed onto their roofs.[13] Craning their necks and focusing their complete attention on the hill, they became filled with dread that the sun would not be regenerated and the world would be destroyed forever.

As the ceremony proceeded, the fire priests focused on the movements of a star group known as Tianquiztli (Marketplace), the cluster we call the Pleiades. As the cluster passed through the meridian, signaling that the movement of the heavens had not ceased, a small fire was started on the chest of the outstretched warrior. The text reads, "When a little fire fell, when it took flame, then speedily the priest slashed open the breast of the captive, seized his heart, and quickly cast it there into the fire."[14] In the

The New Fire Ceremony. (*Codex Borbonicus*, from the E. T. Hamy edition: Paris, 1899)

open chest a new fire was drawn and people could see it from everywhere. To also participate in the sacrifice, the populace cut their ears—even the ears of children in cradles—and spattered their blood in the ritual flicking of their fingers in the direction of the fire on the mountain. The new fire was taken down the mountain and carried to the pyramid temple of Huitzilopochtli in the center of the city of Tenochtitlan. It was placed in the fire holder of the statue of the god. Then messengers, runners, and fire priests who had come from throughout the area took the fire back to the cities, where the common folk, after blistering themselves with the fire, placed it in their homes, and "there was the quieting of many hearts."[15]

This dramatic performance is an outstanding example of what is meant by *worldview*. In this sacrificial ceremony, the world is *viewed*, as the populace sees vividly the procession of *teteo ixiptla*, the city, the darkness, the new fire, and the stars. But the world is also *renewed*! And that is the key to this aspect of the worldview—the world is in dire need of constant renewal. Also called Toxiuh-molpilia (Binding of Years), the ceremony provides a picture of the Aztec commitment to the regeneration of the cosmos that relates astronomy, calendars, child rearing, autosacrifice, war, and human sacrifice together. It also links the capital city with a sacred mountain, and both of these sacred sites to the towns, homes, and populace of the entire empire.

It is important to emphasize how much is observed by the general population. The procession of priests and people wearing the costumes of gods moves along a public passageway through the city and out into the countryside during the day. Thousands of people witness this sacred parade. After the priests and deity impersonators walk the 20 kilometers and climb the ceremonial hill, the populace observes another procession—the celestial procession of the stars through the meridian. Then, there is the public dousing of all fires and the engulfment in darkness. After the horrendous sacrifice, the new fire is lit amid universal rejoicing and bleeding. Everyone experiences a little pain for this renewal to take place. Imagine the impact of living along the lakes and seeing in the darkness from the shores and islands the single great fire roaring on the Hill of the Star and then streaming down the mountain across the lake and into the city. There it lights up the major temple precinct. Then, in a slow version of one of our own fireworks explosions, the fire spreads out in all directions as it is taken to the towns and cities, where it lights up the temples, the palaces, and the homes of the entire populace. That is the renewal of the world through a sacrificial ceremony! This is the Aztec purpose of sacrifice—the renewal of all life.

THE SHAPE AND RHYTHM OF AZTEC TIME

What about the Aztec understanding of time on the cosmic and daily levels? We have already seen how the universe passed through four great eras, each ending in a cataclysm but also giving way to a new cosmos. And we have seen how the Aztecs were careful to mark their important memories with specific dates in the form of day signs. It is very important to know how all these spaces—the four quarters, the center of the world, the dualities, the 13 heavens, and the nine underworlds—revolved, changed, or experienced the passage of time.

The dynamics of the Aztec universe can first be understood in terms of the three kinds of time—the transcendent time of the gods, the active time of the gods, and the time of humans—which all flowed together. We will look at these three kinds of time and then outline the yearly and daily calendar that influenced every part of Aztec life.

Before there was human time or even the time of the creation myths we studied earlier, there was a *transcendent* time of the Dual God who dwelled quietly in the highest heavens. This supreme being existed in peace but provided the original energy and structure of the universe. This primordial time of the gods, when order first appeared out of chaos but did not exist as action, continues to exist in a celestial realm. This existence is reflected in the notion of Omeyocan, the Dual Heaven, where all was in balance and silence.

This peaceful time was broken by a second flow of time, the time when the gods acted out all kinds of events, including creations, abductions, violations, wars, deaths, games, and even the sacrifice and dismembering of other gods in order to make an existence in which humans could eventually dwell. We saw a vivid example of this in the creation of the Fifth Sun in Teotihuacan.

These creative/destructive actions gave way to a third kind of time, the time of humans, which flowed and developed in the middle of the universe—the earth's surface—and the four lower heavens. It was during the second cosmic time, when the supernatural forces acted in all levels of the universe, that the calendar came into being, an invention of the gods to be used to govern and interact with the time of human beings. We know that the calendar was made during the second period, because the creation myths often tell of specific dates of creation. All humans and other significant beings created in the third era have sacred and magical names corresponding to the time of their birth.

What is fascinating and makes the story more complex is that neither the time of the transcendent gods nor the time of mythical action *ceased* after the birth of the time of human beings. In fact, supernatural beings were created who became intimately connected to daily life in human spaces on earth. Also, the forces from the time of the mythic events kept ruling the time of human life on earth through the cycles of nature and the calendar round. We can conceive of these three times as a wheel within a larger wheel within an even larger wheel, even though they don't always turn in the same direction or on the same plane. But each hour and day in earthly time is in touch with the particular forces of the time of the gods and the time of myth. *In this way each human day coincided with a special moment in mythical time and received the imprint of the world of the gods. Each moment of human time was a kind of crossroads where a plurality of divine forces met to determine the kind of day that people lived through.*

The Aztecs had a sacred almanac, a 260-day cycle called the *tonalpohualli,* or "count of days." Twenty day signs ran consecutively from Crocodile through Flower, repeating after the 20th day. These 20 signs interacted with the numbers 1 through 13, which also repeated. This meant that the 20 day signs and the 13 numbers, advancing side by side, yielded a 260-day cycle before starting over again. Each of the 20 day signs were distributed among the four directions of the universe and were associated with a combination of divine forces. Therefore, one of the four directions with its corresponding colors, sacred tree, sacred bird, and deities influenced *every* day in the life of a person. This also meant that the Aztecs had to know their math!

Along with the 260-day cycle, there was also a 365-day cycle, or solar calendar, called the *xiuhpohualli*. This solar calendar was divided into 18 sections or months, each containing 20 days, with five unlucky or empty days, called the *nemontemi,* situated after the 18th month at the end of the year. Each month had a major celebration. What is remarkable is that the 260-day *tonalpohualli* and the 365-day *xiuhpohualli* operated simultaneously, using the same day signs and counting system, and the interaction between these two calendars produced a larger cycle of 52 solar years. As we saw in our discussion of the New Fire Ceremony, the ending and beginning of this cycle were vital moments of cosmic renewal in the Aztec world.

The Sequence of Days in the *Tonalpohualli*

(Numbers in the body of the chart indicate the
postion of the days in the 260-day ritual cycle)

Day Signs *Nahuatl* English	Numerical Coefficients												
	1	2	3	4	5	6	7	8	9	10	11	12	13
Cipactli Crocodile	1	41	81	121	161	201	241	21	61	101	141	181	221
Ehecatl Wind	222	2	42	82	122	162	202	242	22	62	102	142	182
Calli House	183	223	3	43	83	123	163	203	243	23	63	103	143
Cuetzpallin Lizard	144	184	224	4	44	84	124	164	204	244	24	64	104
Coatl Serpent	105	145	185	225	5	45	85	125	165	205	245	25	65
Miquiztli Death	66	106	146	186	226	6	46	86	126	166	206	246	26
Mazatl Deer	27	67	107	147	187	227	7	47	87	127	167	207	247
Tochtli Rabbit	248	28	68	108	148	188	228	8	48	88	128	168	208
Atl Water	209	249	29	69	109	149	189	229	9	49	89	129	169
Itzcuintli Dog	170	210	250	30	70	110	150	190	230	10	50	90	130
Ozomatli Monkey	131	171	211	251	31	71	111	151	191	231	11	51	91
Malinalli Grass	92	132	172	212	252	32	72	112	152	192	232	12	52
Acatl Reed	53	93	133	173	213	253	33	73	113	153	193	233	13
Ocelotl Jaguar	14	54	94	134	174	214	254	34	74	114	154	194	234
Cuauhtli Eagle	235	15	55	95	135	175	215	255	35	75	115	155	195
Cozcacuauhtli Vulture	196	236	16	56	96	136	176	216	256	36	76	116	156
Ollin Movement	157	197	237	17	57	97	137	177	217	257	37	77	117
Tecpatl Flint Knife	118	158	198	238	18	58	98	138	178	218	258	38	78
Quiahuitl Rain	79	119	159	199	239	19	59	99	139	179	219	259	39
Xochitl Flower	40	80	120	160	200	240	20	60	100	140	180	220	260

All local and regional variations of the Mesoamerican calendar in use when the Spaniards arrived were based on a 260-day ritual cycle, referred to in Nahuatl as the *tonalpohualli*. The *tonalpohualli* was organized in 20 periods of 13 days each, which the Spanish priests called *trecenas*. Each of the 260 days was uniquely named by combining one of 20 possible day signs with one of 13 possible numbers or numerical coefficients. The ritual calendar began with the day 1 Crocodile and ended with the day 13 Flower. The progression of days went 1 Crocodile, 2 Wind, 3 House, 4 Lizard, 5 Serpent, 6 Death, 7 Deer, 8 Rabbit, 9 Water, 10 Dog, 11 Monkey, 12 Grass, 13 Reed. Upon reaching the coefficient 13, the first *trecena* was completed and the second *trecena* began using the coefficient 1 with the next day sign, Jaguar. Thus, the count continued with 1 Jaguar, 2 Eagle, 3 Vulture, 4 Movement, 5 Flint, 6 Rain, 7 Flower. After the 20th day sign (Flower), the count went back to the first day sign, Crocodile. Thus, the count continued with 8 Crocodile, 9 Wind, 10 House, 11 Lizard, 12 Serpent, 13 Death, 1 Deer, 2 Rabbit, 3 Water, and so on until all of the 260 combinations became exhausted on the day 13 Flower, after which the *tonalpohualli* would start again with the day 1 Crocodile. (Courtesy of Scott Sessions.)

The calendars marked and regulated the passage of natural and supernatural influences into human life. The numbers and signs of the Aztec calendar, however, were much more than artistic combinations. They had to do with fate—human fate and the fate of all life—and they were used for naming individuals. For instance, as soon as a child was born, the parents invited a day-count reader to the home who was told the exact instant of the child's birth. This calendar priest would open up a divinatory book and examine the paintings associated with the day signs and numbers surrounding the child's birth. A careful study ensued in which the priest identified the particular day sign of the child's birth, but also the other signs related to that major sign. Since each day sign had numerous powers and qualities, the family and the calendar priest looked for the most positive combinations. The numbers 3, 7, and 10 through 13 were fortunate, while 6, 8, and 9 brought bad luck. A combined reading could bring a positive interpretation into the naming of a child even if the basic number was negative. For instance, if a child was born on what was considered a negative day sign, the other associated signs could bring positive influences into the child's life. If the birth date were particularly gloomy, the day-count reader would urge the parents to wait for a favorable day sign and number, which would then become the child's name.

The person's life was forever shaped by the forces and influences of his or her calendar name. One of the most famous Aztecs, Nezahualcoyotl, the ruler of Tezcoco, had the calendar name 1 Deer, a day whose destiny included nobility, fame, and success in war. In fact, he was one of the great poet-warriors of Aztec history in spite of many obstacles. The day 4 Dog brought prosperity to a person, especially if he bred dogs for food. It was believed that his dogs would be healthy, breed well, and live long lives. "It was said: 'How can it be otherwise? The dogs share a day sign with him.'" An unfavorable day was 2 Rabbit, which was associated with the *pulque* gods; it meant that the child had the capacity to become a drunkard. Traders left and returned home on specific days. Wars were started only when the days had strong, positive signs. All events were regulated by this system. An Aztec scholar, Elizabeth Boone, sums up the calendar influences this way:

Even an individual born under the most auspicious day sign, however, could meet disaster if he or she forgot to heed the day signs. The days carried meaning for every activity, and, in the Aztec world, it was crucial that events happen at the right time. Merchants knew that they should only begin their journeys on a few favorable days: 1 Crocodile, 1 Monkey, 7 Serpent, or the best, 1 Serpent, called "the straight way." Approaching home, they would delay on the route to wait for a good day sign for the homecoming. Father Durán was amazed that the Aztecs followed the signs of the days rather than the sign of the fields when it came to harvest. He recalled how the people would not harvest their corn, even though it was ready and in danger of rotting, until the correct day had arrived: "They could have gathered the crop earlier, at their leisure, but since the old sorcerer found in his book or almanac that the day had come, he proclaimed it to the people and they went off in great speed." Father Durán clearly did not understand that timing—doing things according to the auguries of the days—was fundamental to maintaining a balanced world.[16]

It was exactly this search for a balanced world that the ancestral warrior-chief Xolotl was hoping to achieve on that distant morning when he climbed the mountain on the edge of the lakes of Mexico, collected those grasses into a circle, and shot his four arrows into the four directions of the universe. These simple and complex symbols and rituals functioned to give order, balance, and power to the Aztec world. It is now time to enter into the center of that world, the great city of Tenochtitlan, which waits for us, shimmering in the lake like a five-quartered jewel in the middle of the Basin.

NOTES

1. Tim Knab, "Geografía del Inframundo," *Estudios de cultura náhuatl* 21 (1991): 31–57, poem quoted from 46.

2. Miguel León-Portilla, *Aztec Thought and Culture* (Norman: University of Oklahoma Press, 1963), 44.

3. Ibid., 45.

4. Diego Durán, *The History of the Indies of New Spain,* trans. Doris Heyden (Norman: University of Oklahoma Press, 1995), 43–44.

5. Alfredo López Austin, *The Human Body and Ideology: Concepts of the Ancient Nahuas,* trans. Thelma Ortiz de Montellano and Bernard Ortiz de Montellano, 2 vols. (Salt Lake City: University of Utah Press, 1988), 1: 52.

6. León-Portilla, *Aztec Thought and Culture,* 90.

7. Ibid., 107–109.

8. See Davíd Carrasco, "The Sacrifice of Tezcatlipoca," in *To Change Place: Aztec Ceremonial Landscapes,* ed. Davíd Carrasco (Niwot: University Press of Colorado, 1992), 42.

9. Bernardino de Sahagún, *Florentine Codex: General History of the Things of New Spain,* ed. and trans. Arthur J. O. Anderson and Charles E. Dibble, introductory vol. and 12 books (Santa Fe, NM: School of American Research and University of Utah, 1950–82), 6: 25.

10. Ibid., 3: 223.

11. Quoted in López Austin, *Human Body and Ideology,* 1: 328.

12. Sahagún, *Florentine Codex,* 7: 27.

13. Ibid.

14. Ibid., 26.

15. Ibid., 29.

16. Elizabeth Hill Boone, *The Aztec World* (Montreal and Washington, DC: St. Remy Press and Smithsonian Books, 1994), 115.

3

MOUNTAINS OF WATER: TENOCHTITLAN AND AZTEC COMMUNITIES

One of the most vivid descriptions of the Aztec city comes from the eyewitness account of Bernal Díaz del Castillo, a Spanish soldier who participated in the invasion and conquest of the capital. Following a long, difficult journey inland from their landfall on the east coast, during which they encountered a number of hostile communities, the Spaniards crossed mountain passes and descended into the blue-green bowl of the Basin of Mexico. Amid the bustle of the population, who were amazed at the arrival of these strangers, the Spaniards marched into the capital city of Tenochtitlan. The following passages constitute a good introduction to the urban geography of the capital.

During the morning, we arrived at a broad Causeway [a road built up from the shallow lake bottom] and continued our march toward Iztapalapa, and when we saw so many cities and villages built in the water and other great towns on dry land and that straight and level Causeway going towards Mexico, we were amazed and said that it was like the enchantments they tell of in the legend of Amadis [a popular chivalrous romance novel of the day], on account of the great towers and cues [pyramids] and buildings rising from the water, and all built of masonry...the appearance of the palaces in which they lodged us! How spacious and well built they were, of beautiful stone work and cedar wood, and the wood of other sweet scented trees, with great rooms and courts, wonderful to behold, covered with awnings of cotton cloth.[1]

BERNAL DÍAZ DEL CASTILLO

Bernal Díaz del Castillo wrote his account of the conquest of the Aztec capital more than 30 years after the actual events. He was living on his plantation in Guatemala and was afraid that his lands would be taken away if his side of the story wasn't heard and believed in Spain.

One reason the Spaniards thought they were dreaming was because of the exquisite sense of nature they experienced.

We went to the orchard and garden, which was such a wonderful thing to see and walk in, that I was never tired of looking at the diversity of the trees, and noting the scent which each one had, and the paths full of roses and flowers, and the many fruit trees and native roses, and the pond of fresh water. There was another thing to observe, that great canoes were able to pass into the garden from the lake through an opening that had been made so that there was no need for their occupants to land. And all was cemented and very splendid with many kinds of stone [monuments] with pictures on them, which gave much to think about.... I say again that I stood looking at it and thought that never in the world would there be discovered other lands such as these, for at that time there was no Peru, nor any thought of it.[2]

The monumentality of the city also led the Spaniards to think they were dreaming. They found huge buildings, abundant wealth, and an enormous number of people. Great crowds came out to see them, filled the lake, and visited the ceremonial centers and marketplaces. Tenochtitlan, with around 200,000 inhabitants, was one of the largest cities in the world at that time. Seville, the largest city known to most of the conquistadors, had only 60,000 people. London had 50,000 inhabitants, and the largest cities on earth, Paris and Constantinople, had around 300,000. And when the Spaniards learned about Motecuhzoma's daily meals, they found that at each meal more than 30 different dishes were prepared by cooks for him and his entourage. The Spaniards got a bird's-eye view of the Aztec metropolis when Cortés and his entourage were escorted into the heart of the community and taken up to the top of one of the great pyramids of the city. They viewed the statues of the gods, the stone of sacrifice, and other sculptures.

Then [Motecuhzoma] took [Cortés] by the hand and told him to look at his great city and all the other cities standing in the water, and the many others on the lands round the lake.... we turned back to look at the great market place and the crowds of people that were in it, some buying and others selling, so that the murmur and hum of their voices and words that [they] used could be heard more than a league [three miles] off. Some of the soldiers among us who had been in many parts of the world, in Constantinople, and all over Italy, in Rome, said that so large a market place and so full of people, and so well regulated and arranged, they had never beheld before.[3]

The Spaniards also saw the great causeways leading into the island, the bridges constructed along the causeways, and the scores of canoes carrying provisions and trade goods coming into the city. They also saw pyramids and "shrines in these cities that looked like gleaming white towers and castles: a marvelous sight. All the houses had flat roofs, and on the causeways were other small towers and shrines built like fortresses."

We glimpse in this account some of the most important buildings, precincts, and ceremonial centers of the Aztec community. This chapter will explore how the Aztecs achieved their general sense of *orientation* in space and time. We shall see that just as the cosmos had a geometry, a pattern of center and regeneration, so the city that stood majestically in Lake Tezcoco imitated to an impressive degree this geometry and pattern. The controlling idea of this chapter is the *repetition of the archetype.* This notion of human society imitating the ways of the gods is an extremely important idea in the study of any culture and religion, but it is particularly helpful in understanding the Aztec cosmos and its city. An archetype is an

An artist's reconstruction of the urban island settlement of Tenochtitlan and Tlatelolco. From the National Museum of Anthropology, Mexico City. (Courtesy of Salvador Guil'liem Arroyo, INAH)

exemplary pattern or model in the form of an idea, image, or event that is believed to originate in the time of myth, legend, ancestors, and heroes.[4] The ancients, whether gods, supernatural beings, or ancestors, created, discovered, and acted out the models, that is, the essential truths and values of the cosmos, which usually appeared first in the time of myth. These truths, values, and actions constitute archetypes or exemplary patterns. The responsibilities of humans are to *discover, imitate, repeat, celebrate,* and *dramatize* the archetypes as a means of ensuring well-being in their society by modeling it on the archetypes. As we shall see, the Aztec worldview was full of archetypes, which they imitated in their rituals and *materialized* in their buildings. In what follows we will examine the various ways that the Aztecs imitated their archetypes by building their capital city and ceremonial center as a model of the cosmos. We will take a short pilgrimage through the city, starting with the *chinampa* gardens at the edge of the great island, moving on through the neighborhoods, marketplaces, palaces, and temples, and then concentrating on the Great Aztec Temple in the center of the ceremonial heart of the city. This will allow us to see how the Aztecs took their worldview and gave it a material form by building and rebuilding the physical and social world of their city, especially the huge ceremonial center, which became the theater for the acting out of their major ideas and policies.

GARDENS ON SWAMPS

One of the most productive agricultural achievements in pre-contact New World history was the *chinampa* system, consisting of long, rectangular gardens made from reclaimed swampland within or connected to the lakes of the Basin of Mexico. The peoples who migrated into Central Mexico in the 13th century C.E. were expert farmers and learned that the success of the *chinampa* system depended in part on the remarkably fertile soils in and around the lakes. During their early years around Lake Tezcoco, the Aztecs developed their farming and military skills as they sought to attach themselves to the stronger city-states. They were eventually rejected by one of the most powerful communities and were driven off the mainland and forced to live on swamps. They responded by raising *chinampa* fields, which meant piling up vertical rows of mud and vegetation between pylons. Then they dug canals in between these raised gardens and planted willow trees on the margins of the fields so that the extensive roots of the willows would serve as effective walls to the earthen gardens. The Aztecs would dredge the mud out of the base of the canals and reapply it to the garden soils to rejuvenate them with nutrients. Thus, each *chinampa* was a slender, rectangular strip of garden land 10 to 25 feet wide by 50 to 300 feet long. Farming families lived on these earthen platforms in houses made of cane, wood, and reeds. The *Matrícula de Tributos* shows several waterways separating *chinampas*, each with the figure and house of an owner whose name appears as a hieroglyph and a Spanish annotation.

Eventually, this system of gardening required a sophisticated bureaucracy to manage the irrigation, planting, and harvesting of corn, amaranth, squash, and beans. It produced huge amounts of foodstuffs and flowers that contributed significantly to the rise and wealth of the city. One scholar describes some of the work:

All plants except maize spent the early weeks of growth in nursery beds where the seedlings were carefully tended. A layer of mud was spread over part of the chinampa and allowed to harden until it could be cut up into rectangular blocks, then the gardener poked a hole in each block, dropped in a seed and covered it with manure. The absence of cattle in the New World meant that there was no stable-manure, and instead the Aztecs used human dung which was collected from the city latrines for sale to the farmers. The seedlings were watered in dry weather and protected against sudden frosts, then at the appropriate time were transplanted to the main beds and mulched with vegetation cut from the swamps.[5]

This system of farming was so productive that parts of the surfaces of three of the lakes (Chalco, Xochimilco, and Tezcoco) were reduced from open lakes into networks of *chinampas* and canals. This also meant that the produce could be easily loaded from the *chinampas* into canoes and taken directly to the urban markets along the lakes and to the markets in Tenochtitlan and Tlatelolco.

The *chinampa* lands were owned not by the individual farmer or his immediate family, but by the *calpolli*, or clan. On the one hand, the farmer and his family who worked the local *chinampa* could enlarge their holding if, for instance, the family increased in size and the *calpolli* owned vacant ground. On the other hand, failure to cultivate land under a farmer's control resulted, after two years, in a warning that one more year of neglect would mean loss of that land.[6] These farmers paid taxes in the form of foodstuffs, flowers, and cloth woven by women. These taxes went to support local temple schools, governors, ministers, the military, and especially the nobles. When the Spaniards came, they called the *chinampas* floating gardens, a name that has persisted to this day. Visitors to Mexico City today can see and ride in small boats through an impressive remnant of the *chinampas* in the southern district of Xochimilco.

This combination of a raised earthen mound surrounded by water represents one of the most interesting archetypes or symbolic models of Aztec society. It reflects the idea, in miniature, that we discussed in the first chapter: the image of Cemanahuac (Land Surrounded by Water) that expressed the general Aztec view of their world. A plot of land, especially a raised plot of land, was an *altepetl*, or water mountain, from the metaphorical phrase *in atl, in tepetl*, meaning "the water(s), the mountain(s)." But *altepetl*, or mountain of water, was the general term used for "an organization of people holding sway over a given territory," "community," or "city" throughout the Nahuatl-speaking world.[7] It referred to the human and social need to organize life around two aspects of nature: a solid piece of ground and life-giving water as well as human solidarity and agricultural resources. A great pyramid with a spring or nearby water resource was an *altepetl*, as was a social community of extended families and workers. The different *altepetl* were organized into larger units called *tlatocayotl*, small local states that were constantly forming alliances, trading, and fighting with one another. Each *tlatocayotl* organized the agricultural schedule, work, and products of its *altepetl* and regulated the work of the *chinampas*. As we shall see later in this chapter, the competing relations between different city-states caused tremendous tensions and conflicts and provided rich resources for the victors. But winners and losers alike depended upon and lived in terms of the gardens on swamps and the archetype of the *altepetl*.

THE IMPERIAL MARKETPLACE

The *chinampas* surrounded significant parts of the city and were abundant along some of the lakeshores. A sizable portion of the plants grown there was shipped to the many city markets. Markets, called *tianquiztli*, were in every sizable neighborhood within the island community and in every town and most villages in the countryside. Villages had market days at five-day intervals, with inhabitants walking as many as 15 miles back and forth in order to meet friends and family, renew friendships, make deals, exchange information, and trade. As one scholar notes, "Certain towns were famous for their specialties: Acolman for edible dogs, Azcapotzalco for birds and slaves, Cholula for featherwork, and Tezcoco for its textiles and painted gourds."[8]

The great island city was divided into five major sections with four great quarters surrounding the fifth and central section—the great ceremonial precinct. Each section had local markets, but the greatest marketplace was in the northwestern section of the capital at a site called Tlatelolco. Both Bernal Díaz del Castillo and Hernán Cortés wrote about the size and bustle of this market in their memoirs. The latter noted that

it was twice as big as that of Salamanca, with arcades all around, where more than sixty thousand people come... to buy and sell, and where every kind of merchandise produced in these lands is found; provisions as well as ornaments of gold and silver, lead, brass, copper, tin, stones, shells, bones, and feathers. They also sell lime, hewn and unhewn stone, adobe bricks, tiles, and cut and uncut woods of various kinds. There is a street where they sell game and birds of every species found in this land: partridges and quails, wild ducks.... They sell rabbits and hares, and stags and small gelded dogs which they breed for eating.[9]

Everything that was grown or made in the empire could be found in this marketplace, which was under the control of the ruling class.

Motecuhzoma watches over the busy marketplace of Tlatelolco in this Diego Rivera mural at the National Palace in Mexico City. (Courtesy of Scott Sessions)

Sellers had to pay a fee to the market superintendent, while supervisors scouted the scene, checking the quality of the goods and the conduct of merchants and customers. The complex exchanges that took place inevitably led to disputes, debates, and just decisions and rewards. To control the marketplace, the Aztecs built a courthouse at Tlatelolco "where ten or twelve persons sit as judges. They preside over all that happens in the markets, and sentence criminals. There are in this square other persons who walk among the people to see what they are selling and the measures they are using."[10] The marketplace was also the place for odd jobbers. People could hire singers, scribes, carpenters, carriers, and prostitutes.

Trade was entirely by barter, but certain items came to have generally agreed values and were used almost as we use currency. For expensive things the units of exchange were mantles, copper axblades, or quills full of gold dust. Cacao beans formed the everyday small change, and dishonest people sometimes counterfeited them by making copies in wax or amaranth dough. Prices are not easy to calculate: Sahagún says that a good-quality mantle was worth 100 cacao beans, although only 33 years after the Conquest the price is quoted as 240–300 beans.[11]

PALACES AND HOMES

Among the interesting symbols on Aztecs maps are the little footprints indicating the movement patterns of walkers through the community. The Aztec person walking or canoeing through the city would view different types of living quarters, from the large, well-built, multiroomed palaces of nobles to the very simple, commoner houses with one or two rooms. The nobles lived in neighborhoods close to the marketplaces and main ceremonial centers in houses that were built on large platforms that were 10 to 40 feet in height. The walls were made of adobe or stone and covered with a stucco that made them glisten with different hues. Nobles of great distinction had two-story houses, which gave them more living space and social prestige. The noble houses or palaces were built to emphasize the insularity of the family who lived there. All the rooms opened onto principal interior courtyards, but none opened onto the street. The Franciscan friar Bernardino de Sahagún, who interviewed Aztec elders several decades after the conquest about the everyday life of the city, found that these palaces were often surrounded by a walled garden, and contained

The palace complex of Nezahualcoyotl at Tezcoco. Nezahualcoyotl speaks to his son in the throne room (top, center), while rulers from tributary communities sit assembled in the courtyard (center). Other rooms or structures include an armory (top right), judges' chambers (top left), facilities for storing tribute (right), and a great hall for the performance of music and dance (left) with a large drum that has a speech glyph coming from the top. (*Mapa Quinatzin*, redrawn by Scott Sessions)

separate living rooms for men and women, an anteroom, a dining room, a kitchen, servant quarters, and meeting rooms.[12] The doorways were closed by colorful curtains, mats of reeds, or cloth woven with decorative bells.

We know from Spanish accounts that some of these palaces were huge. When they first arrived in the capital, the entire Spanish troop of around 400 men were housed in and around the palace of the ruler, Axayacatl. We have two drawings of royal palaces that give us a basic sense of how they were organized.

One drawing is of the palace of Nezahualcoyotl, the ruler of Tezcoco who collected tributary payments from more than 40 villages and presided over activities in more than 300 rooms. Even
though we cannot tell whether this drawing shows one or two
stories, the king and his son Nezahualpilli (the stargazer mentioned at the beginning of chapter 1) sit in the throne room at the
top. In the large central courtyard are seated the chiefs and lords
of allied towns who paid some kind of tribute (taxes) to Tezcoco.
Other rooms surrounding the courtyard or attached to the throne
room include a warriors' room, a judges' room, storehouses, and
a temple for religious ceremonies. Feet marks lead toward the
two fires in the central patio. One 16th-century European visitor
wrote about visiting a palace: "I walked till I was tired, and never
saw the whole of it. It was the custom to place at the entrance
of all the houses of the Lords very large halls and sitting rooms
around a great patio, and there was one so great that it could hold
three thousand persons."[13]

Aztec nobles, like nobles everywhere, had the means to build
enjoyable environments to live within or adjacent to. There were
gardens, bathing pools, sculpture gardens, and at least two zoos
attached to the rulers' palaces in Tenochtitlan and Tezcoco. Bernal
Díaz del Castillo wrote about Motecuhzoma's "Aviary":

I am forced to abstain from enumerating every kind of bird that was there
and its peculiarity, for there was everything from the Royal Eagle and
other smaller eagles, and many other birds of great size, down to tiny
birds of many-colored plumage, also the birds from which they take the
rich plumage which they use in their green featherwork...and there are
other birds which have feathers of five colors—green, red, white, yellow
and blue...then there were parrots....From all these birds they plucked
the feathers when the time was right....In this house that I have spoken
of there is a great tank of fresh water and in it there are other sorts of birds
with long stilted legs, with body, wings and tail all red.[14]

As we can see, the traveler through the city would pass through
the *chinampas* and the houses of farmers, craftspeople, local temple communities, visit the great marketplace, and get a protected
glimpse of the nobles' homes and the palaces of the rulers. In a real
sense, all roads led into the city of Tenochtitlan, as merchants, allied
rulers, enemy warriors, artists, and poets were drawn to the island
settlement.

TEMPLE PRECINCTS

Some of the most important ritual buildings were the local and central temple precincts, which were usually administered by a core of priests. One important shrine was the Coacalco, which the ruler, Motecuhzoma, had built to house the gods of all the allied communities. In this way, we can say that even the gods traveled to the Aztec capital and had a home there. But the most important humanly constructed sacred space in the entire empire was the immense ceremonial center in the heart of the capital. It measured 440 meters on all four sides and contained more than 80 buildings, including temples, schools, skull racks, sweat baths, priestly living quarters, the Eagle Warriors Precinct, and other buildings. Hernán Cortés described the great precinct in this manner:

Among these temples there is one...so large that within the precincts, which are surrounded by a very high wall, a town of some five hundred inhabitants could easily be built. All round inside this wall there are very elegant quarters with very large rooms and corridors where their priests live. There are as many as forty towers...and the most important of these towers is higher than that of the cathedral of Seville. They are...well constructed in both their stone and woodwork...all the stone work inside the chapels where they keep their idols is in high relief, with figures and little houses, and the woodwork is likewise of relief and painted with monsters and other figures and designs.[15]

A map of the city shows the prominence of this sacred precinct. This map was drawn by Cortés's mapmaker and depicts the four quarters of the city and the grand ceremonial center in the middle of the image. Among the buildings was Tlalocan, a fasting temple in honor of the rain god; the Temple of the White Cinteotl, a corn goddess in whose honor captives with skin sores were sacrificed; the Huitztepehualco temple, where the offering priests scattered the thorns they used in autosacrifice; the Tzompantli (Skull Rack), where severed heads were strung up after sacrifices; Atempan, where child sacrificial victims called *tlacateteuhti* (human paper streamers) were assembled before their deaths; and the Temalacatl, a round circular stone to which the victim was tied before being attacked by a series of Aztec warriors and having his heart extracted. There was also the Tlamatzinco Calmecac, a temple school where the fire priest lived, offered incense, and taught his young students. All these buildings were important, but they paled in comparison to the Great Temple.

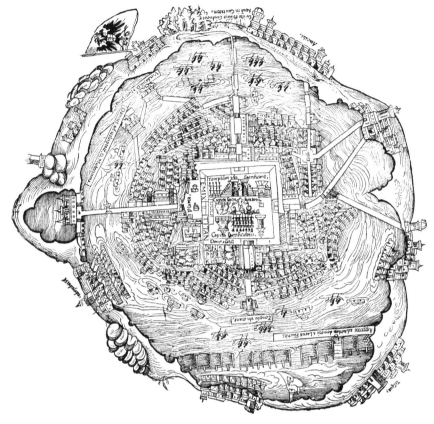

Engraved map of Tenochtitlan, embellished with several European pictorial conventions, from the first edition of Cortés's letters, *Praeclara Ferdi-
nandi Cortesii de Nova Maris Oceani Hispania Narratio* (Nuremberg, 1524).

THE FOUNDATION OF HEAVEN:
THE GREAT TEMPLE

The Aztec poets used to sing praises for their capital. One song
said, in part:

Proud of itself
is the City of Mexico-Tenochtitlan.
Here no one fears to die in war.
This is our glory.
This is Your Command,
O Giver of Life!
Have this in mind, O princes,
do not forget it.

Who could conquer Tenochtitlan?
Who could shake the foundation of the heavens?[16]

The city was celebrated as a proud, invincible place, the foundation of the vertical structure of the cosmos described in the previous chapter. This statement constitutes the idea mentioned earlier: *archetype and repetition*. The city is constructed as an imitation, or at least an image, of the cosmos in this passage, ordered by the Giver of Life and located at the base of heaven as a kind of anchor that steadies the cosmos above it.

The organization of the city is pictured in an image from the *Codex Mendoza* that shows the city at the moment of its foundation. Surrounding the island city is a series of 51 blue boxes, each containing a year sign. This calendar consists of four year signs—House, Rabbit, Reed, and Flint Knife—and 13 numbers depicted as dots. This combination results in a calendar round of 52 years, the number resulting from the four day signs—or, in this case, year signs—interacting with 13 numbers. Within this space are two types of activity: the foundation of the city and the early conquests of the Aztecs. The city is divided into four major sections, with canals crossing at the central area where the god, Huitzilopochtli, is perched on a blooming cactus growing from a stylized rock. Below the rock is a shield covered with seven eagle down feathers and attached to six arrows. Remember how the Aztec worldview emphasized, again and again, that the cosmos was a four-quartered structure organized around a center. That is the archetype. This image shows that the design of the city was a repetition of that exemplary pattern. The site of the eagle on the cactus was where the Aztecs constructed the first shrine to their god Huitzilopochtli (Southern Hummingbird or Hummingbird on the Left). It provided them with a center, an *axis mundi*, a place they could rely on, and it eventually became the greatest temple in the empire, a structure the Aztecs called Coatepec (Serpent Mountain). When the Mexica had arrived at the end of their long migration, Huitzilopochtli reappeared to the people and told them to build their "city that is to be queen, that is to rule over all others in the country. There we shall receive other kings and nobles who will recognize Tenochtitlan as the supreme capital."[17] In fact, the city did become the supreme capital, as Hernán Cortés wrote back to Emperor Charles V: "The great city of Temixtitan [Tenochtitlan] is built on the salt lake, and no matter by what road you travel there are two leagues from the main body of the city to the mainland. There are four artificial causeways leading to it,

Founding of Tenochtitlan. The outlying boxes are year signs, beginning at the upper left-hand corner with the sign 2 House, continuing counterclockwise and ending top center with the sign 13 reed. (*Codex Mendoza*, MS. Arch Selden. A.1, fol. 2r, courtesy of the Bodleian Library, Oxford, England)

and each is as wide as two cavalry lances. The city itself is as big as Seville or Cordoba."[18] According to Aztec myth, the god Huitzilopochtli ordered the people first to divide the city into four main sections, but also to build a central shrine in his honor.

In the image from the *Codex Mendoza*, 10 men are distributed throughout the four sections of the new settlement; each has his name glyph attached to his head with a thread. The leader of the group is immediately to the left of a giant cactus. He is distinguished by his elaborate hairstyle, the speech glyph in front of his mouth signifying that he is the chief speaker, and the woven mat he sits on, signifying political authority. Two important buildings are depicted: the skull rack upon which the decapitated heads of enemy warriors were hung, and the small house above the eagle, representing either the first shrine to Huitzilopochtli or the Men's House, the place of consultation and decision making. Different types of vegetation are scattered around the four quarters.

Two scenes of battle and conquest are below the central image. The buildings are temples that are tipped and burning, each attached to an image or place sign. The place sign on the left is Colhuacan (Curved Hill), whereas the one on the right is Tenayuca (Rampart Hill). The tipped and burning temples represent conquest. These are two of the first communities that the Aztecs conquered. It is interesting that a tipped and burning temple signifies the defeat of not just a religion or group of priests but of *an entire community*. Two proportionally larger Aztec warriors are shown subduing enemy warriors from the two conquered towns by placing their shields on their heads. It is interesting to note that the shields rest on the part of the head where the *tonalli* or soul of the warrior resides. The idea is that the soul, power, or essence of the warrior has been conquered, just as the soul or essence of the town, with its temple in flames, has been destroyed.

THE BIRTH OF THE WARRIOR GOD

To explore the idea of the repetition of the archetype, let us return to the shrine of Huitzilopochtli. This first humble shrine grew to be a massive pyramidal base with two major shrines on top. There is an impressive myth about the origin of this temple that shows how an exemplary event among the gods became a model for ritual imitation among humans.

The Aztecs said that at a sacred site called Coatepec (Serpent Mountain), the mother of the gods, Coatlicue (Serpent Skirt), was

The Myth of Coatepec is presented in these two 16th-century drawings. On the left, Coatlicue gives birth to Huitzilopochtli, who emerges fully grown and ready for battle. On the right, Huitzilopochtli dismembers his sister, Coyolxauhqui, and attacks two other siblings at Serpent Mountain. (*Florentine Codex*, from *Historia general de las cosas de Nueva España*, ed. Francisco del Paso y Troncoso. Madrid: Hauser y Menet, 1905)

sweeping out the temple. A ball of down feathers floated down and landed on the floor. She picked it up and put it in her blouse. After finishing her temple cleaning ritual, she searched for the feathers; discovering that they had disappeared, she realized immediately that they had magically made her pregnant. The news spread that she had somehow become pregnant in the temple, and people became angry.

As she was the mother of the gods, she already had many children. In fact, the myth tells that she had 400 children, a number that meant *innumerable.* One of her children was the female warrior Coyolxauhqui (Painted Bells), who organized the others into a ferocious military party. These brothers and sisters, known as the Centzon Huitznahua (Four Hundred Southerners), decided to prepare for war, march to the temple, and kill the mother goddess. The song went: "They were very angry, they were very agitated, as if the heart had gone out of them. Coyolxauhqui incited them, she inflamed the anger of her brothers, so that they should kill her mother."[19] A description of their preparations and long march includes an episode in which one of Coatlicue's sons, Cuahuitlicac, snuck out of the warriors' camp at night and traveled to the mountain to warn the mother. When he told her that the attack was coming, she became frightened, but a voice from her womb replied to the messenger, "Take care, be watchful, my uncle, for I know well what I must do."[20]

The huge war party marched over several days to the mountain and began its assault. "They were very robust, well equipped, adorned as for war, they distributed among themselves their paper garb, the insignia, the nettles, the streamers of colored paper, they tied little bells on the calves of their legs, the bells called *oyohaulli*. Their arrows had barbed points. Then they began to move."[21] Coyolxauhqui, in a state of berserk anger, led the charge up the mountain and was about to kill Coatlicue when the latter gave birth to a fully grown warrior, Huitzilopochtli, the young god of war. He armed himself with his serpent of fire, then turned and faced the approaching Coyolxauhqui. Swiftly, he beheaded her, dismembered her body, and sent it flailing and rolling down the mountainside. He then turned his divine anger on the other 399 gods. "He pursued them, he chased them, all around the mountain…four times…with nothing could they defend themselves…he drove them away, he humbled them, he destroyed them, he annihilated them."[22] Only a few escaped while he tore the insignia and emblems from the warrior costumes of the defeated and put them on himself.

The texts ends with the claim that the "Aztecs venerated him, they made sacrifices to him…and his cult came from there, from Coatepec, the Mountain of the Serpent."[23] This last claim means that this event was viewed as a model, a kind of blueprint as to how the Aztec warriors and priests were to act in relation to enemies who came to fight against them in Tenochtitlan. In fact, as we shall now see, the entire Great Temple was a replica of this divine drama.

What is this myth telling us about the Aztecs' sense of space, temple, war, and destiny within their general worldview? On one level, the story is about the daily drama of sunrise as understood by the Aztecs. Serpent Mountain (Coatepec) represents the land of the Aztecs. The body of the earth is Serpent Woman (Coatlicue), who gives birth each day to the sun (Huitzilopochtli) by launching a war against the moon (his sister, Coyolxauhqui) and the stars (his 400 siblings, the Centzon Huitznahua), and each day the sun is victorious. In this way, the myth tells of an exemplary pattern in nature. Sunrise is seen as a military conquest of closely related stars. It is also possible that the story tells of an actual war between two groups during the early years of the Aztec culture. If so, the myth tells of an exemplary pattern in history: the Aztec ancestors ferociously conquer their enemies and sacrifice them at the center of the world. Regardless, the Aztecs decided to celebrate this drama at their most sacred shrine, the Templo Mayor. It was an archetypal place where exemplary ceremonies were carried out.

The shrine was called Coatepec (Serpent Mountain) by the Aztecs. It consisted, as noted, of a huge pyramidal base with two stairways leading up to the shrine of Huitzilopochtli on one side and that of Tlaloc the rain god on the other. Monumental serpent heads at the foot of the staircases were connected to the balustrades to give the impression that the serpent bodies extended upward on either side of the stairs. At the top of the southern stairway stood Huitzilopochtli's temple, whose interior walls were covered with murals and with carvings in relief. The shrine held statues of the god. A huge, 11-foot circular stone image of the dismembered Coyolxauhqui lay at the foot of the stairway leading up to the war god's temple. This means that this part of the temple was a *stone replica* of the myth, or what can be called a *material idea*. Huitzilopochtli, the sun, sits triumphantly at the top of the mountain (and the sky), while the dismembered sister, Coyolxauhqui, lies defeated and dismembered at the bottom. This is an example of the repetition of the archetype, the imitation in architecture of a divine drama. As will become apparent in the discussion of human sacrifice, many warriors were killed at this temple, and their bodies were rolled down the stairs in defeat and humiliation just as Coyolxauhqui was in the myth.

THE TEMPLO MAYOR AS A CONTAINER OF EMPIRE

The Templo Mayor was one of the main targets of the Spanish soldiers and priests. They knew that the Aztec rulers and their gods prized the site above all others and that to conquer the city and its people they had to destroy the temple. We have several eyewitness accounts of battles fought on the stairways and the summit of the Great Temple, which the Aztec warriors and priests defended with their lives. When the Spaniards were finally successful at capturing the temple, they took the huge statue of Huitzilopochtli down the steps and buried it somewhere in the Basin of Mexico. Then, using cannon fire and Indian laborers, they had the top four-fifths of the temple blown apart and dismantled. This ragged spot was then filled in with earth and rubble and used as the foundation for Spanish buildings. In fact, part of the rubble from the Great Temple was used to build the Spanish cathedral nearby.

Most of the religious practices and sacred objects of the Great Temple were ignored or forgotten for centuries. A dramatic discovery changed this in 1978, when workers discovered a huge circular stone with unusual markings on it. When archaeologists came to the site and examined the stone, they realized that it was a carved sculpture of Coyolxauhqui, in mint condition, depicting her dismembered body, sacred clothes, precious blood, and magnificent headdress. This was an astonishing moment in American archaeology because the divine songs about the battle between Huitzilopochtli and Coyolxauhqui had been known since the middle of the 16th century, when the Spanish priests were told the sacred prayers by surviving Aztecs. Now, the actual stone carving of the sacrificed goddess had come to light. Equally impressive was what the archaeologists found beneath the stone. Excavating down to the level of the lake bed, they found caches of ritual objects, including masks of gods, human sacrifices, greenstone jewels, animals, urns, and vases. The president of Mexico, whose office was literally next door to the discoveries, ordered the complete excavation of the site, which uncovered the Great Temple itself.

Coyolxauhqui Stone. (Courtesy of Salvador Guil'liem Arroyo, INAH)

MOTECUHZOMA

The director of excavations at the Great Aztec Temple was Eduardo Matos Moctezuma and people often ask him if he is an actual descendent of the last Aztec ruler, Motecuhzoma Xocoyotzin (the Younger), who reigned from 1502 to 1520. Mexicans refer to Matos Moctezuma as Motecuhzoma the Third because the first Motecuhzoma (Ilhuicamina) ruled the Aztecs from 1440 to 1469.

Immediately, under the guidance of Mexico's leading archaeologist, Eduardo Matos Moctezuma, a detailed plan was formulated for the excavation, restoration, and interpretation of the site. Over the next 15 years, the citizens of Mexico and archaeologists throughout the world watched in continuous astonishment as more than seven complete rebuildings and five modifications of the Great Temple were excavated. The Aztecs had rebuilt their temple like a series of superimposed boxes, each one covering the earlier one. Month after month, the archaeologists were amazed as more than 135 buried caches containing more than 8,000 objects were discovered, restored, and eventually put on display at the Museum of the Great Temple adjacent to the site. A series of exhibitions of these objects was mounted in museums around the world, including exhibitions in Rome, Paris, New York, Denver, San Francisco, London, Chicago, and Tijuana. One exhibition at the Denver Museum of Natural History, called "Aztec: The World of Moctezuma," was viewed by more than 800,000 people. The show's organization accounted in part for its success. Like the reader of this chapter, the visitor to the museum was led on a pilgrimage through Tenochtitlan, beginning with a view of the great city from the mountain where Xolotl shot his arrows, moving through the *chinampas* to the great marketplace, past the ruler's visage into the sacred precincts, and finally to the Great Temple, and even the treasures underneath its floors.

CENTER AND PERIPHERY

One of the most vivid and exciting aspects of the excavation of the Great Temple was the discovery of the buried offerings in the floors, stairways, and shrines. These offerings demonstrated that the city and its central shrine were considered, far and wide, to be *the center of the social and symbolic world*. Each *altepetl* and *tlatocayotl* under Aztec control was forced to pay tribute, a kind of tax in the form of

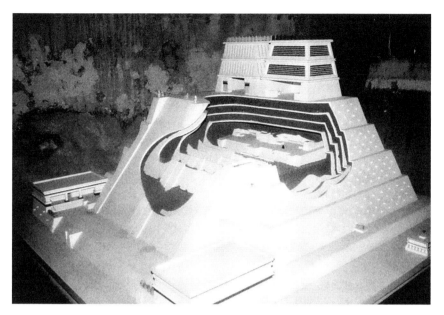

Model depicting the various successive, twin-structured rebuildings of the Great Temple, which served as a container of offerings from throughout the empire. (Courtesy of Lawrence G. Desmond)

foodstuffs, clothes, jewelry, cloaks, warriors' costumes, masks, animals, and more to the capital. Some of the finest objects were actually paid to the gods who resided at Coatepec, the Great Temple. More than 135 offering caches of this symbolic tribute have been uncovered at strategic points around the base of the pyramid at every stage of its construction. When the archaeologists began to explore these caches, they were impressed by the ways in which the Aztecs located and organized the boxes and the objects within them.

The management of the inner space revealed that the Aztecs had used a symbolic language to arrange the contents of these caches. First, it was clear that the offerings were actually gifts given to the gods, especially the great gods, Huitzilopochtli and Tlaloc, who reside at the temple. These included stone masks, statues of various deities, sacrificial knives made of obsidian and flint, miniature houses and canoes, large incense burners, tools, musical instruments, ear spools, nose plugs and breastplates, human sacrifices, animal sacrifices, greenstone necklaces, and much more. Second, it was especially impressive that at least 70 percent of these gifts came from foreign territories at the edges of the Aztec empire. The majority of the objects came from the Gulf Coast region and parts of the present states of Oaxaca, Puebla, and Guerrero. For instance, there were many animals (more than 200 species from among 11 zoological groups), including pumas, dogs, crocodiles, birds, fish, and many different types of shells. Third, and most important, it appears that the cosmic image of three levels was often *replicated* within a single offering, where sand from the bottom of the ocean (underworld) supported animals and human-made objects (human world), which supported animals and symbols representing the sky and the celestial spheres (overworld). Fourth, it is very significant that the offerings not only represented the peripheral communities as well as this sort of cosmic language, but also the Aztec reverence for the honored past—the great Toltec and Teotihuacan civilizations. In a number of caches, the Aztecs buried objects that they themselves had excavated from the earlier ceremonial centers of the City of the Gods and Tula.

In a surprising twist to this pattern of center and periphery, recent archaeological work at the site has revealed that a number of the objects originally believed to have originated in distant towns and workshops and then transported to the Templo Mayor were

Offering excavated at the Great Temple containing coral, shells, ceramic vessels, and stone sculptures. (Courtesy of Salvador Guil'liem Arroyo, INAH)

actually *made within the Aztec capital as imitations of the artistic styles of distant, allied communities*. Yet even with this new angle on these material goods, we see that the center of the world, through imitating the periphery, achieves a form of control over both home and hinterland.

TWIN TEMPLES

Thus far we have noted the prominence of the war god, Huitzilo-pochtli, at the Great Temple and his archetypal role. But there was also a shrine to the great god Tlaloc, the rain god responsible for the agricultural well-being of the entire community. Tlaloc was one of the great creator gods, primordial child of the Dual God, the Giver of Life. Tlaloc also was an old god of Mesoamerica, much older than the Aztecs. In order for them to have a sacred shrine that represented not only their own wandering traditions (Huitzilopochtli), they also needed to appropriate the god of all the *altepetl*, the god of

Tlaloc is depicted on this beautiful ceramic vessel found at the Great Temple. (Courtesy of Salvador Guil'liem Arroyo, INAH)

Model reconstruction of the Great Temple and the ceremonial precinct of Tenochtitlan. (Courtesy of Salvador Guil'liem Arroyo, INAH)

the earth and landscape, who represented the primordiality of the land. One of the most impressive aspects of the excavation of the Great Temple is that there are scores of images of Tlaloc scattered throughout the offerings buried in the site, but not a single image of Huitzilopochtli. Tlaloc vases, urns, and statues are prominent, showing that the visage and power of the god were present everywhere and visible to the people who made offerings to him.

Another remarkable characteristic of the Great Temple related to Tlaloc is the Twin Temples. This feature of having two shrines on top of a pyramidal base appears to be prominent among, if not unique to, the Aztecs. We know from the mythology that, just as Huitzilopochtli's side of the Great Temple was a replica of a mythical mountain (Coatepec), Tlaloc's side replicated another mythical mountain, that of Tlalocan, the paradise where the rain gods lived in perpetual fertility and abundant greenness, dispensing life-giving rains and life-taking floods to humankind. In this way, the Great Temple was the imitation of two archetypes—the mythical mountains of Coatepec and Tlalocan.

THE GREAT TEMPLE AS A MOUNTAIN OF BLOOD

It makes sense that a place that carries the prestige of an archetype, such as the Templo Mayor, will be important not only at the beginning but at the end of a community's life. And so it is with Coatepec and Tlalocan. Two episodes reveal how the destiny and destruction of the Aztec city were tied up with the destiny and destruction of the Great Temple. The first appears in a series of omens that were reported to have appeared in the Basin of Mexico some 10 years before the Spaniards arrived, announcing that the future was bleak. According to the informants of Bernardino de Sahagún (discussed in chapter 1), a series of signs appeared in the sky, lake, and earth warning the people that their world was coming to an end. One omen was a rip in the sky that bled fire onto the city. Another was a comet that flew across the lake in a counter-sunwise direction. Then, a mysterious fire spontaneously broke out in Huitzilopochtli's temple and burned it to the ground, causing great consternation among the priests and rulers. They became frightened that the world was coming to an end, for as noted earlier in this chapter, a tipped and burning temple meant the fall of a community. When some years passed and life went on as normal, the omen was partly forgotten.

But the most impressive example of how the Aztecs used the temple to repeat the archetypes of Huitzilopochtli's myth is found in the account of Bernal Díaz del Castillo that began this chapter. During the military battle for the capital, the Spaniards laid siege to the city. The Aztecs began to starve, and in a desperate move sacrificed a number of Spaniards to Huitzilopochtli at the temple in the heart of the city. Díaz del Castillo witnessed this sacrifice and describes it in his report (which will be examined in detail in chapter 7, where human sacrifice is discussed). He witnessed Spanish soldiers being dragged up the steps of the Great Temple toward the shrine of Huitzilopochtli. Once at the top, they were stripped of their clothes, dressed as Aztec *teteo ixiptla* (images of gods), and sacrificed. He wrote: "And with some knives they sawed open their chests and drew out their palpitating hearts and offered them to the idols that were there, and they kicked the bodies down the steps, and the Indian butchers who were waiting below cut off the arms and feet and flayed the skin off the faces, and prepared it afterwards like glove leather with the beards on."[24]

Some aspects of this amazing ritual, such as the cannibalism and flaying of skin, will be interpreted in a later chapter. But given what we know about archetypes, repetition, the Great Temple, and Coatepec, it should be clear what the Aztecs were up to. Just as in the myth of Huitzilopochtli's birth on Serpent Mountain, when enemies came to attack the temple and its gods, the Spaniards were perceived as the Centzon Huitznahua, the forces of night who had invaded the sacred city and its precincts intent on destroying the Aztec world. And just as Huitzilopochtli appeared, attacked, sacrificed, and dismembered the invaders and threw them down the temple stairs in an act of solar conquest, so the Spaniards were sacrificed at the summit, dismembered, and rolled down the steps, imitating the fate of Coyolxauhqui, who had dared to rebel and attempted to destroy the temple, the city, and its people.

The *altepetl*, the mountain of water, became a mountain of solar conquest and bloody sacrifice.

NOTES

1. Bernal Díaz del Castillo, *The History of the Conquest of New Spain,* ed. Davíd Carrasco (Albuquerque: University of New Mexico Press, 2008), 156.

2. Ibid., 156–57.

3. Ibid., 176–77.

4. Davíd Carrasco, *Quetzalcoatl and the Irony of Empire: Myths and Prophecies in the Aztec Tradition,* rev. ed. (Boulder: University Press of Colorado, 2000), especially chapter 3, which outlines the relations between archetype and imitation. See also Mircea Eliade, *The Myth of the Eternal Return, or Cosmos and History,* trans. Willard F. Trask (Princeton, NJ: Princeton University Press, 1954).

5. Warwick Bray, *Everyday Life of the Aztecs* (London: B. T. Batsford, 1968), 116.

6. Ibid., 117.

7. James Lockhart, *Nahuas after the Conquest: A Social and Cultural History of the Indians of Central Mexico, Sixteenth through Eighteenth Centuries* (Stanford, CA: Stanford University Press, 1992), 14.

8. Bray, *Everyday Life of the Aztecs,* 111.

9. Hernán Cortés, *Letters from Mexico,* ed. and trans. Anthony Pagden (New Haven, CT: Yale University Press, 1986), 103.

10. Ibid., 105.

11. Bray, *Everyday Life of the Aztecs,* 112.

12. Ibid., 104.

13. Ibid., 106.

14. Díaz del Castillo, *History of the Conquest,* 170.

15. Cortés, *Letters from Mexico,* 105–6.

16. Quoted in Miguel León-Portilla, *Pre-Columbian Literatures of Mexico* (Norman: University of Oklahoma Press, 1969), 87.

17. Diego Durán, *The History of the Indies of New Spain,* trans. Doris Heyden (Norman: University of Oklahoma Press, 1995), 43–44.

18. Cortés, *Letters from Mexico,* 102.

19. León-Portilla, *Pre-Columbian Literatures,* 44–45.

20. Ibid., 45.

21. Ibid.

22. Ibid., 47.

23. Ibid., 48.

24. Díaz del Castillo, *History of the Conquest,* 287.

4

EDUCATION AND THE AZTEC LIFE CYCLE: FROM BIRTH TO DEATH AND BEYOND

Niquauhtlamelaoa, tiquauhtlamelaoa = I am a fruitless tree, you are a fruitless tree. This is said when I study something but cannot learn it. It is exactly as if I were a fruit tree that bears no fruit.[1]

From the moment of childbirth, Aztec parents were greatly concerned that their children avoid becoming "fruitless trees" and instead become productive citizens. They believed that infants were exposed to the greatest dangers, and that a child could be invaded by either natural or supernatural sources. In fact, very young children who had not yet eaten corn were considered pure, able to communicate with gods in direct ways. After children had eaten corn, which meant that they had begun to internalize the fruits of the earth and the cultivation of nature by human effort (and also to internalize the forces of death because something of the earth had been killed to feed them), education was the key to gaining strength and knowledge in order to one day become part of the economic and social community. Aztec children would receive both general and specialized instruction from parents, priests, teachers, and other members of the community through a variety of means and institutions.

The direction this education would take was determined early in the child's life, in fact 20 days after birth. At this time, the parents chose what kind of education they wanted their child to have and then took the infant to the appropriate temple or school. The parents of a child destined for the priesthood took gifts of cloaks, loincloths, and food to the priests at the *calmecac,* where they presented the infant. The following prayer was said:

Our lord, lord of the near, of the nigh, [this child] is your property, he is your venerable child. We place him under your power, your protection with other venerable children; because you will teach him, educate him, because you will make eagles, make ocelots of them, because you instruct him for our mother, our father, Tlaltecuhtli, Tonatiuh. Now we dedicate him to Yohualli, to Ehecatl, Tlacatl, Telpochtli, Yaotzin, Titlacahuan, to Tezcatlipoca.[2]

The pact between the family, the gods, and the temple was sealed by incisions made in the bodies of the children. These physical marks were visible signs of a spiritual change. The lower lips of boys were cut open and a jewel was inserted. Girls were initiated when small cuts were made with obsidian blades in their breasts and hips. These incisions signified that they had been initiated into the lifelong educational process upon which their lives depended.

This prayer reaffirmed what all Aztec parents knew and what all Aztec children were required to learn: that their true parents were the gods, that individuals were required to live in relation to the gods and the social group, and that education was the key to bringing about the transformation from childhood to adult responsibility and becoming a "fruitful tree." Another passage says of the schools that "in the *calmecac,* people are corrected, people are instructed, it is the place of a chaste life, a place of reverence, a place of knowledge, of wisdom, of goodness, a place of virtues, a place without filth, without dust."[3] One of the most effective strategies for ensuring that a child would be a "fruitful tree" was to engage in the various rituals, ritual instructions, and periodic *rites of passage* that individuals underwent throughout the Aztec life cycle. These rites of passage not only promoted the controlled development and maturation of Aztec children, but also ensured that physical changes corresponded with spiritual changes and powers throughout their lives.

Rites of passage are fundamental to the cohesive life of any community and will serve as the guiding idea of this chapter on education and the Aztec life cycle. The value of utilizing the rites of passage approach comes from understanding what rituals can do. First, they organize the biological changes of the life cycle into specific, meaningful social events. They give clear order to subtle but vital changes in the human body. Second, they locate these changes within the powers of the cosmos by bringing the human into direct contact with gods and spirits. Third, they relate the elders and their traditional teachings to the evolving humans under their care. Every human being goes through a series of biological and cultural changes. People are conceived, born, given names, taught how to eat and speak; they play, become sexual beings, marry, raise children, fight, grow old, and die. Life is a series of transitions, and it is important to see how a society organizes those transitions through ritual performances. One way is through rites of passage. In what follows we will study a series of biological and social changes, including childbirth, infancy, work, schooling, marriage, parenting, death, and the afterlife.

CHILDBIRTH

In a scene from the *Codex Mendoza* of how a child was treated and named soon after birth, a mother who has recently given birth is seated next to a cradle where her infant lies with four flower symbols above it. Four days after birth, the midwife, who played a major role in Aztec culture, took the naked child to the courtyard of the house, where a ritual cleansing took place. The midwife had prepared a mat of rushes or reeds with a small earthen tub of water, and she bathed the infant. She breathed upon the water, made the child taste it, touched the baby's chest and head with the water and said, "My youngest one, my beloved youth....Enter, descend into the blue water, the yellow water....Approach thy mother Chalchiuhtlicue, Chalchiuhtlatonac! May she receive thee....May she cleanse thy heart; may she make it fine, good. May she give thee fine, good conduct!"

The bath scene has two sets of symbols, above and below the pan of water. The symbols below the bath scene are the female symbols, consisting of a distaff with a spindle, a basket, and a broom, signifying the girl's future role as the keeper of the home. She will be educated into the labor and art of weaving, which was an invaluable part of Aztec life. The act of sweeping, in order to purify and to contribute to good health, was both a practical and a ritual activity associated with women. Aztec homes were extremely clean, as were the temples, where ritual sweeping was done in service to the gods. The spindle was also a fertility symbol associated with the capacity of females to bear children. For instance, two spindles attached to cotton fillets were part of the headdress of a fertility goddess. One

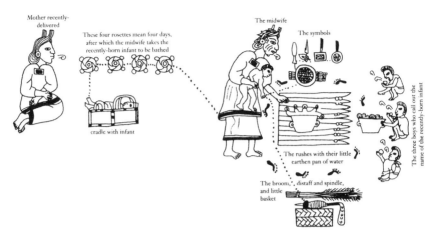

Ritual for newborn infants. (*Codex Mendoza,* courtesy of Frances F. Berdan and Patricia Reiff Anawalt)

Aztec riddle went, "What is that which becomes pregnant in only one day? The spindle." The symbols above the bath scene are the male objects used by the infant's father, which could be a shield and arrows if the father was a warrior, or wood, metal, or feathers if the father was a woodcarver, a metalworker, or a featherworker. There is also the symbol of the painter of books for boys whose fathers were scribes. A little shield with four arrows just above the rushes and pan of water, called *mitl chimalli* (shield and arrows), is an Aztec metaphor meaning war; each arrow represented one of the four cardinal directions of the universe.

When Aztec infants were taken for their first bath, the appropriate symbols were placed in their hands. If the child were a boy, a shield would be placed in his left hand and an arrow in his right hand. After the bath, the midwife would tell the three boys who assisted her to call out loudly the new name of the baby who had just been cleaned. Then the umbilical cord was taken and buried with the symbols the child had carried to the bath. For boys, the umbilical cord and the little shield and arrows were carried to a battlefield and buried in the ground. For girls, the umbilical cord and a female symbol would be buried at home under the *metate*, or stone for grinding corn.

There are four important characteristics in this scene. First, childbirth was an extremely important event, and children were valued deeply in Aztec society. One Spanish priest who had lived among the Aztecs for several years stated that he had never seen another society in which children were so highly valued. The midwife addressed the child with such marvelous phrases as "precious necklace, precious feather, precious green stone, precious bracelet, precious turquoise, thou were created in the place of duality, in the place above the nine heavens."[4]

Second, the Aztecs placed a strong emphasis on birth as the beginning of a lifetime of transitions. The newborn child was moved outside to the patio, cleaned, introduced to the gods, and given a name. A prayer was then offered to Chalchiuhtlicue, the goddess of precious waters, fertility, and life. At this time, children were identified, through the objects they were given, with the roles they would play as adults. The umbilicus, the body organ that linked mother and child, would be taken and buried (planted) in the territory where the infant would experience the most powerful events of his or her life. Also, the key decision as to what type of education the child would receive took place 16 days after the bathing and naming ceremony.

Third, the midwife played a crucial role in the momentous transition of childbirth. It was she, and not the mother, who bathed, announced the name, and addressed the child with information about the gods, the world, and the expectations for the new human being. This suggests the presence of a large family unit where a number of adults would take responsibility for the child's well-being.

Fourth, there is a clear emphasis on gender division at the very first ritual of one's life. At this time, one was clearly designated as male or female and given the appropriate social symbols that strengthened this division between gender roles. For instance, if the child were male, the midwife would give his umbilical cord to the distinguished warriors, "those wise in war," to bury in the midst of the plains where warfare was practiced. If the child were female, the umbilical cord would be buried "there by the hearth, thus she signified that the woman was to go nowhere. Her task was the home life, life by the fire, by the grinding stone."[5] Again and again, the prayers and sayings about the newborn that have come down to us begin: "And if it were a female" or "And if it were a male," with different instructions in each case. Let us explore these four characteristics by focusing on the work and prayers of the midwife during the process of pregnancy and childbirth.

THE MIDWIFE

To understand just how important childbirth was to the Aztecs, consider the preparations made by the parents of the expectant married couple during the final months of pregnancy. During the seventh or eighth month the family held a small feast, and a compatible midwife was sought out who would assist in the birth of the baby. These preparations involved eloquent speeches between the soon-to-be grandparents, who exhorted the midwife to take her job seriously and to realize how much love, compassion, and concern they had for the birth. The midwife responded, "Verily I grasp, I accept your spirit, your word, and your weeping, your compassion with which ye weep, ye feel compassion; with which ye are anguished for the sake of your precious necklace, your precious feather, the little woman who is perhaps your second child, perhaps your eldest, or perhaps your youngest."[6] Again, note the affectionate phrases used to describe children.

MIDWIFE

Did you notice how eloquent the midwife is in her comments? When the Franciscan friar Bernardino de Sahagún lived with the Aztecs he discovered their sophisticated speech patterns. He interviewed numerous elders and wrote down the eloquent speeches of kings, parents, midwives, and many others.

When the birth was imminent the family gathered again for a feast, and the midwife was exhorted to prepare the *xochicalli* (house of flowers), or sweat bath, and to be skillful in helping the young mother prepare to give birth. She responded in an eloquent speech reassuring the family of her diligence, skill, and understanding of the religious power of the event.

When the child was born, or "had arrived on earth," the midwife gave war cries that meant that the mother had fought a good battle like a brave warrior. In this way, childbirth was compared to a warrior taking a captive in battle in the form of a baby! If the baby were a boy, she would call him "my beloved boy, my beloved youth"; if a girl, she would coo, "My beloved maiden, my youngest one, noblewoman, thou hast suffered exhaustion, thou has become fatigued. Thy beloved father, the master, the lord of the near, of the nigh, the creator of men, the maker of men, hath sent thee." Again, the gods are mentioned, only this time it is a god who is the source of the child's life.

The gods sent children to earth for a life of struggle, misery, and joy. The midwife was more specific about the quality of life, and mixed her encouragement with warnings. "Verily, thou wilt endure, thou wilt suffer torment, fatigue, for verily our lord hath ordered, hath disposed that there will be pain, there will be affliction, there will be misery, there will be work, labor for daily sustenance." However, this life of struggle was balanced by delicious food, sexual love, and wonderful clothes: "There is...to be eating, drinking, the wearing of raiment."[7]

The careful detail given to each ritual moment in the early life of an Aztec child cannot be exaggerated. It could be said that the vital elements of the Aztec world—family, the gods, and the past, present, and future—bonded closely together in these critical moments of the transition into life. For example, soon after the child was born, the family summoned a wise man, or soothsayer, to determine the signs under which the child had been born. The soothsayer questioned the family to determine the exact moment of birth, especially in relation to midnight, for that time determined which day sign was active when the child was born. The soothsayers consulted painted manuscripts to study the relationship between the time of birth (daybreak, noon, dusk, night, or midnight) and the sacred forces that every day flowed across the space of human life. The soothsayer might announce, "Good is the day sign on which he was born. He will govern, be a lord, be a ruler...will have wealth...will be brave, an eagle warrior, an ocelot warrior...he will be in the military common...will provide drink."[8] If a child was born on an adverse or unlucky day, the report was negative and frightening: "Behold that which will befall him—vice will be his desert; he will become a thief. Misery will be his desert, his lot. Vainly will he struggle on earth, but that which will be done will fail." But the soothsayer could suggest ways for the family to improve the possibilities for the child, who could be bathed and named on a positive day, even if it meant waiting more than the customary four days. This was often done to bring positive balance into the negative signs of the birthday. The soothsayer was well paid with turkeys, "loads of food," and plenty to drink.

An interesting description of the bathing ritual for little girls shows how ritual was crucial to the well-being of human life. The soothsayers selected a positive day, and the family prepared a little skirt, plus the equipment of the little red basket, the spinning whorl, and the batten. The girl was bathed and raised as an offering in the four directions of the cosmos and then raised up and offered to the gods who resided in the celestial realms. She was given water to drink. Each time the water touched the girl's head, chest, and hands, even when the baby was placed in the cradle for the first time, a short prayer was said: "Here is the coolness, the tenderness of Chalchi-uhtlicue, who is eternally awake.... May she go with thee, may she embrace thee, may she take thee in her lap, in her arms, that thou mayest continue watchfully on earth." Clearly, these children were being brought under the protection of the goddess.

In fact, all these children needed human and divine assistance in the days and years ahead. This assistance would be given by the parents, teachers, and priests, who provided different kinds of education.

CHILDHOOD AND DISCIPLINE

The Aztecs valued love and discipline. On the one hand, children were encouraged to express their feelings and attitudes openly, while on the other hand, they were watched carefully by their parents and given constant correction. When a child reached three years of age, the father began to instruct the boy, and the mother, the girl, in how to be a helpful member of the family and the household. When a child was four years old, the parents became more specific in the tasks they wanted their children to carry out, and girls and boys began wearing different clothes appropriate to their gender. This was the year that children underwent a special growth ritual that was repeated every four years in the month of Izcalli (Growth). Children of both sexes born during the previous four years were purified by fire and had their earlobes pierced and earrings inserted. The ceremony was called Quinquechanaya (They Stretch Their Necks), in which the children were lifted by their foreheads and had their limbs stretched. Another ceremony held every 260 days, on the day 4 Movement, saw the children's noses, necks, ears, fingers, and legs pulled to encourage proper growth during the next 260-day cycle. These two rituals reflect one of the key ideas in Aztec education: the Aztec equivalent of the verb *to educate* was *tlacahuapahua* or *tlacazcaltia*, which meant *to strengthen persons* or *to make persons grow*. This growing and strengthening was accomplished through a series of rituals that incorporated children into the work of the family and society. In these cases the children were introduced to the sacred numbers 4 and 260, which would continue to guide them even after death.

At the age of four, mothers began to teach girls the fundamentals of weaving, and fathers guided boys beyond the confines of the home and had them assist in water carrying. At five, boys helped in toting light loads of firewood and carrying light bundles of goods to the *tianquiztli*, or neighborhood marketplace. This allowed them

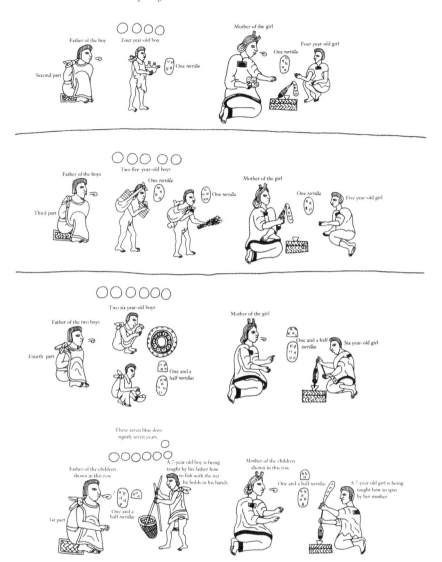

Parents teaching their children, ages four through seven. (*Codex Mendoza,* courtesy of Frances F. Berdan and Patricia Reiff Anawalt)

to greet people, watch the process of exchanges in the market, and meet other children. Girls began to spin with their mothers, learning how to sit, use their hands, and manipulate the cotton. A year later, the *Codex Mendoza* tells us, the parents

instructed and engaged them in personal services, from which the parents benefited, like, for boys, [collecting] maize that has been spilled in the marketplace, and beans and other miserable things that the traders left

Parents disciplining their children, ages 8 through 11. (*Codex Mendoza,* courtesy of Frances F. Berdan and Patricia Reiff Anawalt)

scattered. And they taught the girls to spin and to do other advantageous services. This was so that, by the way of the said services and activities, they did not spend their time in idleness, and to avoid the bad vices that idleness tends to bring.[9]

It is impressive just how close children and parents were during these formative years. In a real sense, the first teachers were the parents, communicating body language, speech patterns, and how to use their clothes to cover and adorn themselves and, in the case of males, to assist in hauling loads.

Between the ages of 7 and 10, boys were given nets to fish with, while girls continued to learn how to spin and cook. Young girls were already proficient in their labor and art by this age and were supervised rather than instructed by their mothers. Apparently, it was during this period of growth that children began to act up and cause problems in the family. The *Codex Mendoza* presents these years as times when parents punished their children for a series of unacceptable behaviors, including laziness, disobedience, rudeness, and boastfulness. There are images of parents "putting before them [the children] the terror and fear of *maguey* thorns, so that being negligent and disobedient to their parents they would be punished with the said thorns." There are scenes of children weeping when presented with these thorns and admonished not to be deceitful. Girls' hands were pierced by their mothers, who used the thorns to punish them for idleness and negligence. Boys who really got out of line had their hands and feet bound, and *maguey* thorns were stuck into their shoulder, back, and buttocks. Such was the price of rebellion by children. These punishments intensified between the ages of 10 and 14 and included being forced to inhale chili smoke or being tied by the hand and foot and forced to sleep on damp ground all night. If a girl was a sloppy spinner or clumsy in her work, she could be beaten by her mother for not paying attention or not concentrating on her work.

Images in the *Codex Mendoza* show that the children got well into line during their 13th and 14th years. Boys were responsible for carrying firewood from the hills and are depicted transporting sedges, bulrushes, and other grasses for the household and fishing successfully in their canoes. Girls would grind maize and make tortillas for their parents and are seen weaving, cooking, and effectively handling the different foods, utensils, and life of the kitchen. In fact, a girl who could grind corn and make the *atole* drink was considered a maiden of marriageable age.

Twelve-, thirteen-, and fourteen-year olds. (*Codex Mendoza,* courtesy of Frances F. Berdan and Patricia Reiff Anawalt)

VERBAL INSTRUCTIONS

It is impressive just how much verbal instruction, in eloquent terms, was given to children by their parents in Aztec society. This was especially true among the noble families, and fortunately we have several of the standard speeches given to the children. Children were instructed on how to appear in public, how to eat, talk, dress, drink, and sleep, and what to avoid in society. Consider these eight instructions given to the children of the elite: First, children, especially teenagers, were required to spend some nights in vigil, that is, stay awake at night. The main point was to train children not to be lazy and sleep too much, but also to periodically pray to the Lord of the Near and the Nigh. During these vigils children had to sweep and offer incense. Second, children were to walk in public with prudence and dispatch. "Do not throw thy feet much, nor raise thy feet high, nor go jumping, lest it be said of thee, lest thou be named fool, shameless." Children were told to walk quickly but with dignity, with their head held high. Third, they were told to speak slowly and deliberately, breathe evenly, and use a soft voice: "Thou art not to speak hurriedly, not to pant, nor to squeak, lest it be said that thou art a groaner, a growler, a squeaker."[10] Fourth, when speaking with someone, especially someone outside of the family, children were not to peer into one's face or stare. Staring at a woman, especially one who was married, was considered a clear sexual advance and was punished, sometimes with imprisonment.

In the fifth instruction, children were sternly warned against gossip and rumormongering: "Ignore it. Pretend not to understand the words. If thou canst not ignore it, respond not. And speak not; only listen, let what is said remain as said." This warning extended to being drawn into plots or plans for bringing harm to someone. "If something evil is told there, that which meriteth imprisonment, that which meriteth death...if thou actest foolishly with others, especially if thou lendest a word...on thee it will be laid."[11] This lesson reflects the widespread parental concern that children, especially teenagers, would be drawn into bad behavior, distracted from social responsibility, and fall into a life of crime.

The sixth teaching was to be obedient and diligent when summoned to do a job. Children should respond immediately, "be not called twice," and if sent as a messenger they should run, get the job done, "like the wind art thou to go." This was particularly important for Aztecs, who loathed laziness, negligence, and haughtiness. A lazy, negligent person was sometimes hit with a club.

The seventh instruction was to dress with dignity and avoid ostentatious or sloppy clothing: "Thou art not to array thyself fantastically...neither art thou to put on rags, tatters, an old loosely-woven cape." Capes were to be carefully tied and to cover the shoulder, or else the person would be thought a buffoon, a mad person, and graceless.

The eighth teaching, concerning eating and drinking, offered one of the strongest warnings. Prudence in the amount and style of eating was exceptionally important. People should not stuff their mouths with food, eat quickly, or make a spectacle by choking on it. Hands and faces were washed before each meal and when eating with others: "Do not quickly seat thyself...and when the eating is over, thou art quickly to seize the washbowls...thou art to wash another's mouth, another's hands."

It may seem that the Aztecs were uptight about everything their kids did. But they perceived life as hazardous and full of dangers that could be avoided if a person was alert, disciplined, prudent, and on the ball. They referred to the dangers in the world in this way: "On earth we travel, we live along a mountain peak. Over here there is an abyss, over there is an abyss. Wherever thou art to deviate, wherever thou art to go astray, there wilt thou fall, there wilt thou plunge into the deep." This meant that acting with discretion, care, and loyalty was the best protection against the many pitfalls, dangers, and temptations in life, which was sure to have a sizable amount of woe in it.

Two of the most woeful aspects of life were sexual promiscuity and drunkenness. Sexual activity before marriage was considered dangerous because it caused diseases of the skin and hair and would lead to death. Drunkenness was considered a companion of crime and led to public humiliation and private misery. The main goal that children, especially teenagers, were taught to aspire to was equilibrium in all things. Excessive eating, talking, looking, running, and especially sex were dangerous because they created disequilibrium in the body and in the interior world of humans.

THE HONOR OF YOUNG WOMEN

When young women reached puberty, known as "the age of discretion," their mothers and fathers spoke to them about how to survive and maintain a life of balance in the critical years immediately ahead. The speeches are eloquent and formal and show the profound concerns and care that parents felt for their offspring. The daughter was addressed as "my precious necklace, thou who art my precious feather...my creation...my blood, my color, my image."[12] The precious image was told to "grasp" why she was alive, why the gods had given her life. First, she was told that life would be a mixture of struggle, hardship, joy, and laughter. The world was difficult and always included weeping and torment. "This is the way things are...the earth is not a good place. It is not a place of contentment." But the gods gave humans laughter, sleep, food, strength, force, and also carnal knowledge so that "there would be peopling."

She was told that people must struggle to become responsible adults, workers, rulers, warriors, and home builders, and raise families. Good marriages were crucial to this development. The girl was reminded that she was chipped from her mother's womb and that she had to be ever mindful of her family's well-being: "Know that thou comest from someone, thou art descended from someone, that thou wert born by someone's grace." The task of the girl was to be devout, to sleep well but rise early to pray to the gods in the proper fashion. "Seize the broom, be diligent with the sweeping." Here began the art of the woman's life, which was care of the home. "The art of good drink, the art of good food, which is called one's birthright" meant to work sewing, grinding cornmeal, and cooking; but, as with everything else, do it in Aztec style. This style included a pronounced emphasis on artistic sensitivity. Young women were encouraged to observe and take in the arts of featherworking, embroidering, and "color-working"—the creation of art.

The crucial message, however, was sexual abstinence. The young woman was a "precious green stone, yet a precious turquoise," who was to be kept clean, pure, and without sexual experience until a husband was chosen. Concerning her heart, she was told to let "nothing [defile] it, it is still untouched, nowhere twisted, still virgin, pure undefiled."[13] In fact, to covet carnal things before marriage was to lead one into a realm of "excrement" and self-destruction. However, when the right young man came along, the one sent by one of the divinities, meaning a match made in heaven, the young woman must not reject him. The message could not be made any clearer than in this admonition:

But meanwhile present thyself well, look well to thine enemy that no one will mock thee. Give thyself not to the wanderer, to the restless one who is given to pleasure, to the evil youth. Nor are two, three to know thy face, thy head. When thou hast seen the one who, together with thee he will endure to the end, do not abandon him. Seize him, hang onto him even though he be a poor person, even though he be a poor eagle warrior, a poor ocelot warrior.... Our lord, the wise one, the maker, the creator, will dispose for you, will array you.[14]

The message was plain: Wait and plan to marry once, knowing that the gods will reward you if you follow this straight and narrow path.

THE RESPONSIBILITY OF YOUNG MEN

Several elaborate Aztec speeches have survived that outline in detail the responsibilities of young men when they reached adolescence. It is clear just how important sexual and social control and dignity were in the educational process. The young Aztec male, like the female, was faced with an ideal image to measure up to. This image was expressed in a series of similes that spoke of perfection. Life was to be lived as a "well-smoked, precious turquoise; as a round, reed-like, well-formed, precious green stone." This meant that one was to strive for a perfect life in sexual and social conduct, to make of one's life a valued example of the divine will on earth. This would result in one of the most highly prized goals—achieving a "good heart." The young man should study the life of devout priests, penitents, chaste men, elders, "keepers of the books," and warriors who brought honor to themselves in war. During his time on earth, the young man was told not to "lust for vice, for filth [illicit sex]; thou art not to take pleasure in that which defileth one, which corrupteth one, that which, it is said, driveth one to excess, which harmeth, destroyeth: that which is deadly."[15]

Rather, the young man was to cultivate a life of courage and be like the ripening *maguey* plant, producing in marriage rugged, agile children who were clean and beautiful. This consistent message of sexual control may strike us as tiresome, but for the Aztecs, a sexual transgression injured not just the person committing the immoral act, but the parents, siblings, and friends of the trespasser as well. This belief was based on the theory that when a human being was thrown out of equilibrium by sexual misconduct, a noxious force would grow and spread among the family like a contagious disease. Thus, if a youth had sex out of wedlock, or if a parent visited a prostitute or had an affair with a married person, the result would be physical and spiritual sickness for the families of the two teenagers or the adulterers. Of course, the same rules were applied to adults and the elderly. Betraying one's family, whether parents or spouse, was considered an aggressive, deadly physical and spiritual violation.

This sense of sexual control and personal discipline was extended to all social behavior. The young man was to get up early in the morning and do his chores either in the family home or in the temple school. This meant sweeping, keeping vigil, praying, and incensing the space. Walking in public was an important social expression of one's dignity and style. As we saw above, the same was true in terms of how one ate, spoke, greeted others, dressed, and studied. The children of the elite often had tutors who accompanied them in public to remind, evaluate, and encourage them to act with dignity and style.

A father sends his 15-year-old boys to different schools. (*Codex Mendoza,* courtesy of Frances F. Berdan and Patricia Reiff Anawalt)

AGE 15—THE BIG TRANSITION

When Aztec children reached the age of 15, they embarked on an important period of transition in their lives: a transition of space, activity, and religious and social responsibility. At this time, parents were required to bring their teenager to a neighborhood school (which they had selected shortly after the child's birth) and initiate the next stage of his or her educational process. From this moment on, children would grow into a new identity that required intense discipline, the strength to face physical and spiritual ordeals, and the capacity to acquire the trusted knowledge of the society. An image in the *Codex Mendoza* gives us a glimpse of this momentous occasion: a father, seated upon a woven mat, instructs his sons about the upcoming changes in their lives. Footprints lead from the youths, dressed in slightly different cloaks, toward two different teachers and two different types of schools.

One kind of school to which parents chose to send their 15-year-old boys was the *cuicacalli* (house of song), although some historical sources suggest that all Aztec children—male and female, noble and commoner—began attending this school between the ages of 12 and 14. These houses of song were a kind of preparatory school found adjacent to temples throughout the city. They were also the residences of the priests and consisted of several large, elaborately decorated buildings arranged around a central patio with surrounding rooms. The courtyard was the scene of songs and dances. Instruction began an hour before sunset, when the boys and girls, under the guidance of the instructors, were taught to sing the sacred songs of the people and to dance the various ritual dances long into the night. These songs contained the most important mythological and historical information about the culture and its worldview. The songs praised the gods and told of their sacred history, the meaning of life and death, and the responsibilities humans had to carry out for the deities. This was a powerful cohesive social experience for Aztec children and their families, who learned and relearned the sacred teachings, dance steps, and stories of their community.

The most rigorous school, however, was the *calmecac* (file of houses), a temple school run by a *tlamacazqui,* or head priest, who trained novice priests in a variety of subjects related to life in the priesthood or in judicial and civil service. Regardless of the final outcome, life in the temple schools was rich in content but rugged in style. This combination is symbolized in the depiction of the youth and the head priest in front of the *calmecac.* The head priest has a painted black body, signifying his austere lifestyle, and his hair is bound and pulled back to expose a bloody smear in front of his ear. This bloody smear refers to his practice of self-sacrifice as a means of enduring pain, building concentration, and offering blood to the gods. The youth facing him has a blackened body and a white cloak, and awaits instructions to successfully begin a career in the school, which will include little sleep, much labor, knowledge of the sacred history and forces of the universe, and ritual instruction on how to bleed oneself.

Education in the *calmecac* included military, mechanical, astrological, and religious training. Youths, both male and female (females had separate schools), were taught from large pictorial manuscripts painted in hieroglyphs telling of the genealogy, history, geography, mythology, laws, and arts of the society. As in the *cuicacalli,* songs and dances were a central part of *calmecac* life. Divine songs telling of the lives of gods, dreams, and the calendar were taught, recited, danced, and sung. Although this school was particularly attractive to noble families, it appears that common folk also dedicated their children to the rigors and riches of the *calmecac*. Key requirements for entering and remaining apparently included good morals, intelligence, discipline, and leading a pure life.[16] Young Aztec men and women who entered the *calmecac* were expected to live clean, peaceful, and chaste lives.

The *Codex Mendoza* shows the kinds of labor young men carried out during their training in the *calmecac*. Duties included the early-morning sweeping of temples, carrying boughs a long distance from the forest for temple decorations, bringing *maguey* thorns for sacrifice, and building fences. It is also clear that these youths were punished and disciplined frequently by piecing their ears, breast,

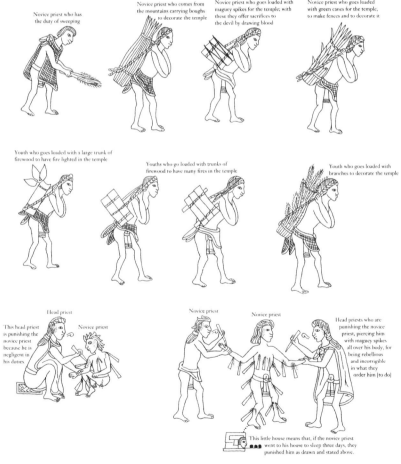

Various duties, labors, and punishments for young novice priests. (*Codex Mendoza*, courtesy of Frances F. Berdan and Patricia Reiff Anawalt)

thighs, and calves. One serious offense was leaving the school to sleep at home.

The education of the novice priests depended, in part, on effective service to the head priest, who transmitted ritual, mythological, and astronomical information to the young students under his charge. This was a demanding, rigorous learning process that included testing one's physical limits. Diego Durán, who lived in Aztec Mexico in the years immediately after the Spanish invasion, wrote of hearing the "eerie, diabolical sound" of conch shells and small flutes that accompanied the nighttime ceremonies and training of young priests. These novices had to bleed themselves, fast for 5 to 10 days, limit their sleep in a ritual called Staying Awake at Night, and go on pilgrimages to nearby mountains to do penance and carry out sacrifices. This involved learning how to incense a shrine with *copal*, acknowledge the four directions of the universe, and use tobacco and magical instruments to communicate with the gods. One of the important nighttime rituals involved playing *teponaztli* drums and other musical instruments and singing to the gods in order to invite their favor and avoid their harmful powers.

It is also clear that Aztec priests taught their students a great deal about skywatching. One of the most interesting images from the *Codex Mendoza* shows a head priest carefully observing the passage of stars to learn when certain ritual duties were to be carried out. The Aztec students learned the names, paths, and powers of numerous stars, constellations, and celestial events. Among the most important celestial bodies was Venus, the Morning Star, called Tlahuizcalpantecuhtli. Venus was considered both dangerous and

Other activities of novice and head priests. (*Codex Mendoza*, courtesy of Frances F. Berdan and Patricia Reiff Anawalt)

benevolent, and the young priests were taught to bleed themselves and others and to flick the blood from their middle fingers and thumbs in its direction. As noted in the previous chapter, Tianquiztli (known to us as the Pleiades) was another crucial celestial pattern Aztecs taught their priests and the populace. This part of the novices' training was related to the vital lessons about the calendar system; teaching the system was one of the chief responsibilities of the priesthood. This took a certain amount of mathematical ability, as the calendar system involved at least two cycles of time—the *tonalpohualli,* a 260-day calendar with 20 day symbols and 13 numbers, interacting with the 365-day solar calendar to form a calendar round of 18,980 days. The record of these numbers, signs, and passages was kept in painted almanacs called *tonalamatl* (book of the day). Rigorous observation over many decades resulted in the transmission of star knowledge that had become precise and complex long before the Aztecs appeared in the Basin of Mexico.

Another important school where many parents sent their 15-year-old boys was the *telpochcalli* (young men's house). The *telpochcalli* was closely related to the *cuicacalli* and was where the great majority of Aztec boys, mostly commoners, were trained for military life and warfare. We know that many young men took to this kind of training easily, and the rewards, as we shall see in chapter 7, were sometimes sumptuous. In the *telpochcalli,* a great deal of time was spent in physical labor, either in the school itself or in community projects such as sweeping, hauling, cleaning, building walls, digging canals, and farming. Other exercises included training in martial arts and transporting large pieces of firewood and branches from the forests to the city to heat and decorate the school. Hauling firewood became a physical test as heavier and heavier piles of wood were loaded on a youth's back to see "whether perchance he would do well in war, when already indeed an untried youth they took him to war." These same youths would soon have to carry shields, food, military supplies, and weapons great distances into huge, open battlefields filled with enemy warriors. This training was designed to drain fear from the youths and to arouse them to be reliable sentinels and scouts, and brave in the attack.

Since the training in the *telpochcalli* involved focused preparation for warfare, the school's instructors demanded from these youths total attention, great physical effort, bravery, and the ability to withstand intense pain. The entire society believed that its well-being depended on the training and courage of its warriors and put major demands on the *telpochcalli* to develop powerful warriors. Therefore, those who strayed from the training were severely punished. One source depicts a teacher beating the head of his student with a fire-brand because he left school to live with a prostitute. Anyone—teacher or student—caught living with a woman during this training period was severely punished; his possessions, adornments, and valued lip pendant were removed and, in an act of public humiliation, his warrior hairstyle was cut off. One passage reads:

Thereafter they beat him repeatedly with a pine stick; they verily caused him to swoon. They singed his head with fire; his body smoked; it blistered…and when they had indeed caused him to swoon, with this they cast him forth;…he just slowly crept away; he left going from one side to the other; he just went confused;…he withdrew forever; nevermore was he to sing and dance with the others.[17]

WOMEN AND THE PRIESTHOOD

Women also played a significant role in the priesthood. In some cases, an infant girl was taken to the temple by her mother a month or so after birth and dedicated to the priesthood. The mother would give the priest a censer and *copal* incense as a sign that the family hoped she would enter a religious vocation when she was older. When she was a mature teenager, she would become a *cihuatla-macazqui,* or woman priest.[18] Priestesses had to be celibate and concentrate intensely on their temple duties and the yearly round of ceremonies they ministered. Some accounts of the sacrificial festivals make it clear that priestesses were essential to the rites. For instance, Ochpaniztli, the feast dedicated to the mother goddess Toci (Our Grandmother), was directed by a woman priest, while an assistant called Iztaccihuatl (White Woman—because she was painted white) was responsible for the decorations, the preparation of the ritual areas, the sweeping of the sacred sites, and the lighting and extinguishing of the ritual fires.

We are fortunate to have some vivid descriptions of these priestesses dressing, dancing, and giving spirit, beauty, and power to the ceremonies. One example comes from the feast of Huey tecuilhuitl, the Great Feast of the Lords, where, we are told,

the women were indeed adorned; they were indeed carefully dressed. All good were their skirts, their shifts which they had put on. Some of their skirts had designs of hearts; some had a mat design like birds' gizzards; some were ornamented like coverlets; some had designs like spirals or like leaves.… All had borders, all had fringes; all the women had fringed skirts. And some of their shifts had tawny streamers hanging, some had smoke symbols, some had dark green streamers hanging, some had house designs.... And when they danced, they unbound their hair; their hair just covered each one of them like a garment. But they brought braids of their hair across their foreheads.[19]

During the sacred ceremony of Quecholli, the young priestesses dedicated to the goddess of maize carried seven ears of corn wrapped in cloth throughout parts of the procession. They were transformed into images of the goddess and wore feathers on their arms and legs and had their faces painted with fertility colors. They sang and processed through the streets until sundown, when they tossed handfuls of colored maize kernels and pumpkin seeds in front of the crowds. The people scrambled to get these seeds because they were signs that the coming year would have a good harvest.

It was possible for a woman to leave the priesthood to be married. But it was necessary that the suitor make the proper approaches to the family, the temple, and the young woman. The details of this possibility reflect what we are beginning to see throughout our study, namely, that the life of women was very much under the control of male authorities and their families. One text tells us that a priestess could get married "if she were asked in marriage, if the words were properly said, if the fathers, the mothers, and the notables agreed."[20]

THE RITE OF MARRIAGE

One of the most meaningful transitions for Aztec youth was the marriage ceremony, which involved families, friends, matchmakers, feasts, soothsayers, and, of course, speeches. Marriages typically occurred when young women reached the age of 15, though the young men were usually older, around 20, when they had finished their formal education. As with all rites of passage, the ritual of marriage involved days and acts of preparation, a special space for the ceremony, elders who imparted sacred teachings and moments, and symbols of the profound change taking place. For to enter into a marriage meant that new responsibilities, new family relationships, and a new, larger identity were being formed. It also meant giving up the intensity of some of the social friendships of adolescence.

One of the most important preparations involved the family consultation with a soothsayer, who helped pick a favorable day for a wedding. Good days for weddings included the day signs Reed,

Monkey, Crocodile, Eagle, and House. Prior to this choice, the prospective bride and groom both had received instructions from their parents on how to prepare themselves for marriage by remaining chaste so that they would have their full sexual potency when the knot was tied. One speech given by fathers to sons included these words: "Take heed, O my son.... For the lord of the near, of the nigh, hath said, thou art ordained one woman for one man...thou art not to devour, to gulp down the carnal life as if thou wert a dog.... Then, thereby, thou wilt become strong in the union, in the marriage;...in thy carnal life thou wilt be rugged, strong, swift, diligent."[21] In the process of arranging marriages, as with most things, Aztec society favored males and gave them more power in making their wishes and choices known.

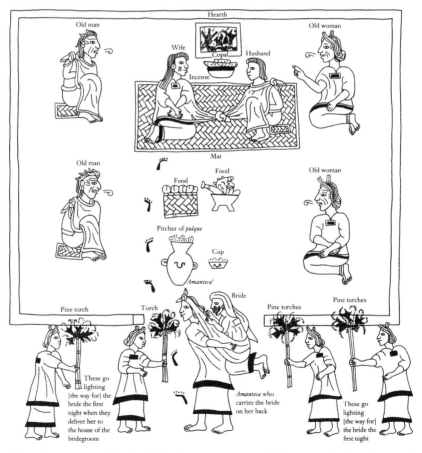

Wedding scene. (*Codex Mendoza,* courtesy of Frances F. Berdan and Patricia Reiff Anawalt)

For instance, when it was time for a young man to marry, as determined by the parents, who deemed him mature, the family of the youth consulted with him as to "which woman they would request." When the choice was determined, a matchmaker, usually an elder woman, was sent to the young woman's home to discuss the possibility with her family. To explore the possibility fully, the matchmaker traditionally visited the family for five days. We know that the parents of young women gave careful thought to their daughters' futures and traditionally asked, "Will she move the humble one, the unembittered one, the unseasoned one? And if at times they will be poor, if her heart will suffer pain and affliction, how will he regard the maiden?" In other words, when difficult days came, how would their daughter be treated? If the match was pleasing to both families, then the wedding day was set and formal preparations began.

Strenuous efforts went into the preparation of a feast that included tamales, corn, cacao (chocolate), sauces, *pulque,* turkeys, tobacco, and many gifts. Most important, perhaps, a wedding space was chosen and laid out around the sacred hearth without which no wedding could take place. All homes and temples had hearths where Xiuhtecuhtli (the fire god) lived, ensuring warmth, cooked food, and the vital soul force of *tonalli,* which emanated throughout the building. Prior to the feast, libations and morsels of food were offered to the fire god.

Formal invitations were sent to friends and family on the day before the wedding feast, and by noon the next day the guests assembled and placed their gifts before the hearth. Elders were permitted to drink *pulque* (also known as *octli*), the fermented juice of the *maguey* plant, in generous quantities; they would inevitably get drunk by sundown, when the wedding ceremony began. One passage about this drinking goes: "And the drinking bowls with which they became besotted were very small: the little black bowls, some drank three bowls, some four bowls, some five bowls. This was sufficient to drink in order for the old men, the old women to become besotted. And that which they drank was yellow pulque, honeyed pulque."[22] In Aztec belief, becoming drunk was a way of communing with the many *pulque* gods who contributed to the fertility of the agricultural fields and human beings. Normally, *pulque*-drinking was controlled by very strict rules that limited it to certain ritual occasions, because the Aztecs knew that it could cause disruption and chaos in society.[23] The privilege of inebriation was restricted to ritual occasions and especially to the elderly during wedding feasts.

RULES

The stereotype of the Aztecs is that they were wild, mean, and blood-thirsty. In fact, they were dedicated to an orderly society regulated by careful rules that guaranteed social cooperation and respect for elders and members of the opposite sex.

As sunset approached, the bride was bathed by the women in her family. Filled with emotion, they washed her with soap, perfumed her, decorated her with red feathers, and sprinkled her face with red or yellow colors. She was covered with a *huipilli* and a head cloth. Following instructions from her elders, she was lifted on the back of a woman who carried her, amid a procession of two rows of people carrying torches, to the groom's house. "And all the woman's kinsmen went in concourse about her; they went surrounding her; it was as if the earth rumbled behind her. And as they accompanied her, it was as if all eyes were fixed upon her; all the people looked at her." A drawing of this procession entering the home of the bridegroom shows the women moving in unison in support of the young woman.

The young woman, who had undergone a steady ritual transformation, taken on a new appearance, and moved to a new social place—then entered into the heart of the ceremony that would give her a new identity. She was placed on a large woven reed mat, facing her husband-to-be, in front of the burning hearth. The mother of the groom placed a new *huipilli* on the bride and gave a similar gift to her mother. The bride's mother tied a cape on the groom and placed a new loincloth in front of him. Then, the matchmakers came forward and actually *tied the knot* by tying a corner of the groom's cape and the bride's new *huipilli* together. The mother of the groom washed the bride's mouth, set out tamales and sauce in bowls, and fed her four mouthfuls. The bride then fed the groom four mouthfuls. The matchmakers then led the young couple to a bedchamber, closed the door for four days, and stood watch outside. On the fifth day, the young married couple came out, and feasting, dancing, and exchanges of gifts by in-laws took place as the newlyweds heard more speeches about their new duties to one another and their responsibilities as adults. The wedding feast came to a close as the families returned to their homes "content...feeling good in their hearts." Education in Aztec society, it seems, never ended.

BACHELOR PARTY

In fact, the new husband had one more major ritual to pass through before fully taking up his duties as a married person. Sometime after the wedding, he organized a feast for a select group of bachelor friends with whom he had served as a youth leader in the school. The feast might include a generous basket of tamales, a turkey, chocolate, and perhaps gifts of capes for his friends. Also, tobacco and perfumes were present to sweeten the occasion. The central gift was a copper ax that the groom would present to his former teacher or to his bachelor friends. Traditionally, the young husband invited the friends and teacher to his home to announce that he would retire from his *telpochcalli* duties as a youth leader in the school and asked for their support and continued friendship. In some cases, the capes he gave his friends were woven by his new wife, who had brought considerable weaving skills to the marriage and demonstrated her talents in the creation of these gifts. In this way, the young man completed the transition from youth leader to a husband who might then go on to become a seasoned warrior, merchant, judge, farmer, ambassador, or other socially responsible person. These careers will be discussed in chapter 5.

Rites of passage accompanied every important transition of Aztec life. Even when merchants set out on a trading trip, they performed small and sometimes complex rites that assisted them in the transition from home, town, and city to the countryside, where surprises, dangers, and sometimes enemies confronted them. Farmers performed rites of passage throughout the year to ensure that the spirits, gods, and powers of the fields, soils, animals, plants, and sky would assist them in their work. Warriors participated in a series of rites to assist them in preparing for and fighting effectively in battle; when a captive was taken, a ritual saying always marked the profound change that had taken place in the potency and destiny of the captor and captive. Women and men periodically took sweat baths to purify themselves, and every stage of the calendar required special actions to assist in the maintenance or recovery of equilibrium.

PUBLIC APPEARANCE

We can imagine, given all this emphasis on decorum, proper behavior, and guided training, that Aztec peoples valued a clean, neat, and attractive personal appearance. Most Aztecs were shorter than people are today. These short and stocky people seldom grew above 5 feet, 7 inches for men or 4 feet, 10 inches for women. One scholar who has studied the record describes them this way: "Skin color varied from dark to light brown, and the typical Aztec face was broad with a prominent and often hooked nose. Eyes were black or brown, almond shaped, and frequently with epicanthic folds at the outer corners, one indication that the ancestors of the Mexicans had migrated into the New World from Asia in the long-distant past."[24]

These people were very hard-working and showed extraordinary endurance in lifting, walking, running, singing, playing, and fighting. As one Spaniard who lived in Mexico wrote about his neighbors, "They are swarthy as leopards, of good manners and gestures, for the greater part very skillful, robust, and tireless, and at the same time the most moderate men known. They are very warlike and face death with the greatest resolution."[25]

Aztec peoples enjoyed bathing and personal cleanliness, and they used the fruit of a soap tree and the roots of certain plants for soap. They took cold baths but were especially committed to steam baths. Many homes had steam bathhouses, some of which have been excavated in the Basin of Mexico. These steam baths were used for ritual purification, during sicknesses, and to help pregnant women, but also as part of daily hygiene.

Aztec women, especially the more well-to-do, shaded their brown complexions with a yellow color extracted from insects and cooking oils. Men appear to have painted their bodies only for certain ceremonies. If women colored their faces too much or before they were old enough, their parents admonished them. Women also used perfumes from plants and used a kind of chewing gum to sweeten their breath. It appears that obsidian mirrors were used in homes so that people could evaluate their personal appearance before going out into the community.

As we shall see, men's clothes, especially those of warriors, reflected experience and valor in the field. But the common man wore a loincloth that was wound around his waist and between his legs, and knotted so that one end hung down from behind and the other from the front. Nobles wore elaborate cotton cloths with colorful embroidered designs. While some poorer workers were limited to these loincloths, most men wore cloaks that were knotted on their shoulders. As we shall see in the next chapter, the clothing of a ruler was astonishing in its color, beauty, and symbolism.

Women wore skirts that reached to their ankles and were tied to their bodies by embroidered belts. Upper-class women wore a blouse over their skirts decorated with certain designs, according to their class or hometown. As Warwick Bray notes, the Aztecs greatly enjoyed ornamenting their bodies and clothes whenever they could:

The Mexicans loved display and were uninhibited in their use of jewelry and such accessories as fans, fly-whisks, and head-dresses made of green or red feathers. Beads were made of rare stones or of gold cast into the form of crabs, scorpions, birds, or sea shells, and necklaces were hung with bells which tinkled when the wearer moved. The same materials were used for pendants and chest ornaments and the limbs of rich young men were adorned with leather or gold bands set with jade and turquoise mosaic. Poorer folk wore ornaments of a similar kind, but substituted shells or less expensive stones for the precious materials used by the aristocracy.[26]

In short, the Aztecs strove for a clean, well-organized, attractive appearance.

THE PASSAGE OF DEATH

One of the most profound and revealing ritual processes in Aztec society focused on death and the destiny of human beings after death. It is difficult for modern Western people to grasp the very different attitudes and practices that native Americans, especially the Aztecs, had about death and the afterlife. One thing is certain: every aspect of the passage from life to death and the destiny of the individual's souls (for the Aztecs believed that each human being had not one but three souls) was marked by rites that assisted in the dangerous and powerful passage. In simple terms, death was a part of life in that (1) it accompanied humans every day of their earthly existence (in a partial way); (2) it was one of the stages of the existence of the human soul; and (3) the states of death and life were parts of the cycle of regeneration. One key to understanding the Aztec view of death is found in the lines of a poem recited by contemporary descendants of the Aztecs who live in the state of Puebla:

we live *here* on this earth
we are all fruits of the earth
the earth sustains us
we grow here, on the earth and flower
and when we die
we wither in the earth
we are *all fruits* of the earth
we eat of the earth
then the earth eats us.[27]

The point is this: humans need to eat in order to live. To eat, humans are forced to kill other beings, including plants and animals. Therefore, when they eat they ingest death into their bodies, and therefore carry death inside them, which also gives them life. Death in the Aztec worldview is intimately tied up with this image of the earth from which and to which everyone, in part, comes and on which everyone depends. Humans have a deep dependency on the earth in two ways. First, they eat the fruits of the earth, especially corn, which is born from the Great Mother. But this food springs from within the earth, which is the region of the dead. Second, in Aztec thought, sexual intercourse was the same as giving oneself to the "things of the earth," that is, to have known the dust, dirt, and filth of the earth. So, when the Aztecs ate or had sex, they were drawing on the forces of the earth, which were forces of life *and* death.

The earth was also thought of as a hungry mouth, cosmic jaws that demanded to be fed by humans. The lords of the underworld, Mictlantecuhtli and Cuezalli, it was said, "have a great thirst for us, they always hunger after us, they keep on panting, always insisting."[28] All human bodies would suffer death, which was a destruction and fragmentation, but also an entrance into another world where another kind of life existed and was regulated by rituals. To understand this coincidence of opposites—destruction and life—it is necessary to refer to our earlier discussion of the three souls of the human body: the *tonalli,* located in the head, which was the soul of will and intelligence; the *teyolia,* located in the heart, which was the soul of fondness and vitality; and the *ihiyotl,* located in the liver, which was the soul of passion, luminous gas, and aggression. All three were gifts from the gods deposited in the human body, but they were also found in animals, plants, and objects. At the time of death, these three souls in the human body dispersed into different regions of the universe. Although the texts about this separation of souls are not always consistent, it appears that the souls could go to one of four places: (1) Mictlan, which was in the underworld, for those who died an ordinary death; (2) the sun in the sky, for warriors who died in combat, people sacrificed to the sun, and women who died while giving birth for the first time; (3) Tlalocan, the rain god's mountain paradise, for those whose death was caused by water or water-related forces like frost or cold sicknesses; or (4) Chichihualcuauhco, which was exclusively reserved for infants who died while still nursing from their mothers, that is, who had not yet eaten from the earth.

Various souls leaving the body of a dead person. (*Codex Laud,* redrawn by Scott Sessions)

It appears that at least one of the souls, the *teyolia,* which resided in the heart, did not leave the body until one was cremated. This was especially true of a dead ruler, who could still be in communication, through the *teyolia,* with his ministers until his body was burned. Remembering the importance of fire in the wedding ceremony, it is impressive that the fire that burned the cadaver carried the soul on its journey to its appropriate place in the afterlife. At this point, rituals were important because relatives made offerings, shed tears, and said prayers at the fire's hearth. These ritual actions protected the soul and gave it strength during its dangerous journey. In the case of some rulers, the servants were sacrificed and cremated on a nearby pyre, but their hearts were extracted and burned on the same pyre as the dead *tlatoani.* These hearts, the *teyolia* of the servants, vessels of invigorating drinks, and clothes accompanied the soul of the ruler and protected it on its journey after death.

After the death of the body, it took extended periods of time for the souls to reach their destination. It took four years to reach Mictlan, which was the lowest of the nine levels, but only 80 days to reach the Sky of the Sun, where the souls of warriors accompanied the solar god on his daily journey. During this time, the mourners carried out ritual offerings to assist the souls. Once the warrior's soul arrived in the Sky of the Sun, or Tonatiuh Ilhuicatl, the mourners could bathe and groom themselves for the first time in 80 days.

In the case of souls destined for Tlalocan, the rain god's paradise, the bodies were not cremated but instead buried in the earth in a symbolic act of planting the flesh as an offering to the gods of vegetation and rain. Fire was not necessary, as burial in the earth was a direct deposit of the souls into the realm of life after death.

Still another funerary ritual was designed to keep some of the souls of the deceased near the living family. Before cremation, locks of hair were cut from the top of the head of the deceased and placed (along with hair cut during the first days of the deceased's life) with an effigy of the person in a box or earthen vessel, which was kept in the home or in the temple of the *calpolli*. This refers specifically to the *tonalli* soul (which resided in the head), which would continue to give vitality and strength to the family for years.

This means that the Aztecs had a practice similar in some ways to the cult of relics we associate with medieval Europe. The bones of rulers and others who had attained a divine reputation while alive were kept in special containers (boxes, vases, or jars) and displayed or buried in temples. A number of these relic containers have been excavated at the Great Aztec Temple in downtown Mexico City in the last 15 years. These containers would receive offerings and, in exchange, the souls of the deceased would lend strength and protection to the community.

A special destiny awaited the souls of women who died in childbirth. These women were considered equal to warriors who died in battle or on the sacrificial stone. They too had made a sacrifice of their own lives so that a new life could come into the world. Their souls ascended into the female side of heaven, where they dwelt together and accompanied the sun from its zenith to its setting. On certain dates these spirits would ascend to earth and haunt the living.

One very interesting belief was that a divine dog who dwelled in the afterlife could assist in the journey of the *teyolia* soul. It was thought that the flames of cremation could "send a dog that would help the dead person cross the subterranean river; the necessary articles to cover himself, to eat, and to protect himself on the road, the offering the traveler could give to Mictlantecuhtli; the gifts captives of war had carried when they were offered on the sacrificial stone; and even the hawk feathers soldiers slain in battle would need to fly before the Sun."[29]

One of the fascinating ideas that confronts us when we study this view of death and the afterlife is the plenitude of the souls of the dead. They can travel to an afterlife, but parts can also remain close to the family, city, or community. They do not conform to the physical limits of the body or its remains. The reason is that souls are animistic forces embedded in material forms, but not always confined to them. The souls of the dead could also become attached to and integrated within gods or goddesses, thus revitalizing them. This was particularly true of rulers, great warriors, and distinguished artists and poets. The one outstanding example was the figure of Topiltzin Quetzalcoatl, who ruled the fabled Toltecs. It is said that when he had himself cremated, his *teyolia* rose up into the sky and was changed into the planet Venus, whom the Toltecs called Tlahuizcalpantecuhtli, the Lord of the House of Dawn.

It is also important to note that the souls of all human beings could become part of lesser gods and divine forces after death. Those who died without distinction from a common disease traveled along the icy paths of the underworld for four years until they arrived at the land of Mictlantecuhtli, where they would become part of his realm. This was a foul-smelling place of torment, to be avoided by living a life of distinction. By living a morally admirable life, a person would be selected by one of the gods who dwelled in another realm of the afterlife. It is also true that accidental deaths not related to human conduct could result in a more favorable afterlife.

Perhaps the best way to end this chapter on rites and learning in the Aztec life cycle is to quote the words of the Spanish friar Bartolomé de las Casas, who witnessed and described the ritual dressing of the dead in another part of Mexico. We see reflected in it the Aztec concern for ritual action that influenced the souls of those children, adolescents, and adults whose life on earth was guided and controlled through education, speeches, and ceremony.

When it was time to bury the dead, people commonly dressed them in the different clothes and insignia of the gods. If it were a child, they clothed it with the insignia of a god they considered to be an advocate of children. If a person died of ulcers, tumors, or a contagious disease, they dressed the body with the insignia of another god. If he were a merchant, he was clothed in one way: if a lord, another way: and if it were a lady, she was clothed differently from women who were poor. If a person died in a war and the corpse was available, they burned it [on the battlefield] without ceremony; and when they returned from war, they brought one of the arrows belonging to the man they had burned and had it as an image of the dead man; and, dressing it with the insignia of the Sun, they burned it. The families of those who had been put to death as adulterers made an image of them composed of the insignia of the goddess called Tlazolteotl, which means goddess of trash and filthiness...because she wished to be worshipped by the commission of vile sins. For those who had drowned, whose bodies they did not have, they made figures of them and adorned them with the insignia of the water god, because, since he had taken them, it might go well with them.[30]

Given all we have learned about Aztec discipline, child rearing, and ritual education, we can now appreciate more fully the meaning of the saying that opened this chapter: to be a tree that bears fruit meant to participate fully in the process of birth, life, death, and rebirth.

NOTES

1. Bernardino de Sahagún, *Florentine Codex: General History of the Things of New Spain*, ed. and trans. Arthur J. O. Anderson and Charles E. Dibble, introductory vol. and 12 books (Santa Fe, NM: School of American Research and University of Utah, 1950–82), 6: 222.

2. Ibid., 3: 51.

3. Quoted in Alfredo López Austin, *Educación mexica: antología de documentos sahaguntinos* (Mexico City: Universidad Nacional Autónoma de México, 1985), 39.

4. Sahagún, *Florentine Codex*, 6: 176.

5. Ibid., 171.

6. Ibid., 158.

7. Ibid., 168.

8. Ibid., 198.

9. *The Codex Mendoza*, ed. Frances F. Berdan and Patricia Rieff Anawalt, 4 vols. (Berkeley: University of California Press, 1992), 4: 120.

10. Sahagún, *Florentine Codex*, 6: 122.

11. Ibid., 122.

12. Ibid., 93.

13. Ibid., 96.

14. Ibid., 98.

15. Ibid., 116.

16. *Codex Mendoza*, 2: 166.

17. Ibid., 178; Sahagún, *Florentine Codex*, 2: 102–3.

18. Jacques Soustelle, *Daily Life of the Aztecs: On the Eve of the Spanish Conquest*, trans. Patrick O'Brien (Stanford, CA: Stanford University Press, 1970), 55.

19. Sahagún, *Florentine Codex*, 2: 98–99.

20. Quoted in Soustelle, *Daily Life of the Aztecs*, 55.

21. Ibid., 167.

22. Sahagún, *Florentine Codex*, 6: 130.

23. An excellent summary of the *pulque* or *octli* cult can be found in H. B. Nicholson, "The Octli Cult in Late Pre-Hispanic Central Mexico," in *To Change Place: Aztec Ceremonial Landscapes,* ed. Davíd Carrasco (Niwot: University Press of Colorado, 1992), 158–83.

24. Warwick Bray, *Everyday Life of the Aztecs* (London: B. T. Batsford, 1968), 28.

25. Quoted in ibid., 29.

26. Ibid., 33.

27. Tim Knab, "Tlalocan Talmanic: Supernatural Beings of the Sierra de Puebla," in *Actes du XLIIe Congrès International des Américanistes, Congrès du Centenaire, Paris, 2–9 Septembre 1976* (Paris: Société des Américanistes, 1979), 6: 127–36, poem quoted from 129–30.

28. Alfredo López Austin, *The Human Body and Ideology: Concepts of the Ancient Nahuas,* trans. Thelma Ortiz de Montellano and Bernard Ortiz de Montellano, 2 vols. (Salt Lake City: University of Utah Press, 1988), 1: 311.

29. Ibid., 324.

30. Ibid., 331.

5

THE SOCIAL PYRAMID: MAINTAINING YOUR PLACE AND THE WORLD

> When the ruler went forth, in his hand rested his reed stalk when he went moving in rhythm with his words. His chamberlains and his elders went before him; on both sides, on either hand, they proceeded as they went clearing the way for him. None might cross in front of him; none might come forth before him; none might look up at him; none might come face to face with him.[1]

This passage describes the appearance and procession of an Aztec ruler in public and introduces us to the principal idea of social stratification that organized and influenced all aspects of daily life. One of the most challenging realizations for students in the United States to confront is that most human societies are arrangements of unequal parts. Sociologists and novelists, for instance, have taught us that inequality and unequal access to privilege, prestige, status, and the goods of life are a common feature of human groups. North Americans, brought up under the rhetoric (though not the reality) that "all men are created equal," may be somewhat blind to the *hierarchical* nature of every human society, or at least every society constructed by urban arrangements. The Aztecs, like many peoples, constructed a pyramidal society, a hierarchical society. In the Aztec case, a basic division between nobles and commoners permeated all social action and was under the direction and sacred influence of the *tlatoani* and his lineage. In the preceding passage the ruler

Attendants dress and adorn an Aztec ruler in this Diego Rivera mural at the National Palace in Mexico City. (Courtesy of Scott Sessions)

emerges from his royal residence poised to direct social life according to the "rhythm of his words," for he is the chief speaker, the central source of the expressed law, wisdom, and will of the gods. As we shall see in chapter 6, the art of words—especially sacred words—was highly valued, and the ruler was the living embodiment of this art. He had been raised, through intense rites of passage, above all human beings, and he was told at his enthronement ceremony, "You are no longer a human being like us, we no longer see you as merely human."[2]

We see this social elevation reflected in the royal servants, chamberlains, and elders who preceded him to clear his path of common people. There is a proper symmetry, a dual symbolism, to this procession, as the ruler is guarded "on both sides, on either hand." One purpose of this protective balance is to ensure the physical and social distance between the ruler and the commoners; it is clear that this distance is both horizontal ("they went clearing the way") and emphatically vertical ("none might look up at him...none might come face to face"). He sits, rules, and walks—regardless of where he is in actual geography—at the symbolic apex of society, and no one except the gods or other rulers can cross his path.

The royal face that looked out or down on the rest of the world was carefully and luxuriously adorned, as the following passage shows. When the ruler danced, he was arrayed as a shining, moving image of beauty, wealth, and sacred wonder.

The [head] band with [two] quetzal feather tassels set off with gold, with which they bound their hair;
   A quetzal feather crest device set off with gold, which he bore upon his back;
   A finely wrought headdress of red spoonbill feathers, with flaring quetzal feathers, and with it a drum [covered] with gold—a device which he bore upon his back as he danced...
   Golden ear plugs, which he inserted in [the lobes of his ears]...
   A green stone lip plug set in gold;
   A long, white labret of clear crystal, shot through with blue cotinga feathers, in a gold setting, which he inserted in his [lower] lip.
   A long, yellow labret of amber in a gold setting...
   A gold lip pendant in the form of a pelican;
   A gold lip pendant in the form of an eagle;
   A gold lip pendant in the form of a fire serpent;
   A gold lip pendant in the form of a boating pole...
   A green stone lip plug in the form of an eagle, fitted at the base in a gold setting...

A lip pendant of gold, in the form of a broad leafed water plant...

A necklace of radiating golden pendants with a thin, green stone disc
set in their midst.[3]

This indeed is a royal head decorated with gold, quetzal feathers,
green stone, and blue feathers, symbolizing the cosmic regions of
the earth and sky, plants and animals, and artists and workers (the
boating pole lip plug), all concentrated in the image of the noblest
of the noble class, who moved through society displaying his cosmic power. When the ruler appeared in public, especially when he
danced, the society was presented with a sacred performance of
the social pyramid at its highest point. Even the drumming and
the drums played were superior—the precious makers of cosmic
sounds. "There were two-toned drums and supports of two-toned
drums, ground drums, golden gourd rattles, and golden bells"
marking out the movements of social triumph and superiority.

But we are led to ask a series of questions, including, "Who d
the work to support this pyramid?" "Who made these objects?" a
also, "How was the social pyramid, which divided the mass of pe
ple into the privileged class and the commoners, held togethe
We see two powerful ideas somehow held together in the ro
procession and dance, namely, a collective commitment by the pe
ple to social differentiation and inequality. As a means of explori
these questions, this chapter is controlled by the idea of *the local
view of the social world of the Aztecs*. A locative view holds that se
ety and the entire cosmos work best when *everything and everyone
find their correct places and conform to the requirements of those places in
the universe*. In this view of the world, it is morally good to fit into
your place, to find and stay within the boundaries of your social
group and your working profession, and to contribute to the overall
balance of society by conforming to the sacred instructions of your
lineage. Doing the right thing means being in the right social place.
The Aztecs were not tolerant of dissent, doing your own thing,
hanging out, or blurring distinctions. Alfredo López Austin sums
it up clearly:

A child grew up in a hierarchical environment in his home and in his
temple-school. The first distinction he learned to make was among the
members of his nuclear family. The rules for internal rank were reinforced
by fear of bodily harm. If a child drank before his elder brother, his growth
would be arrested. If he didn't keep his proper distance from old people,
the vital forces they accumulated with the years could do him harm....
The first objects a child touched were the instruments of his future trade—
gifts from the *calpulli*'s patron god—and while still in the cradle the child

was offered to god in the temple-school to bind him in a definitive way to the institution where he would be taught under the traditional canons of society.[4]

In these ways, people were locked into a social world from the start to the end of their lives and even in the afterlife. This is a locative view of the world. But how does it get constructed? How is this great social pyramid maintained? And why did commoners support a social structure that gave them limited benefits? It is crucial to understand the beliefs and ideas that established and protected social differentiation. Believing in fitting in was essential to the well-being of the social pyramid, and in what follows we will study some of the central ideas, symbols, and actions that *separated and linked* the rulers, nobles, warriors, merchants, and commoners in a world of social difference.

BELIEVING IN FITTING IN

In chapter 2, we learned that the Aztec world was permeated and energized by divine forces that formed an ordered, detailed, and balanced cosmos. Recalling the image of the cosmos from the *Codex Fejérváry-Mayer*, we are impressed by the amount of organized detail of the world of the gods. Each quarter of the universe is precisely organized by gods, sacred birds, colors, and trees filled with the soul forces of *tonalli* and *teyolia*. This precise ordering of the cosmos meant, first, that the gods required human beings to work together in keeping society in a balanced state. Second, this balance meant that certain human groups had specific tasks that focused and limited their social existence in service to the whole of society. Third, each social group, such as the featherworkers, traders, goldsmiths, cape sellers, cacao sellers, clay workers, and tailors, had patron deities who guided their work and social life and whom they honored. One group in particular, the *pipiltin*, was made by the gods and trained to rule the rest of society. Another group, the *macehualtin* majority, was made to work for the benefit of society under the control of the *pipiltin*. Rituals, teachings, social posture, gesture, clothes, and stories all trained people to believe in the need to fit into this overall social model and picture of the universe. It must be emphasized that in the Aztec view of the cosmos and society, failure to conform to your place as a *macehualli* or a *pilli* (and the specific jobs and responsibilities within these two general categories) resulted not only in physical punishment, but also in the release of harmful magical forces that could contaminate one's family and neighborhood. A social outcast who had not effectively fit in to his or her social role could be designated a *tetzahuitl*, a person who sent out harmful forces and created fear, scandal, and danger.[5]

THE SACRED CORD: NOBLES

Children of the precious things, of the jades, of the rings, what is breathed into, what comes from Topiltzin Quetzalcoatl; they acquired life, they were born to their good fortune, to deserve the mat, the chair, to carry what has to be carried, what has to be borne, for this they acquired life, for this they were born, for this they were created there where at night it was determined, ordered, that they be the rulers, that they be *tlatoque*.[6]

This passage does more than tell us that one group was chosen by the gods to be rulers at the time and place of creation—"where at night it was determined." It also tells us that they come from a specific lineage, for it was the Toltec ruler-god Topiltzin Quetzalcoatl who breathed the status of deserving the throne, "the mat, the chair." It also indicates that this is a heavy responsibility to be lifted and assumed through life, "to carry what has to be carried, what has to be borne." Rulership and noble existence were privileges and involved serious restrictions. Let us look at the ideas of noble lineage, privilege, and responsibility associated with nobles.

LINEAGE

When the Aztecs first came into the Basin of Mexico in the 12th and 13th centuries, they were sometimes referred to as Chichimecs or Chichimeca. The word means "lineage or rope of the dogs" and points to the vital importance of family and kinship lineage in Aztec history and society. Nobles were those who were descended, in theory, from either Quetzalcoatl, the Plumed Serpent man-god of the ancient Toltec kingdom, or from Xiuhtecuhtli, the fire god, who was the mother and father of all the gods and therefore the patron god of the rulers and nobles. Thus the nobility carried enormous magical powers that were embedded in their families, bodies, and actions. A noble lineage meant that a person inherited, in his or her body, a name, clothes, traditions, and a moral purity superior to those of a *macehualli*. Recall that the themes of moral purity and upright behavior were preached to children, especially those of the nobility, throughout their upbringing. One common theme was that if you acted immorally, which included everything from walking wildly in the street to sexual misconduct, you were infecting the reputation of your family and its members, both living *and* dead! Consider this speech addressed by a noble to his son:

Listen. And what will ye do on earth? To what purpose were ye born by one's grace? For ye were born by the grace of our lords, the lords, the rulers who have already gone beyond to reside; for ye came to life, ye were born not among the herbs, in the woods. And what are ye to do? Are ye diligent with the staff, with the carrying frame?... Hear ye; here is your task. Take care of the drum, the gourd rattle; ye will awaken the city, and ye will gladden the lord of the near, of the nigh.... And pay attention to artisanship, the art of feather working, the knowledge of things.[7]

The "knowledge of things" meant a knowledge of how the world worked, according to the nobles, and a commitment to following that working world. The great model for the commitment to excellence was the Toltec culture, whose great artistry, knowledge, agriculture, and correct behavior were carried on by the noble lineage of Topiltzin Quetzalcoatl, who ruled over the Turquoise Age, at least before he broke the rules of the nobility and was ruined. Topiltzin had damaged his power and the power of his lineage, and this taught the Aztecs just how potent the magic of lineage was. Sometimes, when a noble committed a crime, he or she was reduced by law to the rank of *macehualli,* as was his or her entire family.

The lineage of the nobles was further strengthened through the successful completion of the educational program described in chapter 4. The increase in knowledge and the experience of commanding workshops, schools, warrior troops, and courts resulted in the heightened reputation and power of the lineage, which was considered morally uplifted. When a noble was particularly successful in leadership or artistic expression, his or her lineage acquired extraordinary magical fire in the heart of the kinship system. The term for this kind of achievement was *yollopiltic,* or "one who has an ennobled heart."

PRIVILEGES

The nobles had superior privileges. Their homes, clothes, food, and access to opportunity were of the highest quality, especially in times of abundance and political stability. They had access to the most valuable goods, including capes, mantles, jewelry, flowers, cacao, musical instruments, and even human flesh. Remember how important the souls of people and things were in the Aztec worldview. Everything was capable of having *tonalli,* the animistic power that resided mainly in the human brain. Nobles had the most direct access to limited forms of human flesh from sacrificial victims, which was considered the flesh of the gods. This flesh contained the vital force of the god's power, which passed to the person who ingested it. Nobles periodically enjoyed small amounts of human flesh in ritual meals. Another way that nobles and *macehualtin* who were elevated to noble status as a result of extraordinary feats on the battlefield acquired magical power was through the ingestion of cacao, the inhaling of burning incense, and the taking of psychotropic drugs such as peyote or hallucinogenic mushrooms. The visionary state that resulted from ingesting these plants was a direct communication with gods and goddesses, who entered into human awareness during these times. It was thought that the nobles became stronger and more effective in their public duties when they ate peyote, cacao, mushrooms, or human flesh. This was a privilege of the noble class, but it must be remembered that the main purpose was to enable them to carry out their responsibilities more effectively. And the noble with the greatest amount of leadership responsibility was the ruler, whose entire life was filled with dignity and privilege.

THE *TLATOANI*: RESPONSIBILITIES, CORONATION, AUTHORITY

We can get the clearest picture of the power and authority of an Aztec ruler such as Motecuhzoma Xocoyotzin, the *tlatoani* who greeted Cortés, by studying the great coronation rituals that taught him and everyone who witnessed them his *place* in the world. The coronation ceremony for the new ruler involved his *social lowering, followed by a social elevation*. The ruler-to-be was first stripped of his noble clothes, dressed humbly in a loincloth, and taken to the base of the pyramid of Huitzilopochtli. Other nobles accompanied him, and he was led by the *tlatoque* of the allied cities of Tezcoco and Tacuba up the steps of the temple. There he was painted black by the chief priests before being adorned with a sleeveless green jacket, a tobacco gourd, and a green cotton incense bag decorated with bones. He was taken by the priests, or "keepers of the gods," before Huitzilopochtli's statue, which he perfumed with incense. Reflecting this chapter's theme of the social pyramid, the texts reads, "All common folks stood looking up at him. Trumpets were sounded and shell trumpets were blown." Then, four nobles dressed in a similar manner, with veiled faces, fasting capes, and the bone design, led him down the temple steps into the house of fasting, which was a military headquarters. There, the nobles and the ruler-to-be underwent four days of fasting and penance. Each day, they would silently ascend the temple of Huitzilopochtli to carry out autosacrifices, bleeding themselves to nourish the god. They bathed to purify themselves each day. On the fifth day, the ruler was escorted to his royal palace and the nobles returned to their homes. The *tlatoani* announced a royal feast, and rulers from all over the realm, including enemy rulers, were invited to receive gifts and food, to dance, and to process with the Aztec nobles.

In this first stage of the coronation ceremony, we see how the ruler learned his place in the world. He was taken *out* of society and magically transformed before reentering society for the second stage of the coronation. He was stripped of his clothes, painted the color of the priesthood, turned into the servant of Huitzilopochtli, whom he fed with incense, displayed from above to the populace, and taken down into a military monastery, where he meditated before ascending the temple four times to give blood and purify himself. His place was a sacred place, and his being was turned into a sacred being, above and below the rest of humanity, greater than humans, *other* than humans, but also among humans, as displayed in the feast. But in this feast, he proclaimed himself ruler of the world, for all the other nobles were required to come and receive his gifts and foods and participate in his dances and processions.

The second phase of the coronation began when the *tlatoani* of Tenochtitlan appeared, now more than a man, before the ruler of the sister city of Tezcoco. For only another sacred king could crown a sacred king. A crown of green stones and gold was placed on the new ruler's head, and his nose was pierced through the septum, where an emerald was inserted. The king was now led to the eagle seat, where he was seated to hear a series of speeches instructing him on his new responsibilities. A sampling of these speeches tells us some surprising things about how Aztecs valued and depended on their rulers.

First we hear the elevated metaphors: "O master, O ruler, O precious person, O precious one, O valued one, O precious green stone, O precious turquoise, O bracelet, O precious feather, thou art present here." Then, the reference to the sacred lineage: "Now, in truth, thy progenitors, thy great-grandfathers, have departed, have gone on to reside." Then, the statement of the weight of the responsibility of rulership: "For they departed placing, they departed leaving the bundle, the carrying frame, the governed-heavy, intolerable, insupportable."[8]

These heavy citizens are without a ruler, and the city lies darkened and abandoned until this very moment, when "our lord of the near, the nigh, causeth the sun to shine, bringeth the dawn. It is thou; he pointeth the finger at thee.... Our lord hath recorded thee, indicated thee, marked thee, entered thee in the books." This choice, this new king, is to be loaded down with an enormous responsibility, for he "will take over the burden": "Thou wilt take the bundle, thou wilt carry the carrying frame for thy progenitors....On thy back, on thy lap, in the arms our lord placeth the governed, the vassals, the common folk, the capricious, the peevish."[9]

Here we see the clear distinction made between the *macehualtin* and the *pipiltin*. The new ruler is warned about coming problems: "In thy time there will be disunity, quarreling in thy city. No more wilt thou be esteemed, no more wilt thou be regarded. Also war will move upon thee." But the ruler is encouraged to stand up to all troubles, for he is the living, present image of the god who governs all things: "Put forth all thy effort, give all, put forth all thy spirit. Sigh, be sad; call out in sadness to our lord, to the lord of the near, of the nigh.... Be not a fool. May thou not speak hurriedly, may thou not interrupt, may thou not confound. Take yet, grasp yet, arrive yet at the truth, for, it is said and it is true, thou art the replacement, thou art the image of the lord of the near, of the nigh."[10]

As the living image of the god who was close to all living things, the ruler's chief job was to ensure order, arrangement, and proper location so that the Aztec way of life could continue in the face of real dangers.

Over there is an abyss, over here is an abyss. Nowhere is it possible, to the left, to the right is the abyss.... Do not become completely enraged.... Retract thy teeth, thy claws. Gladden, gather, unite, humor, please thy noblemen, thy rulers. And make the city happy. Arrange each one in his proper place; establish thy nature, thy way of life.[11]

Following these speeches, the new ruler was transported to the eagle and ocelot thrones in Huitzilopochtli's temple, where he was given a jaguar claw to periodically pierce his ears and legs. In this moment, he again *ascended* upward to the temple of Huitzilopochtli, the sun and war god. Then he was taken to the Coatecoalli, the House of Foreign Gods, where more rites were carried out. At this time he visited the temple containing the gods of other peoples who were conquered by the Aztecs, which were carried by Aztec priests from the enemy towns into the capital city and symbolically imprisoned. In a sense, he was visiting the *horizontal* landscape of the four quarters, the earthly level of social and religious conquest now integrated in the House of Foreign Gods. Then, he was taken to the temple-cave of Yopico, where he communicated with the gods of the earth. In this moment, he symbolically *descended into the earth,* where he offered blood, quail, and incense.

Following this symbolic journey to the above, the below, and the four quarters, the new ruler was taken back to the palace for more speeches by other rulers and nobles; he was reminded of his lineage with Quetzalcoatl, Tezcatlipoca, and Huitzilopochtli. Then, in his first act of generosity, he distributed gifts to friends and allies. Especially important at this crucial moment of the opening of his reign were the gifts he gave to the assembled warriors. For it was said of the new *tlatoani,* "The ruler was known as the lord of men. His charge was war...he determined, disposed, and arranged how war would be made."[12] In fact, each new ruler had to organize and launch a war of conquest as one of the first acts of his reign. Without a successful war of conquest resulting in sacrificial victims and new tributary payments, his legitimacy as ruler would be questioned. Therefore, the warriors were central to his way of life, his arrangement of things. It is to the warrior class and their achievements, ranks, and lore that we now turn.

JAGUARS AND EAGLES: THE WARRIORS OF THE EMPIRE

Nowhere is the theme of fitting into one's proper place clearer in Aztec society than in the ranks and achievements of the warrior class. The surviving documents show us, again and again, that the warriors were crucial to the maintenance and renewal of social life and that they were meticulously ranked according to battlefield achievements. The central importance of warriors was recently demonstrated during the excavations of the Great Aztec Temple in the heart of Mexico City. Archaeologists discovered, immediately adjacent to the Great Temple, a compound containing a series of chambers richly decorated with murals and furnished with long benches showing carved processions of warriors; rich offerings were found in the floors. Flanking one of the doorways were human-size eagle warrior statues showing human beings encapsulated in giant eagle headdresses and deco-

A terra-cotta sculpture of an eagle warrior found at the Great
Temple. (Courtesy of Salvador Guil'liem Arroyo, INAH)

rated with stucco representing eagle feathers. The combination of the eagle warriors and the long carved processions of warriors led the archaeologists to name the entire compound the Eagle Warriors Precinct. The immediate proximity of this warrior compound to the Great Temple testifies to the sacred character of warriors and warfare. And when we remember that one of the two most important shrines in the entire city was dedicated to the war god Huitzilopochtli, who led the Aztecs into the lakes in the 14th century, it is clear that the status of warriors was central and sacred.

There are a number of Spanish eyewitness descriptions of Aztec warriors in combat, including this dramatic account of the battlefield:

It is one of the most beautiful sights in the world to see them in their battle array because they keep formation wonderfully and are very handsome. Among them are extraordinary brave men who face death with absolute determination. I saw one of them defend himself courageously against two swift horses, and another against three and four, and when the Spanish horseman could not kill him one of the horsemen in desperation hurled his lance, which the Indian caught in the air, and fought with him for more than an hour, until two foot soldiers approached and wounded him with two or three arrows. He turned on one of the soldiers but the other grasped him from behind and stabbed him. During combat they sing and dance and sometimes give the wildest shouts and whistles imaginable, especially when they know they have the advantage. Anyone facing them for the first time can be terrified by their screams and their ferocity.[13]

One cannot help but be impressed by the athletic ability, depth of commitment, excitement, and performative exertions of these warriors. But it is important to note that these kinds of wild and powerful displays were organized by a detailed system of rewards, precise tactical plans, and ritual protocol. War was often carried out in specifically designated places. Warriors occupied ranks, achieved a precise set of insignia and costumes, and, when killed, went to a particular heaven. Overseeing this entire system of order and locations was the *tlatoani*, who planned and launched wars, rewarded successful warriors with prizes, and depended on his soldiers to defend the city.

GOING TO WAR

The *tlatoani*, as the supreme warrior, was responsible for launching a coronation war soon after his installation. As in all wars, he was in charge of strategy and battlefield plans. This strategy began when spies were sent out of the city to scan the enemy community. These scouts were charged to return with detailed information in the form of painted images about the layout of the enemy *altepetl*, the surrounding terrain, and the entrances to the town. The military commanders were then summoned to formulate a plan of attack in terms of the time, approach, supplies, and organization of the warriors. Crucial to this stage of the battle preparations, which was almost like an outdoor theater play, were the public display and giving of rich, colorful gifts in the form of quetzal feathers, gold images, and especially shields of high value. The leading warriors were given special uniforms according to their achievements in previous battles. As we shall see, these uniforms were often flamboyant and played a vital role in the hierarchy of warfare. The *tlatoani* also sent out emissaries to allied rulers to build support. This also involved gifts. Consider this description of the building of a psychological and material alliance among the ruler, his warriors, and his allies:

The ruler then adorned and presented with insignia [all the costly devices] all the princes who were already able in war, and all the brave warriors, the men [at arms] the seasoned warriors, the shorn ones, the Otomí, and the noblemen who dwelt in the young men's houses.

And when it had come to pass that the ruler adorned them, when he had done this to the brave warriors, then the ruler ordered all the majordomos to bear their goods, all the costly devices, all the valuable capes there to battle, that the ruler might offer and endow with favors all the [other] rulers, and the noblemen, and the brave warriors.... He presented them all with costly capes, and he gave them all insignia of great price.[14]

The action of battle was tinctured with religious feeling and power. Priests, called "lords of the sun," took charge and directed in war. These "keepers of the gods... they bore the gods upon their backs" (meaning they carried images of gods with them in sacred bundles). They preceded the warriors' march by a day to the edge of the battle area to invoke the magical forces on behalf of Tenochtitlan. Their presence inspired the warriors, helped them focus their attention on the struggle ahead, and gave vigor and courage in the attack.

Battle between warriors from Tenochtitlan and Tlatelolco. (Diego Durán, *Códice Durán*. Mexico City: Arrendadora Internacional 1990 facsimile edition)

These marches could be complex tactical maneuvers involving thousands of warriors of varying degrees of experience as well as youths who carried supplies of food, shelter, and medicines. Once the troops arrived in the area of attack, the commanding generals took over and arranged the warriors in disciplined battle order. It was not unusual for fear to overtake some novices; if their behavior caused confusion among the ranks, they were severely beaten and sometimes executed on the spot. "No one might break ranks or crowd in among the others; they would then and there slay or beat whoever would bring confusion or crowd in among the others."[15] The tension of the moment of attack is described: "And when they already were to rise against the city to destroy it, first was awaited tensely the moment when fire flared up—when the priests brought forth new fire—and for the blowing of shell trumpets, when the priests blew them. And when the fire flared up, then as one arose all the warriors. War cries were raised; there was fighting. They shot fiery arrows into the temples."[16]

The battles were ferocious, noisy, and dangerous physical pandemoniums. The goals were death and capture. The first warrior to be captured was slain on the spot, his breast slashed open with a flint knife. Warriors went in groups and pairs to overwhelm the novices and get to the more experienced warriors, who were attacked and captured if possible. As we shall see, capturing enemy warriors, especially those of high rank, was crucial to elevating one's

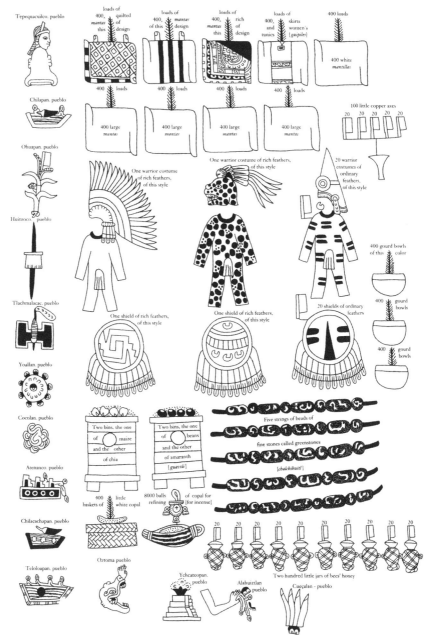

Tribute paid to Tenochtitlan by various communities. (*Codex Mendoza,* courtesy of Frances F. Berdan and Patricia Reiff Anawalt)

place in society. Once a city had been subdued and the main temples burned, there was an immediate accounting of the number of captives as well as the Aztec dead. The *tlatoani* was immediately informed of his own battle dead and those taken captive. Runners were soon dispatched back to Tenochtitlan to "inform all in the homes of those who had gone to die in war, that there might be weeping in the homes of those who had gone to war to die. And they informed those in the homes of the many that had gone to take captives in war that they had received honors there because of their valor."[17] As before the battle, rewards were now given to the successful warriors, including costly capes, foods, chocolate, ear and lip plugs, and other colorful items. Nobles, however, if they had taken captives, received the richest gifts in the form of "honor, fame, and renown" as well as promotions. Those who "had done wrong in battle" were executed on the battlefield by being stoned or beaten to death.

Sometimes disputes broke out among the victorious warriors over who had actually overcome an enemy and taken him prisoner. A special officer called the master of captives, who had already captured at least four warriors in battle, listened to the case and made a

---

WARRIORS

Aztec warfare depended on an efficient road system that linked the cities and towns of Central Mexico. This allowed the Aztec armies, consisting of a few thousand to 100,000 warriors, to march between 20 and 30 kilometers a day.

---

decision. In cases with too much ambiguity, the captive was simply turned over to a neutral *barrio* in the city, where he was eventually presented for sacrifice.

The most important long-term arrangement was the determination of the kinds and amounts of tribute payments the conquered community would supply to the capital and the ruler. These payments included corn, feathers, shields, cacao, capes, green stones, jaguar skins, eagles, and all manner of valuable goods. An Aztec tribute officer was assigned to the conquered town to ensure that the tribute was collected and sent to the capital according to a tight schedule.

WOMEN AND WAR

Although women played secondary roles in the war efforts, their lives were profoundly influenced by many aspects of warfare. Women were seldom warriors, but when necessary they defended their families, homes, and men to the point of death. There is at least one vivid account of women acting as warriors when their community was sorely threatened. Diego Durán, a Dominican friar who conducted research shortly after the conquest of Tenochtitlan, provides the following account of women acting as warriors. During the Spanish siege of Tenochtitlan, the Aztecs were on the defensive.

Cuauhtemoc [Diving Eagle, the Aztec *tlatoani*] now lacked men and strength to defend himself and the city, but, enraged over the death of so many of his people, because so many of his allies had abandoned him, had fled the city, and because of the great hunger they had suffered, he decided not to show weakness or cowardice. He pretended that he did not lack warriors to fight for him and therefore had all the women ascend to the flat roofs of the houses, where they made gestures of scorn to the Spaniards.... When Cortés saw the great number of people covering the flat roofs and filling the streets of the city, he became afraid and feared that he would not be able to conquer Mexico without causing harm to his Spaniards and friends. But he urged the Chalcas, Tezcocans...to take courage and finish with the enterprise. All the men returned to the combat and at this time they realized that the warriors who stood on the roofs

Women defending their community. (Diego Durán, *Códice Durán*. Mexico City: Arrendadora Internacional 1990 facsimile edition)

were women. They sent word to Cortés about this and then began to ridicule and insult the enemy and attack and kill many of them. . . . In the end, though, the Spaniards, greatly aided by their Indian allies, vanquished the Aztecs and made the courageous King Cuauhtemoc flee.[18]

There can be no doubt that this was not the first time that women were used as the last defense of a community under lethal attack, and there are references to women who acted militantly and effectively in combat. But the greatest impact on women was the constant condition of becoming widows through warfare. The many funeral rites held in the *altepetl* for warriors killed in battle or sacrifice also meant that women and their children were now without husbands and fathers. One account tells us that the *tlatoani* would assemble the mourners and address the widows in this fashion:

O my daughter, let no sadness overwhelm you or end the days of your life. We have brought you the tears and sighs of those who were your father, your mother, your shelter. . . . Take courage, show your love for our sons who did not die plowing or digging in the fields, who did not die on the road, trading, but have gone forever, for the honor of our country. They have departed holding each other's hands . . . are now rejoicing in the shining place of the sun, where they walk about in his company, embellished with his light. . . . Therefore illustrious matrons, distinguished Aztec women, weep [for their memory]![19]

These Aztec women, now distinguished by their loss, carried the cloaks of their dead husbands in procession. They wore their hair loose as a sign of mourning and clapped their hands to the beating of the drums; they "wept bitterly and at times they danced, bowing their heads toward the earth. At other times they danced leaning backward. The sons of the dead men also were present, wearing their fathers' cloaks, carrying on their backs small boxes containing the lip, ear and nose plugs, and other jewelry." At times the weeping and wailing was so great that the entire community was filled with fear and trembling.

Women faced another fearful experience if they were captured in war, which was a common pattern. When any community was defeated, the priests and warriors moved in to take booty and to organize a regular tribute payment. Women were often part of immediate and long-term tribute payments to victorious communities. When the Aztecs were victors, they would take captive women, children, and warriors and tie them together with cords drawn through the perforations in their noses. Or, as in the case when the Aztecs defeated the Huaxtecs, "the maidens, daughters of Huaxtecs who had been seized, and the children and little boys who did not yet have their noses or ears perforated wore wooden yokes on their throats, and they were all tied together this way."[20] As in all wars, women were often killed alongside their men and children, especially when real resistance was shown against the Aztecs, or by them.

THE RANKS AND COSTUMES OF WARRIORS

Warriors from both the nobility (*pipiltin*) and the commoners (*macehualtin*) were crucial to the life and success of Aztec warfare. While the military training (which, as noted in the previous chapter, was offered in the *calmecac* as well as in the *telpochcalli*) differed somewhat between these two social classes, it is very difficult to tell whether the rewards for battlefield valor and success were really any different. What follows is a general picture of the ranks and rewards that warriors could expect to find at different levels of the military hierarchy.

A one-captive warrior was a young man who had taken a captive unaided by others. He carried a *maquahuitl*, or club made of well-finished oak. Grooves were cut along both sides, and obsidian or flint stone blades were inserted with turtle dung to make them stick. The warrior was also given a *chimalli*, or shield, without decorations. This feat of taking a captive meant that the warrior had truly embarked on a warrior's career, and he was rewarded with a *manta*, or cloak, decorated with flowers. He also received an orange cape with a striped border, a carmine-colored loincloth, and a scorpion-knotted design cape. The wearing of designs was a valued addition to one's attire.

A two-captive warrior was given the highly valued right to wear sandals onto the battlefield as well as a pointed, cone-shaped cap and a feathered warrior suit with parallel black lines. This is the costume that appears most often in the *Codex Mendoza*'s pictorial program of warrior outfits. In fact, more than 19 culturally diverse provinces sent this kind of costume to the Aztec capital as tribute payment.

One of the most impressive costumes was the four-captive warrior's *ocelotl*, or jaguar, outfit. Ocelots were powerful, stocky animals with great hunting and attacking skills. The body of a warrior was enclosed within an ocelot skin and his head emerged

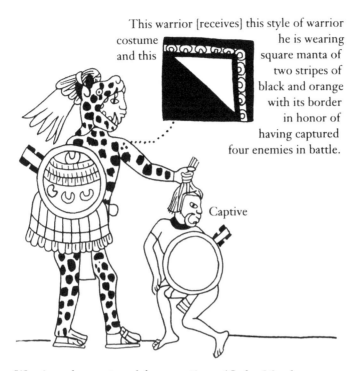

This warrior [receives] this style of warrior costume and this he is wearing square manta of two stripes of black and orange with its border in honor of having captured four enemies in battle.

Captive

Warrior who captured four captives. (*Codex Mendoza,* courtesy of Frances F. Berdan and Patricia Reiff Anawalt)

from the mouth of the animal. These warriors constituted a special unit within the army. Jaguar and Eagle Warriors were respected throughout the empire for their ferocity and bravery. Diego Durán, who grew up in Mexico City soon after the conquest, learned many details about the nature of these warriors and warrior cults:

They were the men whom the sovereigns most loved and esteemed, the men who obtained most privileges and prerogatives. To them the kings granted most generous favors, adorning them with brilliant, splendid weapons and insignia.... When one of these knights performed a great feat in war, capturing or slaying, he obtained these distinctions. As soon as the warrior returned to the court, the king was informed of the brave deed of the knight, who was brought before him. After manifesting his appreciation, the king dubbed him a knight and gave him his honor.... The hair on the top of his head was parted in two, and a red cord wrapped around it; in the same cord was attached an ornament of green, blue, and red feathers...and a red tassel.[21]

These warriors were also used in the famous gladiatorial sacrifices of enemy warriors in the month of the Feast of the Flaying of Men. Four of these jaguar warriors attacked an enemy who was tied to a sacrificial stone, swinging their razor-sharp, obsidian-laced clubs until the captive was killed.

Warriors of extreme distinction were made into generals and were decorated with lavish quetzal-feathered hair ornaments and long, yellow lips plugs made of amber. Their capes were called the "jewels of Ehecatl" (the wind god), and they had awesome titles such as Keeper of the Mirrored Snake, Keeper of the Bowl of Fatigue, Keeper of the House of Darts, or Raining Blood.

All these warriors protected the daily life of the Aztecs, for it was said that they "extended as if made into a wall of men dexterous with arms."[22] These arms formed the protective wall around the city but also reached out, not only to enemy battlefields, as we have seen, but also into the communities that rebelled against the Aztecs, especially those that attacked the Aztec merchants. The rebellious city of Coayxtlahuacan, located far south of Tenochtitlan in the region of Oaxaca, attacked and murdered a large contingent of more than 160 Aztec merchants who were trading in their local marketplace. We have seen what the typical Aztec response, under the guidance of the *tlatoani,* was to this assassination. A war was launched, executioners penetrated the Oaxacan town, and the rebels were executed. But this story introduces us to one of the other key social groups in the pyramidal society of Anahuac, namely, the merchants, called the *pochteca.* Let us turn to the work, symbols, and routes of the great merchants of Tenochtitlan to gain a still broader view of how Aztec society was maintained and renewed.

THE CRY OF THE LAUGHING FALCON: MERCHANTS OF THE CAPITAL CITY

As we have seen, the Aztec city, its ruler, and its peoples were adorned with and accompanied by a wide range of attractive, powerful objects. Many valued objects, including foodstuffs, women's clothes, warriors' costumes, and sacred animals, came from regions and lands beyond the Basin of Mexico. Crucial to the importation and exchange culture of the Mexica were the *pochteca,* the merchants who traveled near and far to trade, spy, make war, and bring goods home.

The dangers and hardships of these carriers of goods cannot be exaggerated. They left home, went out into dangerous terrain, and skirted enemy communities. They traveled through perilous gorges, scaled steep hills and mountains, and crossed treacherous rivers.

They operated in the fear that they would hear the cry of the *huactli*, or laughing falcon, whose noises could signify their doom. If the falcon laughed for a short time during their journey, it was considered a good omen, and success was ensured. But when "they heard that it laughed too long, in a high pitch,—as if its bosom and side tightened; or as if it screamed swollen with joy…they felt that perhaps something woeful would now betide them; they would come upon something perilous."[23] Their labors were heroic, and when successful they brought riches and honor to their ruler, the city, and themselves. The *Codex Mendoza* gives a sense of the material culture that flowed into Tenochtitlan. This was the work of the merchant class, which, true to the idea of a locative view of the world, lived in its own area of the city, worshiped specific gods, and carried out particular sacrifices or debt payments to demonstrate that its *earthly exchanges of goods depended in part on its exchanges with deities.*

Merchant life and history were intertwined with the lifeblood of the Mexica. Merchants were portrayed as being crucial to *every stage of history* that was remembered and revered by the society. For instance, when the history of the rulers was told to the Spaniards, the evolution of trade was intertwined in the narration. Principal merchants are mentioned alongside of rulers, and the growth of trade and the introduction of new trade goods were considered an important part of royal history. We are told that when commerce began, only red arara and blue and scarlet parrot feathers were traded. During the reign of the next ruler, quetzal and troupial feathers, turquoise and green stones, capes and breechcloths of cotton, and skirts of *maguey* fiber were added to the trade list. The next ruler saw new and powerful merchants bringing gold lip and ear plugs, fine turquoise radiating pendants, and the skins of wild animals into the city.

The history of trade was also intimately tied in with wars of conquest and expansion. As the Aztecs spread their interests and power throughout Anahuac, merchants worked as spies, intelligence officers, and warriors. They were part of a frontier communication system. The work of merchants was implicated in the value of captives; for those captives, who "came carrying quetzal feather crest devices; shirts of blue continga feathers, turquoise mosaic shields, golden butterfly-shaped nose plates"—that is to say, the objects brought into any community by merchants—were the most valued.[24] In this sense, *you were what you wore,* or *you were worth what you wore.* When wars were successful, the mopping-up operation was led by the merchants, who went in and assessed the goods, supplies, and production capabilities of the conquered town so that the appropriate level of tribute could be registered. These vanguard merchants would move in and proclaim: "For we came only to seek land for the master, the portent, Huitzilopochtli. And behold the property which we shall have merited, which shall have become the recompense of our breasts and heads, when we come to appear in, when we reach, Mexico; these amber lip plugs, and curved, green pendants with bells, and black staves, and crested guan feather fans."[25] In fact, the *tlatoani* Ahuitzotl took great pains to set up an effective communication system with returning merchants to ensure that the war booty was quickly brought into his royal market. Thus he could benefit from and redistribute the goods, some of which went to the returning merchants as payment for their dangerous, hard work.

A number of orations or *huehuetlatolli,* the rhetorical speeches of the elders, tell of the life and work of the merchants. In general, these ancient sayings and teachings describe three phases of the merchants' existence: the rituals of departure for trading expeditions, the rituals of return, and the practice of sacrificing slaves to the gods. Each phase reflects the central concern of this chapter: the primacy of location in social and geographical space. But we also see how *rites of passage,* similar to those discussed in the previous chapter, were linked to the theme of locative order, for the merchants were deeply concerned about any major *change of place* in their lives. When they left home, they held elaborate preparation ceremonies to build up their magical forces. When they returned, they underwent rites to purify themselves and to reenter the social and sacred world of the city. And they also had to make a final exchange with the gods by paying them back for their safe passage and successful trading, spying, or warring activity.

LEAVING THE HOME PLACE

Thou shalt go into, entering, and leaving, city after city. Thou shalt be in danger; it will not be well with thee.... Thou shalt be long-suffering; thou shalt shed tears.... Perhaps somewhere in a gorge, at the mouth of a canyon, on some high place...at the foot of a tree, shalt thou sleep.[26]

The lives of merchants were lives of ceremony, hardship, and often rich rewards. The act of leaving the home *altepetl* for a trading or spying expedition was an intense, exhilarating, and even frightening event, and merchants could not leave until they participated in elaborate rituals and speeches. As noted previously, the merchant had to live by the calendar signs and could only leave on a good day with a favorable day sign. These included especially

1 Serpent, called the *straight way,* but also the days 2 Crocodile, 1 Monkey, or 7 Serpent. A ceremony was held before a large gathering at a feast organized by the lead or vanguard merchant. The veteran merchants and those going out for the first time were spoken to by an elder merchant, their parents, and other elders who knew the lore and wisdom.

The ceremony began with a ritual cleansing as all the travelers washed their heads with soap and cut their hair. It was understood that they would not wash their heads or cut their hair again until they returned to the city. They would bathe only up to their necks while on the merchant journey. This purification was followed by the decoration of their merchant's staff, which was the symbol and image of their god. They cut papers in a forked style and attached them to the staff with liquid rubber. "They gave it lips, nose, eyes. It resembled a man. Thus did they make a representation of the fire [god]."[27] They wrapped their traveling cane with images of not only Xiuhtecuhtli (the fire god), but also Tlaltecuhtli (the earth deity), Yacatecuhtli (the patron god of merchants), and others. These staffs or staves were the guides and protectors of the merchants.

Now the merchants were ready for a sacrifice, or debt payment, as they called it. Recall that the Aztec worldview put humans in repeated debt to the gods for having given their lives to create the earth, heavens, underworld, and all that existed. At midnight, the merchants placed their canes in a ceremonial pile dedicated to the gods in the courtyard and entered a home, where they stood before the fire in order to increase their *tonalli,* the soul force in their heads. They beheaded quails to feed the fire, then took obsidian blades, pierced their ears and tongues, and flicked their blood into the fire. They returned to the courtyard and scattered their blood toward the sky, the east, the west, the south, and the north, four times each. The blood was also spattered on papers in the courtyard, and then these papers were taken into the house and offered to the fire to give it strength and renewed life. They spoke to the fire: "May it be well with thee, O thou ocelot warrior...O lord of the four quarters! May thou in peace accept thy property, thy possessions, perchance in some small thing I have offended thee."

Then the merchant was supposed to say privately to himself, "He hath been good to me, the master, our lord, I shall indeed reach the place where I am to go."

This is a good example of the sacred bonds between a merchant and the gods. A merchant's bond, a bond of sacred *exchange,* is what being a merchant is all about. He gives to the god, the warrior of the four quarters who lives in the center of the house, temple, and universe, knowing that the god is likely to give him protection on his journey. Of course there is always the possibility the merchant will not be safe, as indicated in the phrase "perchance in some small thing I have offended thee."[28]

Following other detailed ritual gestures, the supporters and elders were assembled and a feast was given, followed by speeches. The traveling merchants were encouraged to face up to the perils of the road with courage, to meet death, if it came, with valor, and to remember that death on the road was like death for the warrior in battle. This meant that they would have a wonderful afterlife in the House of the Sun. They were repeatedly told to work as a tight-knit group, say their prayers, and keep their places. This meant that the elder merchants had to watch over the novices, who were ordered to serve the elders during the journey. Special focus was given to the lead merchant, who heard, sensed, and felt both the compassionate support of his family and comrades and the deep responsibility he had for the merchant troop. The leader ended by saying, "Now we leave

Yacatecuhtli, the patron deity of merchants, at a crossroads. (*Codex Fejérváry-Mayer*, from the Eduard Seler edition: Berlin, 1901)

you; now we proceed to go. For we have received, we have taken, your exhortations, the tears, the compassion which is folded, bound within your bowels, your breasts. For we abandon the entrances and the courtyards. And our aunts, our elder sisters, our parents—may they not forget us."[29] In fact, these departures were full of worries, sorrow, weeping, and some real fear. Family members prayed, sang, and cried, exhorting the merchants to be very careful.

As noted, the life and work of merchants on the road was dangerous. Besides worrying about accidents and the cry of the laughing falcon, they faced ambush, imprisonment, torture, and sacrifice. They had to stick together to garner courage and the magical forces of their walking sticks, gods, and the potent blood within their bodies. Consider this passage about a group of merchants frightened nearly to death on the road by omens, specters of enemies in the shadows, and the formless fears of the night:

And if somewhere night fell, they gathered, joined, crowded, and assembled themselves somewhere at the foot of a tree or the opening of a gorge, and bound and tied, fastened together, and placed on the ground, all their staves, which represented their god Yacatecuhtli. Here, before him, they did penance, bled themselves, cut their ears, and drew straws through them; so that they only yielded to whatsoever might befall them.... If nothing befell them, their hearts were therefore again a little lifted; they raised their heads and revived their spirits; for their fates were so established that fear should no longer be with them.[30]

RETURNING HOME: THE WASHING OF THE FEET

When the merchants returned after their arduous and hopefully lucrative journey, two days were dedicated to reintroducing them to their place, their cultured existence within the city. These two days were filled with feasting, drinking, storytelling, and speechmaking. The merchants returned full of ambiguous potency. On the one hand, if they were successful, they carried highly valued, prestigious objects that had been under their control, observation, and care for some time. One can imagine the temptations and dreams that merchants had, surrounded by those hard-earned riches. On the other hand, they had a kind of dangerous power because they had been outside the social order, in contact with allies and enemies, and subject to the magical forces of the roads, mountains, valleys, and animals. Often, returning merchants brought the painful news of death on the road. They had to report dangers, attacks, and deaths. Therefore, the elders put the returning merchants through a harsh interrogation about the honesty of the expedition, the facts of the encounters, ambushes, meetings, and exchanges, and the intensity of their work.

These interrogations reduced some merchants to tears, we are told, but it appears that these were ceremonial tears, a calculated way of returning to the city. It seems that the merchants were very careful to show humility in the extreme rather than return boasting and displaying their newly gained wealth. The text tells us that the

CACAO

Merchants were associated with cacao beans, which the Aztecs used as currency in the local markets to buy clothing, tools, and jewelry. Cacao was also used to make chocolate, which was valued for its taste and as an energy drink! Columbus was the first European to learn of the bean's importance, but he thought it was a type of almond.

elders "humbled them: they sternly admonished them not to disregard, not to neglect our lord."[31]

Drinking and feasting followed, and the goods were taken to the *tlatoani*, whose assistants recorded them and arranged for their distribution according to the desires of the ruler. Often, merchants were richly rewarded.

PAYING THE DEBT: SACRIFICING SOMEONE ELSE

Since a later chapter focuses on the practice of human sacrifice, it is not necessary to go into any detail about the responsibility the merchants had to sacrifice slaves or purchased victims as a way of paying their debts to the gods for a successful trading campaign. Suffice it to say that following their interrogation, the washing of the feet, and the reception of rewards, they vowed to sacrifice purchased victims in a ceremony called the Bathing. These victims, both male and female, were purchased in a particular marketplace from slave-dealers. The victims were carefully dressed with precious capes, sandals, and lip plugs and had their hair cut in the manner of seasoned warriors. The women were likewise arrayed and decorated, and given tobacco tubes to suck and flowers to carry. Specific rituals designed to transform the victims into the containers of the spirits and fire of the gods were carried out. A great feast was held honoring both the warriors and the merchants. One of the principal purposes of this sacrificial ceremony was the distribution of rich gifts.

All these precious capes and breech clouts mentioned were given as gifts to the great chieftains: the commanding general, the fearless warriors, the lord general…indeed all princes of the reigning family. To these the bather of slaves gave gifts according to their liking. And then he gave gifts to the principal merchants, to those who bathed slaves, and all the distinguished merchants, the spying merchants who entered regions of battle, the slave dealers…. And then he gave gifts to all the women who bathed slaves…. They received as gifts skirts; the one with the heart design, and with whorl or spiral designs.[32]

And then the slaves, now in the form of gods, were sacrificed.

THE BACKFRAMES: THOSE WHO LABORED TO SUPPORT THE PYRAMID

Remembering that the Aztecs constructed an urban society, it is important to give attention to the many ranks, diverse classes of people, numerous social slots, jobs, and laborers who held up the social pyramid on their hands, backs, skills, and abilities. As one would expect, there is much less information about the people who filled out the bottom half of the social pyramid. But it is possible to present some snapshot descriptions of the farmers, stonecutters, carpenters, shopkeepers, clay workers, candle sellers, and weavers. The following word pictures describe these vitally important groups and their work.

The Diligent Farmer

Farmers were divided into two groups—good farmers and bad farmers. The good farmer was most of all energetic and physically powerful, and gave diligent attention to his fields, seeds, soils, and landmarks. A good farmer was thin, a sign of working long hours, eating small amounts, and keeping vigil on the job. Farmers were people of the earth who were skilled at making rows and furrows, breaking up the soil, working particularly hard in summer planting, watering, sprinkling, sowing, thinning the bad corn from the good corn, and timing the harvest. Farmers were the corn people, and, as keepers of the corn, called on the corn gods to assist them in their labor. "He cuts the maize ears, he dismembers them. He shells them, treads on them, cleans them, winnows them, throws them against the wind."[33]

Some farmers were specialists in different types of seeds and trees. Some planters, usually the lead farmers, were specialists in reading the day signs in the pictorial books that told when to prepare the land, plant, irrigate, and harvest. They knew a good deal about the stars and had to synchronize the signs in the books with the weather and the passage of the seasons.

The bad farmer was described as "a shirker, a lukewarm worker . . . one who drops his work . . . noisy, decrepit, unfit . . . who gorges himself."[34]

Carpenters and Stonecutters

The carpenter was described as "one who uses the plumb; who is resourceful. . . . He straightens, evens the edges, planes them, polishes them, makes the edges match." Clearly, these were experts in fitting things into their proper places. Good carpenters were highly valued, especially by the nobles, whose homes, patios, and furniture demanded good woodwork. Bad carpenters, by contrast, were noisy, raising "a clattering din," nonchalant, and broke up lumber and destroyed the wood.[35]

A similar description of the stonecutter tells of powerful, wiry, energetic individuals who had very skilled hands. They were responsible for quarrying the stones, breaking them into large and small pieces, splitting them, curving them, and cutting them with great dexterity, turning them into everything from walkways to houses to monuments. They were draftsmen as well: "he builds a house; draws, sketches a house; draws plans, devises a house, projects house plans." Some of the imperial stonecutters were responsible for the great religious monuments such as the Calendar Stone and other marvelous artistic structures. Unlike the bad or evil stonemason, these individuals did not have a "lame, feeble arm."[36]

The Well-Instructed Craftsmen

Among the many groups of craftsmen, referred to as the *toltecatl*, meaning the keepers of the great Toltec artistic tradition of excellence, were the featherworkers, goldworkers, copperworkers, and lapidaries. The featherworkers were ingenious, imaginative artists whose arrangements of feathers were valued at every level of the social world and especially by the nobles and rulers. They fashioned the feathered shields, capes, and headdresses of the warriors, nobles, and the family of the ruler. They had a good eye for color arrangements.

The gold and copper workers were wise technicians with hands trained for pouring liquid metals, forming molds, shaping the castings, and transforming them into gods, jewels, and other valued symbols. We gain a sense of the intense labor and skill of these workers in this description of the lapidary: "The lapidary is…a creator of works of skill. He is adroit, a designer of works of skill, a gluer of mosaic of stone. He creates, he designs works of skill. He grinds down, he polishes, he applies abrasive stand to stones. He rubs them with fine cane; he make them shine; he glues turquoise. Unlike the bad lapidary, he does not pulverize, damage, or shatter the stones."[37]

Tailors and weavers were widely appreciated at all levels of society, for they made, repaired, and decorated the clothes worn for all occasions. The good tailor knew the art of sewing, stitching, turning hems, measuring, and fitting clothes. He had an artistic ability with designs, ornamentation, and color. Spinning was done mainly by women. As we saw in the description of the upbringing of girls, this art was their territory. "The good spinner is one who forms a thread of even thickness, who stretches it delicately. She put[s] it in her lap. She fills the spindle, stretches the thread…she is persevering and diligent; she works delicately."[38] Weavers were valued if they had steady, dexterous hands. They had the capacity for great sustained focus of attention and needed to use their eyes carefully as they placed and manipulated the templates.

The Sellers of Things

There were a number of types of shopkeepers who sold everything from green stones, feathers, jewelry, capes, obsidian, lime, dyes, glue, candles, bags, baskets, sandals, gourd bowls, smoking tubes, and medicine to amaranth, beans, tortillas, fruit, meat, salt, cacao, and even fine chocolate. Chocolate and cacao were considered wonderful additions to the human diet, and the sellers of these items were esteemed. Chocolate is a good way to end this chapter on the social pyramid of Aztec society; so consider these two short descriptions of a "seller of fine chocolate" and a "bad cacao-seller":

The Seller of Fine Chocolate…is one who grinds…she crushes, breaks, pulverizes the cacao beans.… She drenches, soaks, steeps them…adds water sparingly, conservatively; aerates it, filters it, strains it, makes it form a head, makes it foam; she removes the head, makes it thicken.… She sells good superior potable chocolate; the privilege, the drink of nobles, of rulers…with wild bee honey, with powdered aromatic flowers.[39]

In contrast, the bad cacao seller is a "deluder" who "counterfeits cacao…by making the fresh cacao beans whitish…stirs them into the ashes…with amaranth seed dough, wax, avocado pits he counterfeits cacao.… Indeed he casts, he throws in with them wild cacao beans to deceive the people."[40]

NOTES

1. Bernardino de Sahagún, *Florentine Codex: General History of the Things of New Spain*, ed. and trans. Arthur J. O. Anderson and Charles E. Dibble, introductory vol. and 12 books (Santa Fe, NM: School of American Research and University of Utah, 1950–82), 8: 29.

2. Quoted in Alfredo López Austin, *The Human Body and Ideology: Concepts of the Ancient Nahuas*, trans. Thelma Ortiz de Montellano and Bernard Ortiz de Montellano, 2 vols. (Salt Lake City: University of Utah Press, 1988), 1: 399.

3. Sahagún, *Florentine Codex*, 8: 27–28.

4. López Austin, *Human Body and Ideology*, 1: 385–86.

5. Ibid., 387.

6. Ibid., 392.

7. Sahagún, *Florentine Codex*, 6: 90.

8. Ibid., 47.

9. Ibid., 48–49.

10. Ibid., 50.

11. Ibid., 53.

12. Ibid., 8: 51.

13. Ross Hassig, *Aztec Warfare: Imperial Expansion and Political Control* (Norman: University of Oklahoma Press, 1988), 124.

14. Sahagún, *Florentine Codex*, 8: 51–52.

15. Ibid., 52.

16. Ibid., 53.

17. Ibid.

18. Diego Durán, *The History of the Indies of New Spain*, trans. Doris Heyden (Norman: University of Oklahoma Press, 1995), 555–56.

19. Ibid., 283.

20. Ibid., 327.

21. Diego Durán, *Book of the Gods and Rites and The Ancient Calendar*, ed. and trans. Fernando Horcasitas and Doris Heyden (Norman: University of Oklahoma Press, 1971), 197–98.

22. Sahagún, *Florentine Codex*, 8: 52.

23. Ibid., 5: 153.

24. Ibid., 9: 3.
25. Ibid., 4.
26. Ibid., 6: 63.
27. Ibid., 9: 9.
28. Ibid., 11.
29. Ibid., 15.
30. Ibid., 5: 155.
31. Ibid., 9: 30.
32. Ibid., 47.
33. Ibid., 10: 42.
34. Ibid.
35. Ibid., 27.
36. Ibid., 28.
37. Ibid., 26.
38. Ibid., 35.
39. Ibid., 93.
40. Ibid., 65.

6

AZTEC AESTHETICS: FLOWERS AND SONGS

He hath been able to achieve four hundred.

It is said of one who knows many things—books, painting, or some profession such as the casting of copper, the carving of wood, the casting of gold; all of this he knows well. Hence it is said of him: "He hath been able to achieve four hundred."[1]

When the German painter and engraver Albrecht Dürer first saw a collection of Aztec art objects that had been given by Motecuhzoma to Hernán Cortés and sent to the Holy Roman Emperor, Charles V, soon after the conquest of Tenochtitlan, he exclaimed, "These objects are so valuable that they have been set at a hundred thousand florins. In all my life I have never seen anything that rejoiced my heart so much: I have found an admirable art in them, and I have been astonished by the subtle spirit of the men of these strange countries." This admiration and astonishment in the face of Aztec masterpieces and royal gifts, which brought joy to Dürer's heart, parallels in a remarkable way what the Aztecs themselves felt about the aesthetic (perceiving the beautiful and true nature of the world) creations of their own singers, poets, featherworkers, sculptors, potters, woodworkers, and painters. Their art was about *beauty, heart, and spirit.* As we know by now in our study of the Aztec world, the Toltecs of the 10th to 12th centuries were revered as having invented the great artistic traditions that inspired and decorated Tenochtitlan and signified the spirit of gods in everyday life. Consider this description, outdoing even Dürer's admiration and praise, of how the Aztecs remembered the Toltecs as the sources of art:

The traces of the Tolteca, their pyramids, their mounds, appear not only there at the places called Tula and Xicocotitlan, but practically everywhere—their potsherds, their ollas, their pestles, their figures, their armbands appear everywhere.... And many times Tolteca jewels—arm bands, esteemed green stones, fine turquoise—are taken from the earth.... In ancient times they took charge of the gluing of feathers; and it really was their discovery,... their exclusive property.... In truth they invented all the wonderful, precious, marvelous things which they made.... They went to seek all the mines of amber, of rock crystal, of amethyst, they went to marvel at the pearls, the opals. And these Tolteca were very wise; they were thinkers, for they originated the year count, the day count.[2]

It would be a mistake to think that the central meaning of Aztec art came primarily from the ability to take natural forms and transform them into cultural masterpieces. The Aztecs were excellent craftspeople, painters, and poets. But remember that they understood that their world was infused with divine forces that did not originate in human genius, effort, or imagination. Rather, the world of plants, stones, animals, sky, earth, feathers, and humans was created by gods and existed as something like *the artwork of the gods*. The responsibility of humans was to shape their art as a kind of imitation of the gods' artistic creativity, knowing all the while that they would fall short. Consider this description of the ritual houses or temples built in the 10th century by the ruler Quetzalcoatl as an example of how art and architecture were viewed as imitations of cosmological patterns (in this case, the four quarters of the universe) and truth:

Wherefore was it called a Tolteca house? It was built with consummate care, majestically designed: it was the place of worship of their priest whose name was Quetzalcoatl; it was quite marvelous. It consisted of four abodes. One was facing east; this was the house of gold; for this reason it was called house of gold; that which served as the stucco was gold plate applied, joined to it. One was facing west, toward the setting sun; this was the house of green stone, the house of fine turquoise.... One was facing south, toward the irrigated lands, this was the house of shells or of silvers.... One was facing north, toward the plains...this was the red house; red because red shells were inlaid in the interior walls.[3]

This chapter will explore several of the major artistic traditions of the Aztecs in an effort to appreciate and understand their theory of art and aesthetics. In their view, art was a temporary expression, a technique to (1) open the artist and the audience to divine truth, (2) imitate and approximate the cosmic beauty and pattern of the gods, and (3) communicate and celebrate the gods so that life on earth would be better for humankind. This art was sometimes used in trade and was also part of domestic and political life, royal display, and ritual sacrifice. But the power of the best art came from its ability to reflect and communicate with gods. In what follows we will study the *tlacuilo* (painter of the red and black), the *tlamatini* (wise philosopher-teacher), the sculptor, the featherworker, and other artistic professions.

Stone sculpture of a dog from the National Museum of Anthropology, Mexico City. (Courtesy of Salvador Guil'liem Arroyo, INAH)

THE *TLACUILO*

With flowers You write,
O Giver of Life;
With songs You give color,
with songs You shade
those who live here on the earth.
Later You will erase eagles and tigers,
we live only in Your book of paintings,
here, on the earth.[4]

This poem depicts Ometeotl, the Dual God, as a writer, a singer, and a painter. The Giver of Life is the divine artist who sings and *paints human life into existence in his/her divine book.* The message is also that "those who live here on the earth" are perishable, existing for only a short time. The world is created by the "flowers and songs" of the gods. As we shall see, humans created their own flowers and songs as ways of imitating the divine and communicating with the gods. If gods painted the world in a book, then the human painter, the *tlacuilo,* "he who paints in the red and black ink," was the artist closest to the gods. We see this tie between painting and the gods in this poem about the ideal painter:

The good painter is a Toltec, an artist:
he creates with red and black ink,
with black water....

The good painter is wise,
God is in his heart.

He puts divinity into things;
he converses with his own heart.

He knows the colors, he applies them and shades them;
he draws feet and faces,
he puts in the shadows, he achieves perfection.

He paints the colors of all the flowers,
as if he were a Toltec.[5]

These painters, trained in the priestly schools, were profound stores of knowledge about the mythology, genealogy, and history of the community. The pictorial books of the Aztecs recorded calendars, festivals, mythology, history, conduct of wars, omens, astronomy, coronation ceremonies, and many other aspects of social life. But all these events and patterns were understood to be infused with divine purpose and meaning. To be a true painter, a person had to develop an inward sense of feeling and understanding about the nature and intention of the god. This was called *conversing with one's heart,* which resulted in the painter becoming a *yolteotl,* or *heart rooted in god.* A person who had taken a god into his or her heart could then transfer the images and purpose of the divine reality into the paintings, codices, and murals that were so important to the Aztecs.

We gain a sense of the creative power of these artists, of their hearts and faces, when we gaze at images from the surviving codices and vase paintings. The color, fluidity of line, composition of pages, and the frozen drama of the stories painted on the pages are inspirational even to those who do not understand well the messages being conveyed. On the one hand, they look something like our cartoons, while on the other, they dazzle us with combinations of color and drama. The surviving books are full of images of gods, goddesses, sacred hills, calendar signs, rituals, and the cosmos. We see the Tlaloc gods dwelling in heaven, the four quarters of the universe balanced around a warrior god, rituals of sacrifice, and brilliant calendar signs associated with gods, all with elaborate and symbolic costumes. The bright procession of garments decorating the gestures, gazes, and postures of gods, goddesses, rulers, and animals is full of signs and meanings that are only now becoming clearer to scholars, who for centuries have tried to decipher these scenes. The problem, in part, goes back to the phrase, "He puts divinity into things." It may be difficult for us now to grasp the Aztec concept of divinity or to understand how an artist puts gods, magic, and spirit into paint, wood, stone, feathers, and other kinds of artistic work.

We mentioned earlier in this book the exciting rediscovery of a pictorial manuscript from the 1540s known as the *Mapa de Cuauhtinchan No. 2,* which has recently undergone intensive examination by a group of scholars from different disciplines under the direction of the authors of the present book. This beautiful 3-by-6-foot painting on native bark paper has more than 700 images on it depicting the worldview, pilgrimages, encounters with different ethnic groups, supernatural episodes, and extensive ethnobotanical information of a community that was eventually conquered and integrated into the Aztec empire. The surviving map is actually *stories in pictures*: in fact, it is a large collection of mythical and historical accounts that if written out in European script could be compared to the grand narratives of the *Illiad* and *Odyssey.* For it tells of the long and arduous journeys of the Chichimecs who emerge like Aztec ancestors from the Place of Seven Caves, at the pleading of two Toltec priests (Feather Lip and Serpent Foot) from the great pilgrimage city of Cholula. The pictorial narrative is packed with symbols, events, gestures, colors, places that served as cues and signs for the telling of tales, the singing of songs, the performing of rituals, and the remembering of ancestors and the actions of gods. It is important to understand that this document represents the indigenous way of *writing* history, genealogy, religion, and political solidarity and schism, as well as bringing all these social patterns into contact with the sacred powers of the cosmos. Writing with pictures was not only a way of transmitting information and knowledge but also, as mentioned above, the way of bringing *heart,* that is, the deepest truths of the community and therefore God and the gods, into the viewers' and listeners' minds. This is the power of the painter of stories and the codices, maps, and other paintings of sacred knowledge.

Scenes along the Chichimec migration route in the newly rediscovered *Mapa de Cuauhtinchan No. 2* (1540s). (Photo by Jorge Pérez de Lara. Courtesy of the Mesoamerican Archive and the David Rockefeller Center for Latin American Studies, Harvard University)

THE *TLAMATINIME* AND THE VERBAL ARTS

One of the most refined and powerful art forms was human speech. Throughout the educational experience of children and teenagers, great effort was put into developing eloquent speakers. It wasn't primarily a matter of speaking correctly but of speaking correctly about significant ideas, metaphors, and truth. When the Franciscan friar Bernardino de Sahagún made his extraordinary studies of Aztec life and language beginning in the 1540s, he discovered Nahuatl, a florid, elegant, and meaningful language. Fortunately, he collected many of the formal speeches representing the philosophy of the Aztecs in Book 6 of the *Florentine Codex*. This single volume contains more than 40 elegant prayers, exhortations, and orations spoken by parents, rulers, midwives, and citizens. As we shall see, the Aztecs loved riddles, proverbs, and witty sayings. These sayings and speeches show that the Aztecs developed verbal arts, the most important form of which was called *huehuetlatolli* (ancient words). The individuals who were most highly trained in the *huehuetlatolli* were the *tlamatinime* (knowers of things). Consider this description of these great teachers and speakers:

The wise man: a light, a torch, a stout torch that does not smoke.... His are the black and red ink, his are the illustrated manuscripts, he studies the illustrated manuscripts. He himself is writing and wisdom. He is the path, the true way for others. He directs people and things. He is a guide in human affairs.... He puts a mirror before others; he makes them prudent, cautious; he causes a face [personality] to appear in them.[6]

This passage highlights some of the key qualities of these teachers. First, they are wise people. The Nahuatl word *tlamatini* means *knower of things,* or wise one. This ability to know is compared to the light of a torch that does not smoke, blind, or confuse one, but rather illuminates the truth. The reference to the "black and red ink" means that these *tlamantinime* were the keepers of the books that contained the traditional wisdom of the culture. These books were made from the bark of the *amate* (wild fig) tree or from animal hide folded like an accordion; they depicted the mythology, genealogy, calendar, and history of the people. The art of painting and knowing these books was referred to as the "red and black ink," or the "wisdom of the people." The real teacher, then, *is* the living wisdom, the red and black ink of the community. As living wisdom, the wise teacher is very *active;* he leads people and shows them the way with his stout torch that does not throw smoke in their eyes.

His real art comes from his power to show people their own reality, their truth, by putting a mirror up to them. This is a fascinating image, and it is crucial to understanding the purpose of art and education for the Aztecs. The true teacher is an artist whose abilities *delve into the face (personality) of other humans,* helping them achieve an identity, an understanding of who they are in the world.

These poet-philosophers understood human existence, however, as a difficult reality and as fragile and ephemeral. Consider this poem by the great priest-king Nezahualcoyotl:

I comprehend the secret, the hidden:
O my lords!
Thus we are,
we are mortal,
men through and through,
we all will have to go away,
we all will have to die on earth.
Like a painting,
we will be erased.
Like a flower,
we will dry up
here on earth....
Think on this my lords,
eagles and ocelots,
though you be of jade,
though you be of gold
you will also go there
to the place of the fleshless.[7]

This poem tells us that life is extremely precious and perishable. Jade, gold, flowers, paintings, and humans are transitory and vulnerable rather than solid and with a long-standing foundation. This is the cosmic condition illuminated by the stout torch, which shows that human life is unstable and illusory. How then does one know the truth or reality that exists beyond this world, that is, not just the "place of the fleshless" or the death of Mictlan in the underworld? The answer, in part, is through art, especially the art of poetic words and language. These *tlamatinime* developed a rhetorical strategy aimed at discovering and experiencing the nature of truth, a solid foundation in the world. They believed that there was such a reality beyond human existence, in the region of the gods above and in the region of the dead below. To penetrate these regions and discover a stable reality, they had to devise techniques to open the depths of the human personality to the profound world of truth. The main technique was the creation of *in xochitl, in cuicatl,* or flowers and songs—artistic expression in the forms of words, songs, and paintings that connected the human personality, referred to as the "face and heart," with the divine. The divine or true foundation of the cosmos was understood in terms of a duality that pervaded all levels and regions of the world. Remember that in Nahua culture, the cosmos was originally created and structured by a supreme dual god, Ometeotl. This duality was manifested in the combinations of male-female, hot-cold, left-right, underworld–celestial world, above-below, darkness-light, rain-drought, and life-death. Human beings were also made up of dualities. For the Aztecs, the best instruments for expressing a human duality that reflected and communicated the dual dimensions of the divinity were metaphors that generally consisted of two words or phrases joined to form a single idea, like "flower and song," meaning poetry or truth. In other words, the divine duality of Ometecuhtli and Omecihuatl that together made Ometeotl (Giver of Life) was a *difrasismo,* or two words that meant one thing. Other popular *difrasismos* included the following:

in atl, in tepetl = water and hill = a town

in topan, in mictlan = what is above us and the region of the dead = the world beyond humans

topco, petlacalco = in the bag and in the box = a secret

in cueitl, in huipilli = the skirt, the blouse = the sexual nature of women

The artistic speaker attempted to express his or her heart in flower and song, that is, in poetry that sometimes resulted in the deification of the heart, the sacred inner realization that truth had been achieved through an approximation of the dual nature of the cosmos. This achievement meant that poetry and the human personality became linked to the divine duality above. The most profound truth—that there was a reliable foundation of the cosmos in the form of the Lady and Lord of Duality—was matched or at least *approximated* when great art or great dualities were well expressed in speech or other forms of artistic expressions.

SOME *HUEHUETLATOLLI*

Among the most effective instruments for organizing human behavior in an artistic fashion were the ancient teachings and sayings that were full of *difrasismos* and dual symbolism. These speeches were florid, elegant metaphorical devices that were

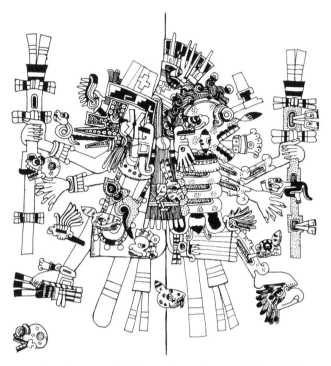

Quetzalcoatl Ehecatl (left) and Mictlantecuhtli (right) representing the duality of life and death. (*Codex Borgia*, from the Eduard Seler edition: Berlin, 1904)

memorized and presented at ceremonial events such as the coronation of a ruler, the entry of a youth into the *calmecac*, the work of a midwife, or a wedding. Such speeches were also used, as we have seen, for the trips of merchants and the gatherings of nobles and warriors. In sum, they showed that life was to be lived as an *art form*, but an *art form* permeated with influences and imitations of the divine, especially the divine duality that was the foundation of all things. Consider this speech given by a nobleman to his son exhorting him to sexual chastity, and notice how elements of *cosmovision* infiltrate the speech and guide its main point. Be especially attentive to the *difrasismos*, or metaphoric couplets (for example, the two opening phrases).

Thou who art my son, thou who art my youth, hear the words; place, inscribe in the chambers of thy heart the word or two which our forefathers departed leaving: the old men, the old women, the regarded ones, the admired ones, and the advised ones on earth. Here is that which they gave us, entrusted to us as they left, the words of the old men, that which is bound, the well-guarded words. They left saying that the pure life is considered as a well-smoked, precious turquoise; as a round, reed-like, well-formed, precious green stone. There is no blotch, no blemish. Those perfect in their hearts, in their manner of life, those of pure life—like these are the precious green stone, the precious turquoise, which are glistening, shining before the lord of the near, of the nigh.[8]

The power of this speech comes from its constant emphasis on balanced ideas and behavior all reflecting the balanced divine order. We hear about "my son...my youth...the old men...the old women...no blotch...no blemish...perfect in their hearts, in their manner of life"—all of which is a reflection of the "lord of the near, of the nigh."

RIDDLES

The art of language was also expressed in wit and word pictures shared by teenagers, children, and adults. Knowing the correct answers to riddles indicated that a person was alert to the concise lessons taught at the school or temple. Here are some of the riddles spoken in the capital when the Spaniards arrived:

> What is a little blue-green jar filled with popcorn? One can see from our little riddle that it is the heavens.
>
> What is that which is a stone of red ochre which goes jumping? The flea.
>
> What is that which is a hill whence there is a flow? Our nose.
>
> What is that which says: You jump so that I shall jump? This is the drum stick.
>
> What is that which is a small mirror in a house made of fir branches? Our eye.
>
> What is it that follows along the gorge, going clapping its hands? The butterfly.
>
> What is it that has a tight shift? The tomato.
>
> What is that which we enter in three places and leave by only one? It is our shirt.
>
> What is a tiny colored stone sitting on the road? Dog excrement.
>
> What is it that bends over us all over the world? The maize tassel.[9]

These were some of the instruments used by *tlamatinime* to help people clearly see the things and relationships of the world and develop a "face and heart," that is, a strong personality. Besides these riddles, the Aztecs also enjoyed using proverbs to educate and inspire each other through language arts. Among some of the most interesting are the following:

Ipal nonixpatlaoa = Because of him my face becomes wide. This is said when someone's child—a boy or girl—or else someone's pupil, was well-taught, well brought up.

Yollotl, eztli = Heart, blood. These words were said of chocolate because in the past it was precious and rare. The common people and the poor did not drink it. They also said it was deranging and it was thought to be like the mushroom, for it intoxicated people.

Naztauh, nomecaxicol = My heron feather, my cord jacket. That is, when the city gave me a task, I thereby became a slave. If I should harm it, if I should endanger something, I should be imprisoned.

In ie tlecujlixquac, in ie tlamamatlac = Already at the edge of the fire, already at the stairway. This saying was said of those who were about to be put to death, who already had been brought up to die: or they had already been placed at the edge of the fire; it was time for them to die.

Mixtitlan, aiauhtitlan = In the clouds, in the mist. This saying was said of the highly esteemed, the very great; of those never before seen, of those never before known, nor anywhere seen in times of yore. So here in all Mexico it was thus said that the Spaniards came emerging from within the clouds, within the mist.

Anjtlanammati, anjtlatamati = I heed no mother, I heed no father. This was said of him who was admonished many times. He heeded not, he disregarded the discourse.[10]

SACRED STONES

The Mexica sculptors were guided by certain principles of carving that required a magical act of illuminating, for those who had eyes to see, the sacred forces hidden in nature: "What is carved should be like the original, and have life, for whatever may be the subject which is to be made, the form of it should resemble the original and the life of the original.... Take great care to penetrate what the animal you wish to imitate is like, and how its character and appearance can best be shown."[11] In fact, Aztec stonework, both monumental and miniature, reveals that the natural world of squash, grasshoppers, snakes, butterflies, monkeys, frogs, fleas, and birds was observed in minute detail, and that such objects were viewed as passageways for the sacred forces of the gods into the world. The representations of these animals and insects appear in

obsidian, basalt, shells, amaranth dough, and other natural medi-
ums. Sometimes they are impressive combinations of the natural and the supernatural, as in the two magnificent stone images
known to us as the Calendar Stone and the statue of Coatlicue (Serpent Skirt). Let us turn to these two huge pieces of art to gain more
insight into the Aztec theory of art.

THE CALENDAR STONE

Remembering our earlier discussion of the myths of the suns,
we saw how the repeated creation and destruction of the universe
was central to the cosmovision and worldview of the Aztecs. That
dynamic worldview was carved into a huge monolith, the so-called
Calendar Stone, which illustrates how the potent elements of nature
and the imagination of nature were combined and expressed in art
forms. The purpose was to *reflect and participate in the original creation so that it could be repeated and maintained.*

This stone was discovered on December 17, 1790, when workers were leveling and repaving the central plaza of Mexico City.
A huge irregular mass of basalt was found just below the surface. When the stone was raised up, investigators were surprised
to find a series of concentric circles filled with complex symbols.
The disk was more than three and a half meters in diameter. The
stone was set upright to facilitate viewing and eventually lodged
in the southwest tower of the Cathedral of Mexico until 1885. In
the years immediately after its discovery, important studies were
made by the Mexican scholar Antonio León y Gama and the German scientist Alexander von Humboldt, the "scientific discoverer
of the New World." The stone has become the second most popular image of Mexico, next to the image of the eagle and the serpent
on the Mexican flag and, in the words of one prominent scholar,
"unquestionably . . . the best known work of art produced by Native
Americans before the arrival of the Europeans."[12] It appears that
the huge stone was used as a *cuauhxicalli* (eagle vessel), a ritual
receptacle for offerings of sacrificed hearts, blood, and other gifts
to the gods.

The great stone has an image moving from the inner to the outer
circles. In the inner circle is the face of the sun god with an open
mouth and a distended tongue. The god wears a headband stud-
ded with three jewels of precious greenstone. There are two circular
flanking jewels and a central jewel of a thimble-like image containing four leaves. A double curving band flanks the eyes and hair, the

Aztec Calendar Stone. (Reprinted from Raúl Noriega, *Tres estudios sobre la Piedra del Sol.* Mexico City: n.p., 1954)

latter indicated by five curving parallel strands on each side of the face. A long nose bar is tipped with jewels, and circular ear spools with greenstone jewel signs descend from the centers.

In the center, a tongue emerges from an open mouth, appearing as a *tecpatl,* or sacrificial knife, decorated with the usual "demon face" depicted on many Aztec monuments. This is the creator sun god, Tonatiuh, who draws his creative power from the sacrifices carried out by gods and humans. This stone knife/tongue image is featured on many Aztec sculptures and also appears near the bottom of the Calendar Stone, emerging from the mouths of the two huge fire serpents whose bodies encircle the entire scene.

Referring back to the earlier quote concerning the principles of carving Aztec sculpture, one way of getting "like the original" is to put the original in the center. Tonatiuh, at the hungry center of the universe, is surrounded by another circle. In it is a giant *ollin*

(Movement) sign consisting of four boxes, each in turn containing cosmic symbols of the ages that have collapsed—Jaguar, Wind, Fire, and Rain. A huge sun dart protrudes from the top of Tonatiuh's head, while the tips of the feathers appear below the two quincunx (five-part design) symbols below his chin. On each side of the god's face, almost like huge ears, are two images identified as "demon-faced" claws clutching human hearts.

Surrounding that is a narrow band of the 20 day signs circling the central core of the stone. Here we see how the sculptors have integrated signs of nature and the supernatural into the cosmic image. Starting at the top and moving clockwise are the signs for Crocodile, Wind, House, Lizard, Serpent, Death, Deer, Rabbit, Water, Dog, Monkey, Grass, Reed, Jaguar, Eagle, Vulture, Movement, Flint Knife, Rain, and Flower. These are major signs of nature and culture, things made by the gods, and things made from things made by the gods. Surrounding this series of signs is a series of boxes with the quincunx, the five-part sign that represents in miniature the balanced images of the center and the four quarters. These are interrupted by and attached to rays of the sun.

The outer image is the body of some kind of animal or insect that has fire symbols in boxes along its body. The tails appear at the top as darts pointing toward a box that has the year sign 13 Reed. The body of the animal or insect curves down to the bottom, and the heads face each other as gaping serpent jaws from which are protruding two faces, each with a stone knife tongue. There are two different opinions about what kind of animal or image this is. The traditional view is that these huge images are fire serpents, as indicated by the huge serpent heads and the images of fire that cover their bodies. Fire serpents were often depicted in Aztec art to indicate the power of the solar god or a weapon of the solar god. But a more recent interpretation, offered by Karl Taube, suggests that these images are not serpents at all, but giant caterpillars representing the transformation and rebirth of the warrior as the sun, emerging in the center of the image in the shape of a great butterfly.

THE LADY OF THE SERPENT SKIRT

In 1791, just a few months after the discovery of the Calendar Stone, another monumental sculpture, depicting the Aztec goddess Coatlicue (Serpent Skirt), was uncovered in the central square of Mexico City. Standing more than eight feet tall, this statue is one of the most astonishing pieces of sculpture ever found in the New

World. You will remember from chapter 3 that this goddess played
a central role in the birth of the Aztec patron deity Huitzilopochtli,
the sun and war god. Like the Calendar Stone, this sculptural image
of Coatlicue is a composite of gods, signs, animals, and meanings.
This is not monotheism. But it does reveal, in still another way, that

Monumental stone sculpture of Coatlicue from the National Museum of
Anthropology, Mexico City. (Courtesy of Salvador Guil'liem Arroyo, INAH)

basic charge entrusted to the Aztec carvers to give life to the stones, to make them like the original. Well, what an incredible formula of originality we have here!

The Coatlicue statue challenges any Western conception of beauty and truth usually associated with simplicity of line and reasonable balance. She has a huge head consisting of two rattlesnakes facing each other, which together create the illusion of one great snake looking directly at the observer. This reflects our earlier discussion of duality and unity. Myth tells us that these two snakes actually represent streams of blood emerging from her neck after her head had been severed. Across her chest, she wears a great necklace of human hands and hearts, indicating that she receives the body parts of sacrificed gods and humans. Her belt is a two-headed serpent (duality again) bound at the front by a human skull pendant. Below this terrible collection of symbols is an expertly carved skirt of intertwined serpents, which identifies her. Her feet are the talons of a raptorial bird, perhaps an eagle, but with eyes. Seen from the side, her arms, raised up as though she is lurching forward, consist of two giant serpent heads with fangs ready to strike and a jutting tongue sensing the air. Even the bottom surface upon which she stands, probably never seen by the populace, had a carved image of an earth goddess with a devouring mouth, understood by some to be the entrance to the underworld.

It is important to consider the variation and diversity of Aztec art, for the Coatlicue statue exemplifies another dimension of the Aztec artistic cosmos, different from the *tlamatinime* who gave humans a heart and face, a personality. She hungers for, takes, and transforms hearts, faces, and hands into the insatiable needs and powers of the gods. Not all gods were like this, but one of the fundamental rules of Aztec creation was that the gods must be fed continually and directly with the body, blood, and energy of other gods and humans. Carving this image must have been one of the greatest challenges in the history of stonework.

Aztec stonework, however, was not limited to monumental and frightening images such as this. In fact, when the Mexican excavators opened the 135-plus caches buried at the Templo Mayor, they found beautiful alabaster stone images of deer, sun darts, flowing water, and obsidian jewels.

FEATHERWORK

The Aztec artists were as fascinated with perishable, vulnerable natural elements as they were with permanent, invulnerable stones.

Nowhere is this commitment to the fragile more evident than in the florid featherwork that adorned rulers, warriors, gods, and people at all levels of the Aztec empire. Consider this description of the featherwork of the town of Amantlan given to Sahagún by native informants:

In their hands were taken apart indeed all the precious feathers. They displayed well, they made attractive, the precious feathers, thereby preparing artistically all the splendid shields which were the gifts of the rulers; nothing common; all covered, pasted over, with precious feathers...painted, decorated, designed with those of the blue cotinga, the hummingbird, the red spoonbill; with gold tufted with parrot feathers on the border, rimmed with hanging ornaments; with pendants, radiating from the lower rim, with eagle down, with quetzal feathers, with those of the troupial, with those of the red spoonbill.[13]

The art of featherwork was immediately evident to the Spaniards when they met the ruler Motecuhzoma Xocoyotzin in 1519. Not only was he wearing a magnificent headdress, but he gave one to Cortés, which today resides in the Museum für Volkerkunde in

A replica of the quetzal-feathered headdress Motecuhzoma gave to Cortés, from the National Museum of Anthropology, Mexico City. (Courtesy of Salvador Guil'liem Arroyo, INAH)

MOTECUHZOMA'S HEADDRESS

It is believed that one of Motecuhzoma's headdresses was taken to Europe in the 1520s and today it is on permanent display in a museum in Vienna. Its whereabouts before Austria purchased it in 1880 are unknown. Today the Mexican government is trying to have it returned to Mexico.

Vienna. This gift consisted of 500 green and gold quetzal tail plumes and blue and red feathers, fastened with gold disks and clasps. The quetzal feathers originated in faraway Guatemala and had to be imported into the Basin of Mexico and brought to the royal market. The blue feathers came from what the Aztecs called the *xiuhtototl*, or turquoise bird, which lived in the hot lowlands of the eastern and southern regions. Parrots and scarlet macaws provided the red feathers, all of which were tied together by *maguey* thread to a coarse-meshed fabric onto a wicker frame in order to appear and be enduring. The Aztecs were careful observers of birds, and we have a number of detailed accounts of how birds looked, flew, nested, ate, and sang. The transformation from the bird to the headdress or other objects depended on the skills of the featherworker, described as "accomplished, ingenious."[14]

The good featherworker is imaginative, diligent; meritorious of confidence, of trust. He practices the featherworkers' art; he glues, he arranges the feathers. He arranges different colors, takes measurements, matches feathers.

The bad featherworker is a hypocrite, a destroyer of good work—heedless of others, dull, uncouth. He is stupid, torpid. He can do nothing; he harms, damages, wastes feathers.[15]

As this passage notes, the featherworker was a craftsperson skilled in measurements, sensitive to the relations of color, light, and the texture of feathers, and no doubt trained in the theory of symbolism, that is, the overall meaning of colors, shadows, and arrangements of both. The featherworkers depended on the scribes for help, because the designs of the feather devices of the rulers, especially for important ceremonial occasions and dances, showed evidence of their skill. One text says: "They who first drew [the pattern] were the scribes. When [the featherworkers] had seen how it was designed, that it was well done, that the painting was sufficiently detailed, then on a *maguey* leaf they reinforced cotton; they strengthened it with glue."[16] Clearly, feathers were not only valuable, but were understood to carry the power and beauty of the bird into the very object, whether a headdress or a shield. And it is significant that the Aztecs had a law forbidding the wearing of certain feather articles called the Shadow of Lords and Kings unless the ruler granted permission. Featherwork was a highly valued art, and many nobles took up the honorable career of featherworker. This work was considered a protection during hard times. One father instructs his sons and daughters to pay attention to "the art of featherworking" so that in the time of "suffering, when misery dominates, the artisanship will be a rampart, a buttress."[17] Several feather shields have survived, indicating that in battle warriors were not only meant to appear intense and dangerous, but beautiful and florid.

GOLDWORKING

Three other activities related to artistic expression are goldworking, ballplaying, and game playing. In the first case, we know that the *cuztic teocuitlapitzqui,* or goldworkers, took the regular supplies of gold from the provinces who paid tribute and reworked them into jewelry and decorations worn by rulers, nobles, merchants, and deity impersonators. The Indians got their gold, which was not desired in great quantities, simply by panning the rivers; sometimes they found gold "as big as grains of maize." The Nahuatl name for gold is quite interesting, as it means "the excrement of the gods," from *cuitlatl* (excrement) and *teotl* (god). Gold was considered "wonderful, yellow, good, fine, precious. It is the wealth, the riches, the lot, the possession, the property of the rulers, our lords."[18] Gold was understood to seep out of the earth. Its first appearance was compared to diarrhea, and so it was called either the excrement of the sun or the excrement of the gods. But its ritual and costume use depended on the labor of the goldsmith, as this description of the method of goldworking shows: "I excavate gold. I pulverize sand. I wash sand. I blow sand. I wash gold. I purify sand. I make something clean. I cast gold. I melt something. I form, I prepare the gold. I cast, hammer, make gold bowls, gold cups, gold eagle vessels, gold jars for water.... Thus I make things beautiful; thus I make things give off rays."[19]

THE BALLGAME

Though they are not necessarily artworks, the games of *patolli* and *ollamaliztli,* the ballgame, depended on the craftsmanship of

The Ballgame. Two players face each other in the I-shaped ballcourt. (*Codex Maglibechiano,* redrawn from the 1903 Zelia Nuttall facsimile edition)

artists and the art of their performances. Let us consider the latter first. Archaeologists have found *tlachtli* (ballcourts) all over Mesoamerica, and this game was also enjoyed by the Aztecs. The Mexica rulers and nobles supported these games, and they became sites for gambling by the noble classes. The ruler who played "caused the ball to enter...the ballcourt rings.... Then he won all the costly goods, and he won everything from all who watched there in the ballcourt."[20]

The court was shaped like a thick capital *I* turned on its side and was surrounded by tall walls. On each side, a stone ring was set in the wall. A player scored by sending a hard rubber ball through a small opening in the opposing team's ring. Hands could not be used, nor could a player use his feet, calves, or arms. He could strike the ball with his knees, thighs, and buttocks. According to Diego Durán, who witnessed the ballgame after the Spaniards arrived, the ball was extremely lively: "Jumping and bouncing are its qualities, upward and downward, to and fro. It can exhaust the pursuer running after it before he can catch up with it."[21] According to Durán, some players were so skillful that they could play for an hour and

Two individuals playing *patolli* on a game board that reflects the importance of the four cardinal directions and the center in Mesoamerican
cosmology. (Diego Durán, *Códice Durán*. Mexico City: Arrendadora
Internacional 1990 facsimile edition)

the ball would never touch the ground! Durán also described the
physical danger the players faced:

On seeing the ball come at them, at the moment that it was about to touch
the floor, they [the players] were so quick in turning their knees or buttocks to the ball that they returned it with an extraordinary swiftness.
With this bounding back and forth they suffered terrible injuries on their
knees or thighs so that the haunches of those who made use of these tricks
were frequently so bruised that those spots had to be opened with a small
blade, whereupon the blood which had clotted there because of the blows
of the ball was squeezed out.[22]

PATOLLI

Finally, *patolli*, though not actually an art, was used to win valuable
pieces of jewelry and other expressions of value and beauty. In this
game, beans were placed on a board divided into squares, the object
being to be the first to move six beans through the entire course.
There were moments of high tension and excitement in *patolli*, for if
a player threw the dice beans so that one landed and stood up on its
side, it was regarded as a triumphant moment and the thrower was in
a winner-take-all position. The game has been compared to parcheesi
or backgammon. Here is a succinct description of how it was played
on a mat painted with a big X made out of liquid rubber:

Within the arms of the X, lines were drawn so as to form squares. Twelve
pebbles—red and blue—were used in these compartments. Bets were

made on the player who could best handle the dice, which were five or six black beans, each of which had a number painted on it. The game invariably drew a large crowd. Onlookers and gamblers pressed each other around the mat, some waiting to play, others to place bets.[23]

The winner won some of the precious objects we have studied in this chapter, showing that what we have called art (the gifts and the imitations of the gods) was also sought after in games of chance or gambling, which were very popular among the Aztecs.

He who won in playing *patolli* won all the costly goods: golden necklaces, green stone, fine turquoise, bracelets on which were round, green stones or fine turquoise, quetzal feathers, slaves, houses, fields, precious capes, mats, large capes, green stone lip plugs, golden ear plugs, duck feather capes. But even here, in the gambling dens of the Aztecs, the spirits of the gods could be present and pushing themselves through the thin, permeable membrane that divided the seen from the unseen world. For we are told, "And he who played *patolli,* who cast the beans, if then he made one of them stand, if the bean stood up there on its thicker end, it was taken as a great omen; it was regarded [as] a great marvel."[24]

NOTES

1. Bernardino de Sahagún, *Florentine Codex: General History of the Things of New Spain*, ed. and trans. Arthur J. O. Anderson and Charles E. Dibble, introductory vol. and 12 books (Santa Fe, NM: School of American Research and University of Utah, 1950–82), 6: 224.

2. Ibid., 10: 165–68.

3. Ibid., 166.

4. Miguel León-Portilla, ed. and trans., *Native Mesoamerican Spirituality: Ancient Myths, Discourses, Stories, Doctrines, Hymns, Poems from the Aztec, Yucatec, Quiche-Maya and Other Sacred Traditions* (New York: Paulist Press, 1980), 244.

5. Quoted in Miguel León-Portilla, *Aztec Thought and Culture* (Norman: University of Oklahoma Press, 1963), 172–73.

6. Ibid., 10.

7. León-Portilla, *Native Mesoamerican Spirituality*, 241–42.

8. Sahagún, *Florentine Codex*, 6: 113.

9. Ibid., 237–40.

10. Ibid., 227, 241–56.

11. Quoted in Inga Clendinnen, *Aztecs: An Interpretation* (Cambridge: Cambridge University Press, 1991), 226.

12. H. B. Nicholson, "The Problem of the Identification of the Central Image of the 'Aztec Calendar Stone,'" in *Current Topics in Aztec Studies: Essays in Honor of H. B. Nicholson*, ed. Alana Cordry-Collins and Douglas Sharon (San Diego, CA: San Diego Museum of Man, 1993), 3.

13. Sahagún, *Florentine Codex,* 9: 89.

14. Ibid., 10: 25.

15. Ibid.

16. Ibid., 9: 93.

17. Ibid., 6: 90.

18. Ibid., 11: 233.

19. Ibid., 234.

20. Ibid., 8: 29.

21. Diego Durán, *Book of the Gods and Rites and The Ancient Calendar,* ed. and trans. Fernando Horcasitas and Doris Heyden (Norman: University of Oklahoma Press, 1971), 316.

22. Ibid.

23. *The Codex Mendoza,* ed. Frances F. Berdan and Patricia Rieff Anawalt, 4 vols. (Berkeley: University of California Press, 1992), 2: 230.

24. Sahagún, *Florentine Codex,* 8: 30.

7

WHERE THE JAGUARS ROAR: AZTEC HUMAN SACRIFICE AS DEBT PAYMENT

Let us face the fact that many people think of the Aztecs in terms of the images of human sacrifice that have come down through the centuries. We think of Aztec culture as committed to high pyramids, bloodthirsty priests, human sacrifice, and some cannibalism as well. This image comes in large part from the Spanish accounts of the conquest of the capital city, Tenochtitlan. For instance, one of the last narrative views of the Great Aztec Temple before it was partially dismantled by cannon fire comes from Bernal Díaz del Castillo, who gave this hair-raising account of the human sacrifice of Spanish soldiers to the war god Huitzilopochtli while he and his cohorts were being driven out of the city by Aztec warriors:

We had retreated near to our quarters and had already crossed a great opening where there was much water...when again was sounded the dismal drum of Huichilobos [Huitzilopochtli] and many other shells and horns and things like trumpets and the sound of them all was terrifying, and we all looked towards the lofty Cue [Pyramid]...and saw that our comrades whom they had captured when they defeated Cortés were being carried by force up the steps and they were taking them to be sacrificed. When they got them up to a small square in front of the oratory, where their accursed idols are kept, we saw them place plumes on the heads of many of them and with things like fans in their hands they forced them to dance before Huichilobos, and after they had danced they immediately placed them on their backs on some rather narrow stones which had been prepared as places for sacrifice, and with some knives they sawed open their chests and drew out their palpitating hearts and offered them to the idols that were there, and they kicked the bodies down the steps, and the Indian butchers who were waiting below cut off the arms and feet and flayed the skin off the faces, and prepared it afterwards like glove leather with the beards on, and kept those for the festivals when they celebrated drunken orgies, and the flesh they ate in *chilmole*.[1]

When we, as students of Aztec thought and culture, combine this highly biased account of Aztec ritual killing with our understanding of Aztec aesthetics, child-rearing, and education, we are presented with a fractured image that emphasizes human care and genius juxtaposed with human aggression and violence. This raises questions of the most profound and emotional sort. For instance, how could a people who conceived of and carved the uniquely marvelous Calendar Stone and developed one of the most accurate calendrical systems of the ancient world spend so much time, energy, and wealth in efforts to obtain and sacrifice human victims for every conceivable feast day in that calendar? Why did a people so fascinated by and accomplished in sculpture, featherwork, craft industries, poetry, and painting become so committed to cosmic regeneration through the thrust of the ceremonial knife? The image that glares at us through the evidence is one of startling juxtapositions.

In this chapter, we will attempt the difficult task of answering these questions about this fractured Aztec image by presenting descriptions and interpretations of the practice of human sacrifice. It is vitally important for the reader to remember the earlier chapters on worldview and "mountains of water" so that a *contextual* understanding of ritual sacrifice can be achieved. By *contextual* is meant the different forces, ideas, symbols, and meanings that were *woven together* in Aztec culture and which presented a convincing worldview that was based, in part, on the need to sacrifice people so that the world could be renewed and healthy. The reader is not being asked to embrace or support human sacrifice, but rather to take up the challenge of understanding what in the world the Aztecs thought they were up to.

When thinking about the powerful and painful practice of sacrificing human beings, a practice that all adults knew about and witnessed, it may be helpful to think about some of the group or crowd behaviors of the past century that involved violence against other humans. How was it possible to mobilize millions and millions of men to leave the comfort of their homes and families and travel long distances to fight to the death with strangers on waste-land battlefields in World War I or II? Why have many women, who have been physically abused by men throughout much of human history, apparently accepted an ideology that males belong in all the positions of political leadership? How could so many Europe-ans participate, to one degree or another, in the systematic deporta-tion, torture, and incineration of millions of Jewish people during what we now call the Holocaust? How could Christian churches by the hundreds support the slavery of African peoples when Christians declared that to love one's neighbor was at the heart of their religion? One simple answer, reflecting the title of chapter 2 in this book, is that each of these societies constructed a world-view, a view of the natural and divine order of the world, that jus-tified, legitimated, and persuaded people to do extreme violence to other human beings. Once you get human beings to *internalize a worldview and believe it as cosmic truth*, they can be motivated to do anything. Of course, the same point can be made for mobilizing crowds of people to do helpful, healthy, and caring things such as cleaning up the environment, struggling for racial justice, helping the poor and hungry, or organizing to stop wars. In approaching human sacrifice, be attentive to three things: (1) Remember that in Aztec philosophy, the human body was understood to be the most vital container of sacred forces in the world. The heart and the head were receptacles of the most potent cosmic sources of power and renewal in nature. (2) Aztec religion and daily life were based on two ideas: repeating the creative/destructive work of the gods and nurturing the gods through providing gifts of sacred energy. (3) The Aztecs were a militaristic and agricultural people. The Aztec nobility organized their society and educational system to extend their dominion over various Mesoamerican communi-ties to obtain more tribute, wealth, and offerings for themselves and their gods. This meant intense and unstable relations with allied and enemy kingdoms, resulting in warfare with enemies, some near by, others at a distance. Their agricultural worldview, emphasizing the cycle of life and death, led their nobles, warriors, and many artists to believe that giving birth and taking the power from other human lives were two parts of an intimate process of creativity. A short discussion of human sacrifice in world religions follows. We will then focus on the Aztec case by reviewing the Flowery Wars and the places, paraphernalia, and practices of sac-rifice. We will discuss in detail two sacrificial festivals, the sacrifice of Tezcatlipoca (Smoking Mirror) and the Feast of the Flaying of

Men. This will help us understand what the Aztecs were trying to accomplish in that sacrifice of Spaniards described at the beginning of this chapter.

HUMAN SACRIFICE IN OTHER CULTURES

Human sacrifice means the killing of human beings and the use of their bodies and blood for ritual intentions that include some purposeful communication with the gods. In fact, human sacrifice has been a widespread practice throughout history, as evidence from India, Hawaii, Japan, China, Europe, South America, and North America shows. In China, for instance, an entire company of soldiers, charioteers, human companions, and horses was sacrificed and buried with the supreme ruler around 1500 B.C.E. In their worldview, kinship existed between the living and the dead, who together formed a state bureaucracy. This meant that in the afterlife, a host of servants worked for the deceased ruler and his family just as they had in their earthly existence. The dead received salaries in the form of human sacrifices for working as intercessors between the king and the High God.[2] Just a few years ago, a 2,500-year-old tomb containing nearly four dozen victims of human sacrifice were uncovered in an excavation in eastern China. The coffins of the sacrificed people were neatly laid next to each other in rows and excavators also found beautiful and precious gold and bronze artifacts as well as silk gowns. Most impressive was a black, gold, and blood-red sword inscribed with pictures of dragons. Interestingly, this sacrifice took place in the same era when the great philosopher Confucius lived.

Another example of human sacrifice occurs in the Bushido cult of the Japanese samurai of the 17th to 19th centuries. In this worldview, warriors were required to give complete loyalty to their lords, including self-sacrifice or *seppuku* (ritual suicide), if it was demanded. *Seppuku* involved enormous self-control while the warrior slashed open his own belly with a special knife, after which he was decapitated by an assistant. This type of self-sacrifice was carried out for various reasons, including payment for certain transgressions against a lord, avoiding capture in war, the death of one's lord, or as an act of selflessness in order to force a wayward lord to act in accordance with the correct moral order. A dramatic example of *seppuku* was carried out in full public view in 1970 by the flamboyant and prolific Japanese writer Yukio Mishima. Mishima and four Shield Society members seized control of the commanding general's office at the military headquarters near downtown Tokyo in protest of the Japanese government's post–World War II military politics. Mishima gave a 10-minute speech to a large assembly of soldiers and then committed *hara-kiri* (disemboweling oneself) and was decapitated by a follower.

There are many other examples in world history of societies who condoned, practiced, and criticized human sacrifice. Although the practice may seem strange according to modern sensibilities, extreme conditions of poverty, warfare, terrorism, and fanaticism often produce sacrificial actions. For instance, on November 18, 1978, a total of 914 members of the People's Temple, a California-based cult, who had moved to Jonestown, Guyana (South America), took their own lives by drinking a cyanide-laced fruit drink. These people practiced a form of Christianity and were motivated by a collective sense of martyrdom, believing that their lives in this world were corrupted by outside influences and that a better, utopian life awaited them on the other side, in some heavenly place.[3] In a similar, more recent case, 39 followers of a group known as Heaven's Gate carried out a collective suicide at a mansion in Rancho San Diego, California, a few days before their bodies were found on March 26, 1997. Believing that beings in a spaceship traveling behind or associated with the highly visible Hale-Bopp comet would transport them to what they called the Kingdom—a level beyond human—the followers took their own lives and were found lying in their beds, dressed in black, with purple shrouds over their heads. Like the Aztecs, these people decided to choose the time, place, and form of their own deaths in the belief that their sacrifice would result in a better afterlife.

PLACES OF AZTEC SACRIFICE

It must be understood that human sacrifice among the Aztecs was carried out within a larger, more complex ceremonial system in which a tremendous amount of energy, wealth, and time was spent in a variety of ritual festivals dedicated to a crowded and hungry pantheon of divine entities. This dedication is reflected in the many metaphors and symbols related to war and sacrifice. Human hearts were likened to fine burnished turquoise, and war was referred to as *teoatltlachinolli* (divine liquid and burnt things). Death on the battlefield was called *xochimiquiztli* (flowery death). This may be similar to one of the claims made about death in modern wars that it is *good and noble to die for one's country.*

Portion of the stone skull rack at the Great Temple. (Courtesy of Jose B. Cuellar)

   This crowded ceremonial schedule was acted out in the many ceremonial centers of the city and empire. The greatest ceremonial precinct, which we studied in chapter 3, formed the axis of Tenochtitlan and measured 440 meters on four sides. It contained, according to some accounts, more than 80 ritual temples, skull racks, schools, and other ceremonial structures. Book 2 of Sahagún's *Florentine Codex* contains a valuable list with descriptions of most of these buildings, including the Great Temple, which stood "in the middle of the square...very large, very tall...and...faced toward the setting of the sun." We also read of a temple where "Motecuhzoma did penances...there was dying there; captives died there." Also, there was the main high school of the city, called "Mexico Calmecac: there dwelt the penitents who offered incense at the summit of the pyramid Temple of Tlaloc. This they did quite daily." There was a temple from which men were thrown into fires and burned to death. Nearby stood the Great Skull Rack, where the heads of sacrificial victims were hung up for display. Another temple was dedicated to the corn goddess, where a young woman impersonating the goddess 7 Snake was sacrificed at night. "And when she died, then they flayed her...the fire priest put on the skin." There were also cooking temples, such as the one where they "cooked the amaranth seed dough for the image of Huitzilopochtli." Another temple related to cooking and eating human flesh was described where "they gathered together the sacrificial victims called Tla-locs…when they had slain them, they cut them to pieces there and cooked them. They put squash blossoms with their flesh…then the noblemen ate them, all the high judges; but not the common folk—only the rulers."[4]

These place names and short descriptions show us that Aztec sac-rifice was a special kind of violence carried out in specific ceremo-nial centers to help the Aztecs communicate with particular deities, forces, and sacred beings. These sacred places served to limit the action to a certain ritual space and also provided mental and emo-tional focus to the practitioners carrying out the sacrifice.

THE GENERAL PATTERN OF AZTEC SACRIFICE

Though important variations of ritual activity were carried out at these temples, schools, skull racks, and bathhouses, the general pattern of human sacrifice was as follows. Most Aztec rituals began with *nezahualiztli,* a preparatory period of priestly fasting, usually lasting four (or a multiple of four) days. An important exception was the year-long partial fast by a group of priests and priestesses known as the *teocuaque* (godeaters) or the greatly feared *in iachhuan Huitzilopochtli in mocexiuhzauhque* (elder brothers of Huitzilopochtli who fasted for a year). This preparatory period also involved *tozo-hualiztli* (nocturnal vigils) and offerings of flowers, food, cloth, rubber, paper, poles with streamers, as well as *copaltemaliztli* (incens-ing), the pouring of libations, and the embowering of temples, stat-ues, and ritual participants. Dramatic processions of elaborately costumed participants, moving to music ensembles and playing sacred songs, passed through the ceremonial precinct before arriv-ing at the specific temple of sacrifice. The major ritual participants were called *teteo ixiptla,* or deity impersonators. All important ritu-als involved a death sacrifice of either animals or human beings.

The most common sacrifice was autosacrifice, or the sacrifice of oneself. This involved the use of *maguey* thorns or other sharp instruments to pierce one's earlobes, thighs, arms, tongue, or, in the case of sinners and priests, genitals in order to offer blood to the gods. The most common type of killing was the beheading of animals like the quail. But the most dramatic and valued sacrifices were those of captured warriors and slaves. These victims were ritually bathed, carefully costumed, often taught to dance special dances, and sometimes either fattened or slimmed down during the preparation period. They were elaborately dressed to impersonate specific deities to whom they were sacrificed.

The different primary sources reveal a wide range of sacrificial techniques, including decapitation, shooting with darts or arrows, drowning, burning, hurling from heights, strangulation, entombment, starvation, and gladiatorial combat. The ceremony, which often lasted as long as 20 days, usually peaked when splendidly attired captors and captives sang and danced in procession to the temple, where they were escorted (often unwillingly) up the stairway to the *techcatl,* or sacrificial stone. Victims were quickly thrust onto the stone, where a temple priest cut through their chest wall with a *tecpatl,* or ritual flint knife. The priest grasped the still-beating heart, called "precious eagle cactus fruit," tore it from the victim's chest, offered it to the sun for vitality and nourishment, and placed it in a carved circular receptacle known as a *cuauhxicalli* (eagle vessel). In many cases, the body, now called "eagle man," was rolled, flailing, down the temple steps to the bottom, where it was dismembered. The head was cut off and the brains taken out. After being skinned, the skull was placed on the *tzompantli,* or skull rack, consisting of long poles laid horizontally and loaded with skulls. In some cases, the captor was decorated, for instance, with chalk and bird down, and given gifts. Then, together with his relatives, he celebrated a ritual meal consisting of "a bowl of stew of dried maize called *tlacatlaolli*...on each went a piece of the flesh of the captive."[5]

About 30 years ago, a heated debate broke out in academic and popular journals about the extent and purpose of Aztec cannibalism. Some argued that the Aztecs ate large numbers of people as a source of protein necessary for survival. The Aztec state was called "the cannibal kingdom" by one anthropologist, who, unfortunately, did a very limited study of the evidence. The opponents of the protein argument stated that cannibalism in Aztec Mexico was primarily a ritual need to feed the gods and renew their energy, not a gastronomic need of humans to feed themselves. This meant that in the Aztec understanding of sacrifice and cannibalism, it was the gods who ate humans through the ritual offerings of blood and human flesh. In addition, the Aztecs had abundant protein sources in the animals and plants of their environment, and it is important to note that the surviving evidence shows that Aztec peoples, primarily the nobles, consumed very small amounts of human flesh, and only on relatively rare occasions during ritual meals.[6]

THE SACRIFICE OF TEZCATLIPOCA: LORD OF THE SMOKING MIRROR

Let us now turn to a specific sacrifice to see how the human body was viewed as the source of sacred potency and how the Aztecs turned the enemy warrior into one of their own gods. Let us imagine how the sacrifice would appear to an observer who lived in the city of Tenochtitlan and witnessed the entire process of a sacrificial festival. Our observer, the 17-year-old scribe-in-training Nauhmitl (Four Arrows), has been chosen to draw and paint this year's festival of Toxcatl for his *calmecac*'s library. As he is preparing for this year's festival, he describes what he saw, felt, and learned as a novice priest when the Smoking Mirror sacrifice was carried out a year ago.

I, Four Arrows, have been asked by my *calmecac* teacher, the high priest Precious Serpent (Quetzalcoatl), to record in paintings the most sacred festival, which we call "Dry Season" (Toxcatl). Precious Serpent, my stern but helpful teacher for three solar years, told me he was impressed by the energy of my heart and the way I can paint the spirit of ritual events onto the sacred pages. Last year he asked me to watch closely all the details of this royal ceremony in preparation to paint this year's festival. I have worked long into the night and risen early in the morning for three years now and feel honored to paint the red and black truths of the festival for the Smoking Mirror (Tezcatlipoca), whom Precious Serpent says is our "god of gods." When I saw this ceremony last year as a member of the priestly school, I was amazed by the physical beauty of the enemy warrior who was killed at the end of the festival. This seasoned warrior, whom we change from a human into the god Tezcatlipoca, can have no blemish upon his body, and he is treated like our most royal family member during the long year leading up to his sacrifice. During that time he is given all the finest luxuries from the nobles' storehouses, including foods, clothes, teachers, women, and instruction. He walks among us as a living god, and I was impressed and felt pride for my *altepetl* when the younger people stopped their work or play and were mesmerized by him and his entourage of servants and guards as they strolled through the city or rode in the canoes along the canals. Many of us become attached to this living god, and a terrible sadness comes over some of the women when, at the end of the year, he is taken to Chalco and dismembered in public view. Let me share with you my images and memories of what happened last year when I followed his every movement. It will help me prepare my paintings in the book of sacred history.

We have been taught in the *calmecac* that all these festivals in which a human person is killed are *nextlaoalli,* or "debt payment" to our gods for their lives, which were taken away in the time of legends so life could develop in Anahuac. This debt payment is a yearlong ceremony that begins when Precious Serpent goes to the house where a special group of captive warriors are kept under guard for several months before the festival begins. Last year when I went with him and the royal guards, I was impressed with the extraordinary, athletic bodies of these warriors. They have to be perfect according to our standards, because Tezcatlipoca represents perfection to us. When the guards led us into the viewing area, Precious Serpent studied the men closely, and I remember he recited the following chant before choosing the new *teotl ixiptla*:

> We seek a perfect body, a bold warrior of fair countenance, slender, reed-like, long and thin, a man like a stout cane, like a stone column, hard all over. And a man who is intelligent and alert to the gods. He must be smoothed like one of our tomatoes, like a pebble, round and hard, or like one sculpted from the cosmic tree. He cannot have curly hair or a rough forehead or a long head. His eyelids cannot be swollen or large. He cannot have a flat nose, or a wide nose, or a concave nose. He cannot have thick lips or gross lips or big lips. He must speak perfectly and not stutter and he must learn Nahuatl before he pays the debt. He cannot have buckteeth or large teeth or yellow teeth or ugly teeth. He must have teeth like seashells. He cannot be cup-eyed or round-eyed or tomato-eyed or have a pierced eye. And his hands, yes the hands, must be perfectly formed. He cannot have a long hand or be one-handed or fat-fingered. His torso must be balanced. He cannot be skinny or fat or big-bellied or have a protruding navel and certainly not a hatchet-shaped navel or a wrinkled stomach or shrunken stomach. And his butt must be perfect. He cannot have a hatchet-shaped butt or a long butt or a twisted butt. Today I seek such a man of perfect order. And if we find such a man, who has no flaw, who has no bodily defect, who has not one single blemish or mark, then we will teach him how to be a god, how to blow the flutes and play the whistle like a divine musician. We will teach him to be the best of who we are and he shall know how to walk like a god and hold the sacred flowers and smoke the smoking tube and be among us as the perfect Smoking Mirror.[7]

Then a careful examination was made, and Precious Serpent pulled two warriors aside and took them into another viewing area. After consulting with his assistants he chose one of them—a very impressive figure whose name was Xiuhitl, which means grass, time flowing, renewal. When this perfect specimen of a warrior was taken back to the royal apartments, he entered a long training period, under constant scrutiny of his guards, which eventually changed him into one of our great artists. He was trained to play the divine songs on the flute, speak eloquently like a *tlamatini*, hold our most precious flowers like a noble, and walk like a ruler through the city.

In fact, and this is one of the most interesting parts of our great yearlong festival, the Tezcatlipoca *ixiptla* was never stationary for long. Very great care was taken that he would be very circumspect in his discourse, that he talk graciously with the people he met. He was daily in the city, walking about, displaying himself, playing his music, and greeting people who stopped to offer respect. When people saw him, they sighed at his beauty and said, "Our Lord, we bow before you and take our wet fingers and rub them along the earth, taking the dust from the land that gives us life and we lick it off our fingers in respect of you." We call this the Earth Eating Ceremony, which means that we are not worthy of Tezcatlipoca, for we are of the earth and death and decay.

I remember vividly the day when Tezcatlipoca, after having learned the arts and having displayed his ability to process around the city, was taken to meet our most revered *tlatoani*, Motecuhzoma Xocoyotzin. All the nobles were gathered in their colorful regalia, the drums beat thunderously,

During the festival of Toxcatl, a captured enemy warrior is ritually transformed into an *ixiptla* or impersonator of the god, Tezcatlipoca. (*Florentine Codex*, from *Historia general de las cosas de Nueva España*, ed. Francisco del Paso y Troncoso. Madrid: Hauser y Menet, 1905)

the flutes played high notes, and all eyes turned toward the meeting of our ruler and his god. Motecuhzoma brought out the divine clothes and dressed Tezcatlipoca in beautiful jades, feathers, breechcloth and cape, and gold and presented him with gifts that our merchants had brought back from their distant journeys. It was at this ceremony that I came to realize how far above the common people the ruler was in terms of riches, glory, and beautiful things. But I was also impressed by how much the ruler looked up to the living god Tezcatlipoca.

We pause here for a moment to make some observations before continuing with Nauhmitl's narrative. Sahagún's informants provided the details of this further transformation into the ruler's god. Eagle down feathers and popcorn flowers were pasted on the head of the chosen captive. He was arrayed with "the flowery stole."[8] Golden shell pendants were placed on his ears and turquoise mosaic earplugs were inserted in the earlobes. A shining seashell necklace and white seashell breast ornament were draped on his neck and chest. A snail shell lip pendant was inserted in his lip.

Hardly an area of his body escaped transformation. Golden bracelets covered his upper arms, while turquoise bracelets covered almost all of his forearm. A wide-meshed net cape with a fringe of brown cotton thread hung above his elaborate breechcloth, which reached to the calves of his legs. His legs were covered with gold bells above obsidian sandals with ocelot skin ears.

This living image of physical, cultural, and imperial splendor presented himself to the pathways of the city once again, where the citizenry beheld the ruler's "beloved god."

Then, during the 20 days prior to the sacrifice, two major transformations took place. First, the "image" shed these luscious ornaments, and his hair was cut in the *tochyacatl* style of a seasoned warrior, with only a forked heron feather ornament and a quetzal feather spray attached to his head. Second, he was given four wives, and "for only twenty days he lived lying with the women, that he lived married to them."[9] The symbolism of this ceremonial coupling was meaningful, as each of these wives was also a *teotl ixiptla* representing the goddesses Xochiquetzal, Xilonen, Atlatonan, and Huixtociuatl. The five of them sang and danced in public for five days and distributed food and gifts to people at a series of specific locations, including Tecanman, then at a place where the image of Titlacahuan was guarded, then at Tepetzinco in the middle of the lagoon, and on the fourth day at Tepepulco. We now return to Nauhmitl's narrative.

I cannot overemphasize to you how much the entire mood of the long ceremony changed suddenly and with finality after these visits to the sacred places in the lakes. Tezcatlipoca and the beautiful women *ixiptla* were set off in a boat but now the women began to sing sad, sorrowful songs that made those of us who watched and listened from the shore shiver in fright. They were consoling him for the awful moments ahead. With these dirges in the air, they circled out in the lake and then came back, and the women embraced him intensely and said good-bye. Last year the guards had to step in and tear one woman away from him, as she had become so deeply attached to Tezcatlipoca and could not bear to think he would be killed, beheaded, and his heart removed. Even though she went into the ceremony knowing that this was the inevitable fate of the man-god, her passions burst out, and she was carried away in shame and sorrow. I must say that this display of emotion rattled me and later that night I confessed to Precious Serpent my experience. He told me in no uncertain terms that this display of doubt was a profound breach of the rules that went against all our educational training and that it could not be tolerated in a young priest like myself. When I looked into his eyes, I felt afraid that he would punish me with the thorns and obsidian bleeding blades that I had suffered the year before. But I also saw that he understood my weakness, that he must have had the same thoughts long ago when he was a young priest. There was a knowing look in his eyes but also a warning never to speak of this again.

Now Tezcatlipoca was all alone on the shore except for the guards, who began to stiffen up and close in so he would not try to escape in the confusion. Then the death walk began as he and the entourage made their final, bold display to our people who gathered along the shore and walkways to watch him go to the temple of sacrifice in Chalco. I cannot describe for you the looks of awe, fear, and respect that came over the faces of the men and women who stood and gazed at this god going to his killing. The drums beat slowly; the whistles blew in high, shrill notes; and a chorus of song filled the air during the entire three-mile route to the southern part of the community.

I was so surprised the first time I accompanied Precious Serpent to Chalco when I saw the temple where Tezcatlipoca was killed. It was not a majestic, multicolored holy house, as I had anticipated, but a small temple with less than ten steps. Each step, however, was important in what happened next. All was silent as Tezcatlipoca stood at the foot of the stairs, guards nearby and the High Priests awaiting with knives and blades at the top. Tezcatlipoca, after several minutes of intense concentration, began to ascend the temple by himself, of his own free will, going up to die at the top. He would take a step up and stop, lift one of his flutes to the heavens and then break it into pieces. Another step, another broken flute, another broken whistle. It was very slow until he reached the top and suddenly everything sped up like the rapids in one of our nearby rivers.

The offering priests seized him with great force and threw him upon his back on the sacrificial stone. He was surrounded by six men, five of whom held down his four limbs and head; the sixth gave out a wail and then cut open his breast with one diving thrust of the sacred knife. A terrible, awesome cry filled the air and everyone stiffened and shook. Then, Precious Serpent stepped in and took out his heart which we could barely see was still pumping blood and he raised it in dedication to the sun. A song was sung as the heart was placed in one of our holy bowls, the *cuauhxicalli,* where it began to feed the god whose face was carved within.

The first time I saw this, I began to faint with amazement but was steadied by my comrade, Cuauhtemoc. Then Tezcatlipoca's body was carefully lowered from the temple so his perfect body would not be injured. His head was severed from his body and, after the brains and eyes were removed, it was carried by a special messenger to the Great Skull Rack back in the heart of the city where it was hung up for all to see.

Emotionally exhausted and physically drained, I followed the group of priests back to the center of the city, where we gathered to hear some solemn words from Precious Serpent. He stood there near the Skull Rack

Sacrifice of the Tezcatlipoca *ixiptla.* (*Florentine Codex,* from *Historia general de las cosas de Nueva España,* ed. Francisco del Paso y Troncoso. Madrid: Hauser y Menet, 1905)

and held out his hand, pointing to the skull of Tezcatlipoca, and sang a message I will always remember: "This betokened our life on earth. For he who rejoiced, who possessed riches, who sought, who esteemed our lord's sweetness, his fragrance—richness, prosperity—thus ended in great misery. Indeed it must be remembered: 'No one on earth goes exhausting happiness, riches, wealth.'"[10]

I must tell you as I close these thoughts that I learned so much from being a part of this grandest of rituals. In particular I learned that Tezcatlipoca *is* really everywhere. He is in the beauty of our bodies and in the decomposition of our lives. Now I understand why we call him "the enemy on both sides," for while we can live for a while in peace and happiness in the middle, we are surrounded by the gods who demand of us our lives in sacrifice, in payment of the debt.

And now I feel that I am ready to paint this year's Toxcatl ceremony so that the next group of students in the *calmecac* will hear and see the glorious story of the Smoking Mirror.

Nauhmitl's remarks reveal the following points: In the Aztec descriptions of what they were up to there is very little emphasis on the actual sacrifice. For them, it was a public ceremony of (1) transforming a man into a god, (2) the luxurious display of this sacred captive, (3) the sacralization of the spaces and places he went and visited, and (4) the ultimate message that life on earth is not the real life, the important life. It is the giving of life that leads to the renewal of the gods that is important. Let us look at a more militant example in order to address the problem of the eating of the gods.

THE FEAST OF THE FLAYING OF MEN: THE CITY AS IDEAL BATTLEFIELD

In the previous example, the movements of Tezcatlipoca's *ixiptla* mark out the ritual theater for the sacrificial ritual, and his perfect body becomes a moving sacred space. In the example that follows, we will see how the city becomes an *ideal battlefield*, the battlefield where nothing can go wrong for the Aztec warriors. In other words, the battlefield *out there*, which can be a place of victory or defeat for the Aztecs, becomes the perfect battlefield *in here, in the city*, where there is only public victory for the Aztecs. Before turning to this ritual, a short summary of the Flowery Wars will help us understand the relations of war and human sacrifice.

One of the most important ritual and political institutions of the Aztec empire was known as the Xochiyaoyotl (Flowery Wars), which lasted from 1450 to 1519 and consisted of a series of scheduled battlefield confrontations between warriors of the Triple Alliance (the governmental alliance between Tenochtitlan, Tezcoco, and Tlacopan) and warriors of the Tlaxcala-Puebla Valley kingdoms. These wars were, in part, substitute wars, that is, battles arranged by the rulers of these competing kingdoms when there were no pressing crises to provoke actual wars. They were similar to modern war games, only much more serious, as actual killing and sacrificial prisoners were part of the action. They involved the elaborate training of warriors, the organization of supplies, long marches of armies and supporters, the designation of battlefields, and the battles themselves. Tactics, heroism, capture, wounding, killing, war booty, and triumphal returns were essential to the Flowery Wars.

FLOWERY WARS

One of the most puzzling aspects of Aztec warfare are the Flowery Wars. After years of study scholars still are not sure of the real political and ritual purposes of these wars. Were they to provide sacrificial victims? Maintain the political balance of powers? Keep warriors in tip-top shape?

There is a strong debate among scholars over the causes and significance of the Flowery Wars. According to the Aztecs, they launched these wars to obtain sacrificial victims for ritual festivals and to keep the warriors in training during times of peace. It also appears that between 1450 and 1454 the Aztecs suffered a devastating famine that was interpreted by the priestly elites as a sign of angry gods who needed a greater supply of warrior sacrifices. According to a 16th-century chronicler, Diego Durán, the Flowery Wars were instituted for the specific purpose of supplying victims for the Great Temple of Tenochtitlan. Tlacaelel, the chief advisor to several *tlatoque*, compared a warrior going to the Flowery Wars with a merchant going to distant markets to purchase luxuries. The god and his army went to the battlefield to purchase blood and hearts, the luxuries of the temples.

Recent research has expanded our understanding of the Flowery Wars by revealing that these military confrontations resulted not just in the capture of warriors for temple sacrifice but in large-scale battlefield killing that left the competing armies depleted and in disarray. In these cases, the Flowery Wars reflected true warfare conditions between states, not simply the acquisition of warriors for sacrifice in the capital. Further, it is certain that during periods of truce between these ritually warring kingdoms, rulers of enemy territories were invited to witness the theatrical sacrifice of warriors in the ceremonial center of Tenochtitlan. Hidden behind special canopies, these visiting lords witnessed the ritual devastation of allied and enemy warriors. This was done in order to intimidate and fill with fear both the allies and the enemies of the Aztec *tlatoque* and their nobles so that psychological superiority could be maintained.

One of the most remarkable sacrificial festivals associated with the psychology and politics of war was Tlacaxipehualiztli, the Feast of the Flaying of Men. It is important, in part, because it included the eating of small parts of the victim's body. We will look at three aspects of the festival: (1) preparations for sacrifice, (2) the gladiatorial sacrifice, and (3) the gifts to the gods and the captors, that is, ritual cannibalism by gods and men.

Preparations

During this festival the people honored the god Xipe Totec (Our Lord the Flayed One). One of the central acts was the sacrificing and flaying of captive warriors who were led through an elaborate series of rituals in different neighborhoods and in the main ceremonial center of Tenochtitlan. Prior to the actual sacrifice and flaying, the warriors were transformed into god images. In one account, captive warriors were bathed, purified, and dressed as *teteo ixiptla,* living images of Xipe Totec, 40 days before the feast day, and were then displayed in public in each of the city's *barrios.*[11] Their bodies were painted with long red stripes following an all-night vigil during which hair was taken from the crown of their heads. This hair was guarded by the captor as a potent piece of an "eagle man" whose destiny after the sacrifice was to be "taken upwards" into the heavens to dwell "in the presence of the sun." This hair would guarantee honor, flowers, tobacco, and capes; "his valor would not in vain perish: it was as if thus he took renown from the captive."[12]

While the captive was being changed into a god image, the captor was taken to the temple of Tecanman, adorned with white turkey down, covered with chalk, and given gifts. The captor was given the names Sun, Chalk, and Feather because he "had not died there in war, or because he would yet go to die, would go to pay the debt in war or by sacrifice." This means that he was declared a potential sacrificial victim.

Deity impersonator of Xipe Totec watches over the gladiatorial sacrifice of a war captive by a jaguar warrior. (Diego Durán, *Códice Durán.* Mexico City: Arrendadora Internacional 1990 facsimile edition)

The Gladiatorial Sacrifice

The central drama of the gladiatorial sacrifice began with the entire city present at the spectacle. They saw the captives and their captors march to the gladiatorial stone following eagle and ocelot warriors who danced, pranced, and displayed shields and obsidian-bladed clubs raised in dedication to the sun. Amid the sounds from conch shells, singing, and whistling, the sacrifice began when the captor seized the captive by the hair and led him to the sacrificial stone, where he raised *pulque* four times and drank it with a long hollow cane. A quail was beheaded for the captive and cast away. The captive was made to drink *pulque* and forced up on the round stone, where a priest called the Old Bear, dressed in bear skin, tied him by the ankle or waist to the center of the stone with the "sustenance rope."[13] Given a war club decked with feathers, the captive was attacked by a dancing jaguar warrior armed with a war club filled with obsidian blades. The text reads:

Then they fought each other; they kept menacing each other; they threatened each other. They looked at each other well to see where they would
smite each other, would cut each other in a dangerous place, perchance in
the calf of the leg, or in the thigh, or on the head, or in the middle. And if
some captive was valiant, courageous, with great difficulty he surpassed
his adversary. He met all four of the ocelot and eagle warriors; he fought
them. And if they could not weaken him, then there went one who was
left-handed.
  Then this one wounded his arms; he felled him; he felled him flat. This
one appeared as the god Opochtli. And although the striped one already
faltered, already weakened, also he acquitted himself as a man; he still
acquitted himself as a man. And when one only went faltering, only went
on all fours, went fainting, only went undone, only vainly, only impotently,
they snatched his war club. Thus the one who striped him, the striper,
confronted him. And on the other hand there was the one who no longer
did anything, no longer defended himself with them, no longer attended
to it, no longer took the trouble, no longer spoke. At once he faltered, he
fainted, he fell on the surface, he threw himself down as if dead, he wished
that breath might end, that he might endure it, that he might perish, that
he might cast off the burden of death.[14]

Some captives were not killed in this way but rather were taken
the next day by offering priests who seized them by the hair
on the tops of their heads and forced them to climb the pyramid to the temple of Huitzilopochtli. Some captives resisted
or fainted, but ideally the victim "did not act like a woman; he
became strong like a man, he bore himself like a man, he went
speaking like a man, he went exerting himself, he went strong of
heart, he went shouting...he went exalting his city.... 'Already
here I go: You will speak of me there in my home land.'"[15]
  The captive was stretched out on the sacrificial stone by six offering priests who extracted his heart, called "precious eagle-cactus
fruit," and offered it to the sun (the text says that it "nourished"
the sun) before it was placed in the eagle vessel. The slain captive
was now called eagle man, and his body was rolled down the steps:
"breaking to pieces, they came head over heels...they reached the
terrace at the base of the pyramid."
  Other people—strangers to the city—were also present. Foreign
rulers and nobles "from cities which were his enemies from beyond
(the mountains)...those with which there was war, Motecuhzoma

secretly summoned" to the ceremony and placed behind an arbor of flowers and branches so that they would not be seen by the citizens of Tenochtitlan.

Gifts of Nourishment for the Gods and the Captors

After the enemy warrior/god image was killed at the gladiatorial stone, a frightening figure called the Night Drinker sacrificed the captive, extracting his heart, saying, "Thus he giveth the sun to drink." These words followed the action of an offering priest who set a hollow eagle cane in the captive's breast cavity. These gestures, the submerging of the hollow cane in the blood and the raising of the blood toward the sun, meant that "he giveth the sun to drink."[16]

Then the captor, dressed in his warrior's insignia, took the eagle bowl filled with the captive's blood to "every place…nowhere did he forget in the calmecas, in the calpulcos. On the lips of the stone images…he placed the blood." After visiting the neighborhoods and schools, the captor left his insignia at the palace.

The fragmented body was carried by *calpolli* elders to the local temple where the captor had previously vowed to bring a captive. The body was flayed and then taken to the captor's home, where it was cut up for a ritual meal, "and it was said that they [those who ate of it] would be considered gods."[17] One piece of flesh was eaten by the blood relatives of the captor in a bowl of dried maize stew. At one point in the drama, a revealing ritual relationship was acknowledged, when the captor, who could not eat any part of his captive, said, "Shall I perchance eat my very self?" For when he had captured the enemy, he had said, "He is as my beloved son," with the captive answering, "He is my beloved father." One thigh bone was sent to Motecuhzoma as a gift, while the other thigh was kept by the captor as a trophy and put up on a pole in the captor's house 20 days later.

Remarkably, the captors' friends and assistants took turns wearing the flayed skins of the sacrificed victims and traveled in groups around parts of the city in order to accomplish two tasks. First, they would enter into skirmishes with other younger warriors-to-be who attempted to snatch a piece of skin under their fingernails as a sign that they were brave and participated symbolically in the capture of the enemy. Second, these men wearing skins traveled from door to door collecting food for themselves and for the owners of the skins, that is, the captors. These movements through the neighborhoods were considered provocative displays, and they often resulted in boisterous, unruly mock battles between the

Warriors wear the skins of sacrificed war captives in the festival of Tlacaxipehualiztli. (*Florentine Codex,* from *Historia general
de las cosas de Nueva España,* ed. Francisco del Paso y Troncoso.
Madrid: Hauser y Menet, 1905)

young Aztec warriors and the *xipeme* who were wearing the skins.
The young skinless warriors snatched at the navels of the men
wearing skins, trying to get a piece of skin, in order to "bring out
their rage, their anger."[18]

The skin wearers chased their attackers through the ceremonial
area, beating warriors with rattle sticks, arousing anger. This group
was followed by the Night Drinker, who menaced the warriors, occasionally capturing them and holding them for ransom at a temple
for turkey hens or mantles. In this ritual called Neteotoquiliztli, or
the Impersonation of a God, some warriors added an extra layer of
their insignia to the image of Xipe Totec as it paraded in the streets.
This begging ritual involved skirmishes, mock battles, and visits to
family homes, where ears of maize were given by the common people, while nobles offered clothes, feathers, and jewels. According to
Durán, women would bring children out to the *xipeme,* who took
them into their arms, spoke special words, circled the courtyard of

the house four times, and returned the children to their mothers, who gave gifts to these living images of Xipe Totec.[19]

The head of the captive was carried during the dances, and it was said, "They dance with the severed heads." The visitors from cities with whom the Aztecs were at war dispersed as the dancing, feasting, and adorning continued on late into the night near the great palace.

On the third day, the scene began at the great palace with more lavish displays as Motecuhzoma danced into the ceremonial center, leading the rulers from Tezcoco and Tepaneca. According to Motolinía, these rulers wore the skins of the most important flayed victims. After a long, eloquent speech, Motecuhzoma distributed presents of cloaks and food to the warriors for their accomplishments.

On the 20th day, the captor gave a banquet for kin and friends. The captors and the men wearing skins went dancing, jumping, stinking, wearing the skins through the streets to Xipe Totec's temple, where the dried, crackling, disintegrating human skins were placed in a basket and buried in a cave at its base. The *xipeme* bathed themselves and returned to the captor's courtyard, where the captor took a thigh bone and planted "a pole of the flaying of men signifying that he had flayed a captive." At the top of the pole was a "sleeveless knotted cord jacket and [a] small spray of heron feathers." He wrapped the thigh bone in paper and gave it a mask and this was called "the god-captive." The captor held a feast for his friends and kin, at which the old men and women became intoxicated; a man dressed in the captor's insignia offered white *pulque* in four places, singing, until the month came to an end. The text reads: "Here they finished when he had done similarly in all places. It was done in no more than one day. But song did not end in the song house until they went ending when it was the feast of Huey tocoztli."[20]

OTHER FESTIVALS AND THE MASS-SACRIFICE SOCIETY OF THE SPANIARDS

Eighteen yearly festivals involving the public sacrifice of human beings are described in detail in Book II of the *Florentine Codex*. Among the most remarkable was Atlcahualo, which involved the paying of debts to Tlaloc, the rain god. On this day, children (called *tlacateteuhti*, human paper streamers) with two cowlicks in their hair and favorable day signs were dressed in costumes—some set with pearls—of dark green, black striped with chili red, and light blue, and were sacrificed on seven different mountain tops around the Basin of Mexico. The flowing and falling of their tears ensured the coming of rain.

Another astonishing festival was Ochpaniztli, which was celebrated in honor of the mother goddess Toci (Our Grandmother). A young woman whose physical appearance resembled the goddess's features was transformed into her *teotl ixiptla* by being arrayed with rich, feminine ornaments. She was dressed and cared for by an entourage of women, especially midwives and medicine women. The girl was not told that she was going to be sacrificed, because it was believed that if she became sad or depressed, the potency of the sacrifice would be nullified. She was led, dancing and singing through the streets, eventually to the house of the ruler or another noble. She had sexual intercourse with this royal man, whose potency was believed to be increased through lovemaking with a goddess. Then she was taken to the pyramid temple and suddenly grabbed by a priest who, standing back to back with her, bent over forward so that she was stretched out. Her head was quickly struck off, her body was flayed of its skin, and her heart was extracted and placed in the *cuauhxicalli*. Then a young man put on her skin and processed through the city, receiving gifts and participating in more dances and rituals.

Regardless of how hard we try and how far our understanding advances, it is difficult not to be amazed and somewhat repulsed by these ritual forms of violence. The Aztecs carried human violence to an extraordinary degree in human history, and this fact alone makes it important to study and understand them. But it should also be pointed out that when the Europeans came to the Americas, other, distinctive forms of violence were unleashed on the native population that had never been equaled in the New World. Within 100 years, over 85 percent of the native population died as a result of "microbe shock," murder in warfare, cruelty in the mines, fields, and towns, and massacres. In Mexico, there were close to 25 million people in 1500, but by 1600 only 1 million native Mesoamericans were still alive. The majority of the indigenous population who died during the 16th century were the victims of diseases transmitted by the "lethal handshake"—physical contact with Europeans, including the baptisms performed by Catholic priests. As one writer has put it, the Aztecs had a sacrifice society, but the Europeans brought a mass-sacrifice society, a massacre society, to the New World. One Franciscan priest, Motolinía, compared the devastation of the indigenous populations with the 10 plagues sent by God to chastise the Egyptians in the Old Testament. The first plague was smallpox: "They died in heaps, like bedbugs." The second plague was the death by Spanish weapons. The third was the famine that accompanied the Spanish destruction of Indian harvests. The fourth plague was the vicious overseer who tortured the natives. The fifth plague was the taxes in the forms of lands and goods levied on the natives. The Indians were under such pressure that when they had no goods they were forced to sell their children to the Spaniards, and eventually to sell themselves. The sixth plague was the mines, in which the Indians were forced to work long hours in dangerous conditions, sometimes carrying loads as heavy as 250 pounds up steep underground ascents. The seventh plague was the building of the city of Mexico, during which scores of Indians died in falls or were crushed by falling beams or by buildings being torn down. The eighth plague was the slavery of the mines. Slaves were branded by the letters of all those who bought and sold them. In some cases slaves were tattooed with brands on many parts of their bodies. The ninth plague was the open graveyards around the mines. One eyewitness wrote, "For half a league around these mines and along a great part of the road one could scarcely avoid walking over dead bodies or bones, and the flocks of birds and crows that came to feed upon the corpses were so numerous that they darkened the sun."[21]

The 10th plague involved the in-fighting, factions, and scapegoating among the Spaniards. Their internal social problems often led to frustrated excuses for executing large numbers of Indians without legal or rational justification. Consider, for instance, this unbelievable report by Bartolomé de las Casas. One day, after a picnic, a group of Spaniards decided to test whether their swords were sharp.

A Spaniard, in whom the devil is thought to have clothed himself, suddenly drew his sword. Then the whole hundred drew theirs and began to rip open the bellies to cut and kill those lambs,—men, women, children, and old folks all of whom were seated, off guard and frightened, watching the mares and the Spaniards. And within two credos, not a man of all of them there remains alive. The Spaniards enter the large house nearby, for this was happening at its door, and in the same way, with cuts and stabs, begin to kill as many as they found there, so that a stream of blood was running, as if a great number of cows had perished.[22]

In thinking about this mass-sacrifice society brought by the Spaniards, it is also important to say that there were many priests, nuns, and others who not only strove to understand and appreciate the nature of Aztec society, but who also struggled, sometimes at serious personal risk, to stop the abuse, killing, and exploitation of native peoples. And it should be admitted at the end of this chapter on sacrifice and warfare that the worldview the Spaniards brought to the Americas elevated their own humanity and degraded the human value of the Aztecs in a way that justified, in their minds, the excessive cruelty they practiced and believed in.

NOTES

1. Bernal Díaz del Castillo, *The History of the Conquest of New Spain,* ed. Davíd Carrasco (Albuquerque: University of New Mexico Press, 2008), 287.

2. Kay A. Read, "Human Sacrifice: An Overview," in *Encyclopedia of Religion* (2nd ed.), ed. Lindsay Jones (Detroit, MI: Macmillan, 2005), 6: 4183.

3. Jonathan Z. Smith, *Imagining Religion: From Babylon to Jonestown* (Chicago: University of Chicago Press, 1982), 102.

4. Bernardino de Sahagún, *Florentine Codex: General History of the Things of New Spain,* ed. and trans. Arthur J. O. Anderson and Charles E. Dibble introductory vol. and 12 books (Santa Fe, NM: School of American Research and University of Utah, 1950–82). See the appendix to book 2 (*The Ceremonies*), especially 175–93.

5. Ibid., 49.

6. Human sacrifice and cannibalism have been the subject of heated controversy over the years. The now-discounted position of Michael Harner, "The Ecological Basis for Aztec Sacrifice," *American Ethnologist* 4 (1977): 117–35 and Marvin Harris, *Cannibals and Kings: The Origins of Culture* (New York: Random House, 1977), has been ably summarized and critiqued by Bernard R. Ortiz de Montellano, "Counting Skulls: Comment on the Cannibalism Theory of Harner-Harris," *American Anthropologist* 85 (1983): 403–6. See Peggy Reeves Sanday, *Divine Hunger: Cannibalism as a Cultural System* (New York: Cambridge University Press, 1986). Also see Davíd Carrasco, "Cosmic Jaws: 'We Eat the Gods and Gods Eat Us'" and "Give Me Some Skin: The Charisma and Sacrifice of the Aztec Warrior," in *City of Sacrifice: The Aztec Empire and the Role of Violence in Civilization* (Boston: Beacon Press, 1999).

7. This chant has been paraphrased from Sahagún, *Florentine Codex,* 2: 66–68, which provides an elaborate description of the requisite attributes of this *teotl ixiptla.*

8. Ibid., 69.

9. Ibid., 70.

10. Ibid., 71.

11. See Alfredo López Austin's focused discussion of human sacrifice in *The Human Body and Ideology: Concepts of the Ancient Nahuas,* trans. Thelma Ortiz de Montellano and Bernard Ortiz de Montellano, 2 vols. (Salt Lake

City: University of Utah Press, 1988), 1: 375–80, especially 376, where he writes that the *teteo imixiptlahuan* were "men possessed by the gods, and, as such, died in a rite of renewal. It was not men who died, but gods—gods within a corporeal covering that made possible their ritual death on earth."

12. Sahagún, *Florentine Codex*, 2: 49.

13. Ibid., 52.

14. Ibid., 53.

15. Ibid., 48.

16. Ibid., 53.

17. Ibid., 54.

18. Ibid., 50. Another account of this ceremony appears in Sahagún, *Florentine Codex*, 8: 85, where the skirmishes in the streets are described in some detail: "And then the chieftains started forth and fell upon the *tototecti*: they pinched their navels. Very swiftly they pinched them, and then they took after them and went skirmishing with them there in the place where they were, a place called Totectzontecontitlan."

19. Ibid., 8: 85, gives interesting details of this penetration of domestic spaces by the impersonators: "Thereupon the *tototecti* visited house after house. Nowhere did they omit a house or one's home. Indeed everywhere they entered; and the common folk, seasoned to this, awaited them in order to offer them the things with which they expected them—bunches of ears of maize, tortillas made of uncooked maize, and tamales of maize, amaranth seed, and honey mixed together. For the whole day they went from house to house, [thus treated with] esteem."

20. Ibid., 2: 60.

21. Quoted in Tzvetan Todorov, *The Conquest of America: The Question of the Other,* trans. Richard Howard (New York: Harper and Row, 1984), 138.

22. Ibid., 141.

8

THE TWO TONGUES: THE AZTECS ENCOUNTER THE EUROPEANS

It was a woman, Marina, an Indian like him, from his own land, who actually defeated him, although she did use two tongues. It was she who revealed to Cortés that the Aztec empire was divided, that the peoples subjugated by Motecuhzoma hated him and hated each other as well, and that the Spaniards could grasp opportunity by the forelock.

—Carlos Fuentes[1]

One of the most interesting problems facing the student of Aztec history is this: How could the Aztec empire, with its powerful military tradition, complex religious institutions, and long-range trading and spy system in good working order, fall to a conflicted group of Spanish invaders in the short period of two years, and on home ground? We remember that the Aztecs appeared to have a supreme confidence in themselves, as witnessed in this poem about the city:

Proud of itself
is the City of Mexico-Tenochtitlan.
Here no one fears to die in war.
This is our glory.
This is Your Command,
O Giver of Life!

Have this in mind, O princes,
do not forget it.
Who could conquer Tenochtitlan?
Who could shake the foundation of the heavens?[2]

In fact, between Easter Sunday 1519 and August 13, 1521, the Aztec capital, religious system, cultural practices, noble classes, farmers, poets, and artists had their world completely shaken and profoundly transformed. One Mexica poet wrote about the devastation of the city and its people in these moving but pitiful phrases:

Broken spears lie in the roads;
we have torn our hair in our grief.
The houses are roofless now, and their walls
are red with blood.
Worms are swarming in the streets and plazas,
and the walls are splattered with gore....
We have pounded our hands in despair
against the adobe walls,
for our inheritance, our city, is lost and dead.
The shields of our warriors were its defense,
but they could not save it.[3]

In what follows, we will trace the key events of the high drama of what has been called the conquest of Mexico by focusing on (1) both the Aztec account of the arrival of the Spaniards and the Spanish account of their march and entry into Tenochtitlan, (2) the identification of Cortés with the man-god Quetzalcoatl, and (3) the battle for the capital. We will see that the so-called conquest was much more a rebellion by the indigenous enemies of the Aztecs, who formed crucial alliances with the Spaniards and supplied thousands of indigenous warriors that served under Cortés's leadership. We will also meet one of the most interesting figures in American history, the native woman who served as the translator between the Aztecs and the Spaniards, Malintzin, also known as doña Marina and Malinche. We begin with a short description of the reign of Motecuhzoma Xocoyotzin, the famous Aztec ruler between 1502 and 1520.

THE REIGN OF MOTECUHZOMA XOCOYOTZIN

The *Codex Mendoza* gives a detailed description of the talents and successes of this Aztec ruler, who came to power after the death of King Ahuitzotl in 1502 and met Cortés in 1520. Motecuhzoma (Angry Lord, from *tecuh*[*tli*] = lord, *mozuma* = to frown from anger)

Xocoyotzin (the Younger, from *xocoyo*[*tl*] = younger child, *tzin* = revered) "was by nature wise, an astrologer, a philosopher, and skilled in all the arts, civil as well as military. His subjects greatly respected him because of his gravity, demeanor, and power; none of his predecessors, in comparison, could approach his great state and majesty."[4]

According to the native informants who helped draw, paint, and write the *Codex Mendoza,* Motecuhzoma enjoyed the adoration of his people: "And he was so greatly feared by his vassals, and by his captains and leaders, that when they negotiated with him out of the great esteem and fear that they had, none dared look him in the face, but they kept their eyes on the ground and their head bowed and inclined to the ground."[5] In fact, most descriptions of this ruler's reign support this image of success and adulation, at least until the Spaniards arrived. We get the following picture of his time on the throne.

He was 34 years old when he ascended the Aztec throne and was already famous as a military leader. He had attained the high military position of a *tlacatecuhtli,* or great lord, and spent the greater part of his reign consolidating the many conquests of his predecessor. When he first came to the throne, he led a very successful war of inauguration (remember that each ruler had to initiate a war for his own coronation ceremony) into the far southern regions of the empire. These triumphs continued; the *Codex Mendoza* pictures an astonishing 44 conquests during the period 1502–20. It was during his reign that the Flowery Wars, discussed in the last chapter, escalated. It also appears that there were a growing number of rebellions against Aztec hegemony (or dominance over many of the communities of Mexico) that played an important role in the different ways that the Spaniards found allies.

Motecuhzoma's extravagant lifestyle included taking many wives—one account mentions more than 200. These marriages were, in part, political arrangements that consolidated the ability of the Mexica to form and maintain military and economic alliances with nearby and distant city-states. They also resulted in a large number of children who became members of his royal entourage and government. We are fortunate to have several European eyewitness descriptions of this now very famous man. Bernal Díaz del Castillo, a foot soldier in Cortés's troop who later wrote a massive memoir of the conquest, which he titled *The True History of the Discovery and Conquest of New Spain,* tells us that the emperor was neat, clean, slender, tall, and well built. He put on fresh clothes more

Motecuhzoma Xocoyotzin, the ninth *tlatoani* of Tenochtitlan who reigned from 1502 to 1520, depicted with 16 of his 44 conquests. (*Codex Mendoza*, courtesy of Frances F. Berdan and Patricia Reiff Anawalt)

than once a day. Hernán Cortés in his letters to the king of Spain described the life of the court: apparently, every day at sunrise, more than 500 noblemen and their attendants would arrive at the palace and spend the day walking, talking, and planning governmental events. Hundreds of servants would fill the courtyards and streets near the palace.

This crowd was more than equaled at mealtime, for when the ruler ate, more than 300 servants brought dishes of meat, fish, fruit, and vegetables, placing them in a great room where Motecuhzoma ate while sitting on a "finely made, small leather cushion." Díaz del Castillo described the meal:

> I have heard it said that they were wont to cook for him the flesh of young boys, but as he had such variety of dishes, made of so many things, we could not succeed in seeing if they were of human flesh or of other things, for they daily cooked fowl, turkeys, pheasants, native partridges, quail, tame and wild ducks, venison, wild boar, reed birds, pigeons, hares and rabbits, and many sorts of birds and other things which are bred in this country, and they are so numerous that I cannot finish naming them in a hurry.[6]

Four very beautiful women attended the ruler, who placed a gold-encrusted wooden screen before him so that no one would watch him eating. Sometimes other chieftains ate with the ruler, who sometimes drank a chocolate drink from a cup of pure gold. Often, according to the Spaniards, the emperor enjoyed the singers, dancers, and buffoons who entertained him, sometimes giving them portions of the food and drink he and his entourage had not eaten.

SPANIARDS BEFORE CORTÉS

It is a common misconception that the first Spaniards to make landfall in what is now Mexico were led by Cortés in 1519. In fact, Díaz del Castillo's famous memoir tells us that he participated in a small slave-hunting and exploring expedition that left the Spanish settlement of Cuba in 1517 and, after some nights of terror caused by storms, landed in the area known today as Yucatán. After being attacked and nearly slaughtered in ambushes on the beaches and in a Maya town, they heard the word *castilan* (Castilian) spoken over and over. In fact, these Maya already knew who the strangers were, because a few Spaniards who survived a shipwreck in 1511 had crawled ashore and been placed at the mercy of the local inhabitants.

When Cortés arrived eight years later, again with Díaz del Castillo in the group, he found out through an interpreter that two of the shipwrecked Spaniards were still alive and living elsewhere on the island of Cozumel. Searching, he found one of the men, Gerónimo de Aguilar, who now spoke Mayan as well as recalling his native Spanish and could still recount the trials and tribulations of the shipwrecked survivors. Aguilar told Cortés how the rest of them had either died of hunger or disease or been sacrificed, except for another man, Gonzalo Guerrero, who had become a Maya war chief in another town. In fact, while Aguilar seemed happy to be rescued, his contrasting story of Guerrero shocked the Spaniards. Guerrero had married an Indian woman, had children with her, gotten tattooed in the native style, become a war captain, and even organized an attack on certain Spanish explorers.

In the incredible drama that followed, Aguilar was to aid the Spaniards by translating crucial information for them as they attempted to form alliances with native city-states who harbored deep antipathy for the Aztecs. Amazingly, Guerrero stayed on the Maya side, helping them resist and fight against the Spaniards at all costs. It appears that his tattooed body was found among the Indians killed in a fight with the Spaniards in 1535 south of Yucatán. He had led a canoe attack against the Spaniards and had died in the battle.

THE THREE TONGUES

The subsequent defeat of the Aztec nobles, warriors, and ruler was accomplished by many forces, including the power of language. As the quotation that opens this chapter suggests, the conquest of the Mexica capital would not have taken place without the work of translation and especially a native woman. The Aztecs and the Spaniards spoke two entirely different languages—Nahuatl and Spanish. It is almost always overlooked how difficult communication was between these two people and how Cortés relied on not two but three languages to figure out what and where the Aztec empire was, to communicate with the great Motecuhzoma, and to organize his assault on Tenochtitlan.

The key person, however, was neither Motecuhzoma nor Cortés, but an Indian woman named Malintzin who became known to the Spaniards as doña Marina. She grew up as a Nahuatl-speaking daughter of a *cacique,* or chieftain, in the Gulf Coast region of the Aztec empire. When her noble mother remarried, it was decided that a newborn son should be first in the line of royal succession rather than Malintzin, so she was sold into captivity among Maya peoples. She grew up in a Maya community near Cintla. After the Spaniards won a battle against the local Indians, she was given, along with some other native women, to Cortés. She became one of Cortés's mistresses and bore him a son, Martín, who appears to have been his favorite. Speaking at least two Indian languages, Chontal Mayan (the language Aguilar had learned) and Nahuatl (the language of the Aztecs), doña Marina became Cortés's interpreter. She would take information from the Nahuatl-speaking representatives of Motecuhzoma and translate it into Mayan for Aguilar, who would then translate it into Spanish for Cortés. She accompanied the Spaniards during their march to the central plateau and was present and played a crucial role during the initial meetings between Cortés and Motecuhzoma. Although her name was Malintzin, both she *and* Cortés, in part because they grew so close, were popularly referred to by the name Malinche. Today in

Doña Marina serving as interpreter. (*Florentine Codex,* from *Historia general de las cosas de Nueva España,* ed. Francisco del Paso y Troncoso. Madrid: Hauser y Menet, 1905)

Mexico she is known as La Malinche and has been the subject of both derisive books about her as a traitor to the natives and admiring books about her intelligent and shrewd tactics of bridging the cultures that made up Mexico.

MALINCHE

Malinche, Malintzin, or doña Marina, as she is variously known, has become a cause célèbre of Latina and other writers who value her as an exemplary, creative, courageous woman who managed to straddle two divergent, antagonistic cultures and become the symbolic mother of Mexico.

THE AZTEC ACCOUNT OF THE CONQUEST

In 1959 Miguel León-Portilla, one of the finest scholars of the Aztecs, published a book called *Visión de los vencidos* (Vision of the vanquished), known in English as *The Broken Spears: The Aztec Account of the Conquest of Mexico*. This book became popular around the globe and has been translated into over a dozen languages. It contains a collection of descriptions of the Spanish arrival on the eastern shore of Mexico, early encounters with Aztec spies and traders, the identification of Cortés with the returning priest-king-god Quetzalcoatl, the march to Mexico, the meetings of Cortés, doña Marina, and the Aztec ruler, the ferocious battles for the city, the death of Motecuhzoma, and the fall of the capital. A concise summary of these critical events follows, using both the Aztec views and information from the two most important Spanish documents relating the same events, Hernán Cortés's "Second Letter" to Emperor Charles V (the king of Spain) and Bernal Díaz del Castillo's *The History of the Conquest of New Spain*. This will help you to appreciate the pathos, tragedy, and drama of this most incredible encounter.

THE OMENS AND THE GOD

When the Aztecs told their version of the events of the conquest 20 years after the fact, they had a preface. They said that 10 years before the Spaniards arrived, a series of omens warned them that something catastrophic would happen to their daily life and imperial power. The first omen was "like a tongue of fire, like a flame…piercing the heavens," while the second omen was a fire that "of its own accord" burned down the temple of the war god, Huitzilopochtli. It was a magical fire, for "when they cast water upon it, all the more did it flare up." Then the fire god's temple was struck by a lightning bolt, and a comet traveling from west to east flew across the sky, "showering glowing coals," and upsetting the populace. The water in the lakes foamed up, "boiled up with a cracking sound," and flooded the houses of the city. These signs of celestial and terrestrial attacks on the place "where no one fears to die in war" were followed by a crying woman who haunted the people at night, yelling out, "My beloved sons, now we are about to go!" The seventh omen, which followed this cry of doom, was the appearance of a brown crane who had on its head a round, circular mirror that was pierced in the middle. When the ruler looked into the mirror, he saw "people coming massed, coming as conquerors, coming girt in war array. Deer bore them upon their backs." Finally, the eighth omen was the discovery of some men with two heads who suddenly vanished when Motecuhzoma saw them.[7]

What is the meaning of the Aztecs beginning their account of the conquest with these omens? They are saying that in looking back over the events of the end of their empire, they realize that the celestial and terrestrial forces of their own cosmos, and not primarily the Spanish soldiers, were responsible for the collapse. The celestial powers of comets and lightning, the terrestrial magic of boiling floods, and the appearance of magical animals and haunting humans warned them that their end was near.

The Aztec account moves on to describe the early reports of the Spaniards on the seashore, exchanges of gifts sent by Motecuhzoma, and the immediate fears that the ruler developed. One of the most amazing and puzzling aspects of this account is that when the Aztec ruler received descriptions of the strangers on the shore, he thought that the Toltec ancestor was returning: "When he heard of it, then he speedily sent messengers. Thus he thought—thus was it thought—that this was Topiltzin Quetzalcoatl who had come to land. For it was in their hearts that he would come, that he would come, that he would come to land, just to find his mat, his seat. For he had traveled there [eastward] when he departed."[8]

This passage has become one of the most controversial statements in the entire history of European-Indian relations in the Americas. For it suggests rather strongly that the Aztecs, in this case the Aztec ruler himself, thought of Cortés and the Spaniards as ancient Toltec ancestors returning to fulfill a prophecy and take

Cortés and Spaniards arrive on the Gulf Coast of Mexico. (Diego Durán, *Códice Durán.* Mexico City: Arrendadora Internacional 1990 facsimile edition)

over the Aztec throne. The passage "it was in their hearts that he would come...just to find his mat, his seat" refers to an indigenous prophecy that Topiltzin Quetzalcoatl, the great king of the mighty Toltecs, would return and take over the rulership that he had lost centuries before.

Remember that the famous ruler who was the human representative of the god, Quetzalcoatl, left his kingdom in disgrace and went to its eastern shore, where, according to two different traditions, he either sacrificed himself in a funeral fire and was transformed into the planet Venus, or sailed away on a raft of serpents to the east, whence some predicted that he would return one day. In one of the amazing coincidences of history, the Cortés expedition arrived in the year 1519, known to the Aztecs as the year 1 Reed (Ce Acatl), which was the birthdate and calendar name of Topiltzin Quetzalcoatl. As we shall see, this identification of Cortés with Quetzalcoatl and the prophecy of return reappears later in the story. Some scholars reject the importance of this prophecy and these passages in the actual political events of 1519–21, claiming that these references were invented by the Spaniards as a way of enhancing their own triumphal story of the conquest. Others, however, see evidence of a deeper Mesoamerican tradition at work, reflecting how indigenous people saw and in some cases still see the drama of this encounter.

The Aztec ruler sent Cortés four elaborate costumes of their gods, one of Tezcatlipoca and Tlaloc and two of Quetzalcoatl. This apparently whetted the Spanish appetite for native riches and brought the Spaniards inland. Both the Aztec and Spanish accounts trace, in slightly different ways, the progress of the Spanish advance. But the general outline goes like this: The Spaniards advanced inland and Cortés, through his interpreters, gained an understanding of indigenous religious belief and mythology and learned of the central symbolic importance of the giant *ceiba* tree. In an act of political and symbolic defiance, he gathered his troops in the central square of the town where a *ceiba* stood. Claiming the land and community for the king of Spain and the Christian religion, he took his sword, made three cuts into the bark of the tree, and ordered his carpenters to attach a cross to the tree as a sign of the replacement of Christianity for indigenous beliefs. Soon afterward the Spaniards arrived at the town of Cempoala, where Cortés made a shrewd political move. Discovering that the local peoples hated the Aztecs after years of being dominated by them, he convinced the Cempoalan rulers to imprison the imperial tax collectors sent by Motecuhzoma. Impressed with Cortés's boldness, the Cempoalans formed an alliance with the Spaniards. Then, in the dark of night, Cortés secretly released the tax collectors, sending them back to Tenochtitlan with a message of friendship and alliance with the Aztecs. Thus, he formed two alliances, pitting the natives against each other.

Cortés and the Spaniards then marched a long distance to Tlaxcala, a large, prospering kingdom that had successfully resisted Aztec domination for many years. Fighting alongside the Cempoalans, the Spaniards launched a series of attacks against the Tlaxcalans and after many bloody encounters and significant losses Cortés persuaded the Tlaxcalan rulers to form a new alliance with them against the Aztecs. The Aztecs grew fearful that a Spanish-Tlaxcalan alliance would pose a real threat to them, so they sent

Battle between Spaniards and native Mesoamericans. (Diego Durán, *Códice Durán*. Mexico City: Arrendadora Internacional 1990 facsimile edition)

ambassadors to woo Cortés and his men away from Tlaxcala. Cortés, having manipulated this entire political situation, took his body of troops, now greatly enlarged with Cempoalan and Tlaxcalan warriors, into the region of Cholula, one of the greatest pilgrimage ceremonial centers of central Mesoamerica. The invaders attacked the city and committed a terrible massacre, remembered in Mexico to this day, killing more than 4,000 citizens, including women and children, throughout the famous pilgrimage city.

The Aztec accounts tell us that these developments sent Motecuhzoma into a panic; he sent magicians into the Spanish path to try and cast spells and deceits in their way. Roadblocks were also set up, but none of these tactics could stop the Spanish advance. One passage on their approach to the capital reads:

[The Spaniards] came grouped, they came assembled, they came raising dust. Their iron lances [and] the halberds seemed to glisten, and their iron swords were wavy, like a watercourse. Their...helmets seemed to resound. And some came all in iron; they came turned into iron; they came gleaming. Hence they went causing great astonishment; hence they went causing great fear.[9]

In an interesting twist, the Spanish perspective as expressed in Díaz del Castillo's memoir presents a different Motecuhzoma and royal entourage during the Spanish march. Motecuhzoma appears concerned but politically effective, constantly monitoring the alliance building of the Spaniards while continuing to rule the capital's institutions with calm.

The growing military troop of Spaniards and thousands of native warrior allies arrived in the city of Tenochtitlan. Both Cortés and Díaz del Castillo wrote of their utter astonishment at the sophistication, order, and luxuries of the capital and have provided us with invaluable eyewitness accounts of the people, clothes, buildings, aromas, sounds, and daily life activities. The Spaniards led the way in while their indigenous allies were asked to stay in the background. When Cortés was greeted by Motecuhzoma; according to both the Spanish and Aztec accounts, the ruler made a speech welcoming Cortés as a returning lord. The Spanish captain was told through his interpreter, doña Marina, that according to ancient teachings he was expected to return and assume his throne, which the Aztec ruler had only been guarding for him. The other rulers, including Motecuhzoma's great-grandfather, Motecuhzoma Ilhuicamina, "departed maintaining that thou wouldst come to visit thy city, that thou wouldst come to descend upon thy mat, thy seat. And now it hath been fulfilled; thou hast come.... Visit thy palace."

Today there is a real debate about the meaning of these passages. Some scholars are intensely skeptical about the accuracy of these passages as to whether they represent actual Aztec attitudes toward the Spaniards. Others argue that they represent the Aztec myth and prophecy of Quetzalcoatl's kingdom, departure, and return. That is, they argue that for a short period of time the Aztecs, especially Motecuhzoma, believed that Cortés *was in fact* a representative or descendant of Topiltzin Quetzalcoatl who had returned to reclaim the throne. Further, they argue that this belief influenced the Aztec policy toward the Spaniards, allowing Cortés and his men to gain a foothold in the capital, thus contributing to but not causing the Spanish military success. Other scholars take a very different position. They claim that this entire story was invented by Cortés and other Spaniards during and after the conquest to make Cortés look extravagantly effective and to portray Motecuhzoma as a political and spiritual weakling. The main goal of this ruse, these scholars say, was to impress the king of Spain, to whom Cortés wrote immediately, that the Spanish captain was a brilliant military and political genius able to conquer great territories for Spain.[10]

Whatever the actual case, the Aztec ruler provided the Spaniards with first-rate accommodations in a royal palace and gave his visitors a grand tour of the city, showing off the temples, gardens, zoo, and great marketplace. After getting settled, Cortés became aware that Moctecuhzoma was forming his own secret alliances against the visitors and realized that he was actually surrounded by thousands of Aztecs in his luxurious accommodations. Then, in an incredibly bold move, Cortés took Motecuhzoma hostage in his own palace, warning him that if he did not cooperate with this kidnapping he would be killed immediately. In an attitude of royal dignity, the Aztec king continued to rule his city and visit his usual temples and retreats, giving the outward appearance of continuity of rulership and urban order. Word that he was in fact a prisoner leaked out, causing anger and a crisis of confidence among the Aztec nobles. Some blamed the ruler for allowing the Spaniards into the city and royal compounds. Others fled in fear of being captured themselves.

Then Cortés left the city and rushed to the coast to intercept another group of Spaniards who had been sent to arrest him and stop his military campaign. A disaster followed when Cortés's second-in-command back in the Aztec capital, Pedro de Alvarado, massacred a large group of unarmed warriors and priests during one of their most holy ceremonies. The Aztecs rose up in rebellion, and guerrilla war erupted in the city. Motecuhzoma was murdered—some say by the Spaniards, others say by the Aztecs—in retaliation for his poor leadership. The dead ruler's brother, Cuitlahuac, who had earlier urged resistance against the Spaniards, led a massive attack, and on a rainy night in June 1520 drove the Spaniards out of the city. In what is today known in Mexican history and memory as the Noche Triste (Night of Sadness), more than 500 Spaniards and 2,000 Tlaxcalan warriors were killed in the battle, their bodies filling the canals to such a depth that it was said that one could walk across the water on top of them. Around 400 Spaniards, all of them wounded, barely escaped the city and, humiliated in defeat, dragged themselves out of the Basin of Mexico and back to Tlaxcala. There they recuperated for five and a half months and began to build reinforcements. Cortés planned a siege that would eventually starve the Aztecs into submission.

European microbes, however, also came to Cortés's aid and proved to be the most effective warriors of all. During this five-month period, an epidemic of smallpox swept through the Aztec population, killing warriors, commoners, and nobles. Cuitlahuac, the new ruler, died after two months. The Aztecs later remembered:

There was hunger. Many died of famine. There was no more good, pure water to drink—only nitrous water. Many died of it—contracted dysentery, which killed them. The people ate anything—lizards, barn swallows, corn leaves, salt-grass; they gnawed...leather and buckskin, cooked or toasted: or...adobe bricks. Never had such suffering been seen; it was terrifying how many of us died when we were shut in as we were.[11]

Interestingly, one Spaniard wrote that the starving Aztecs never ate the flesh of their own people but only that of enemy warriors captured in battle.

To insure the success of the Spanish siege Cortés made two effective decisions. First, he ordered the construction of 13 small ships by Spanish and Tlaxcalan carpenters back in Tlaxcala. The ships were constructed in parts and then transported to the city of Tezcoco and assembled. Meanwhile, Cortés took an effective troop of warriors and circumambulated the lakes surrounding the Aztec capital, weakening Aztec allies and building alliances with Aztec enemies who would play crucial roles in the upcoming siege and attack of the island city.

The populace of the city was in weakened physical and spiritual condition when the three-month siege began. The Spaniards not only halted food supplies and transportation into the city, but also attacked at every chance, using their cannons and catapults to weaken the capital further. Several major communities in the lake area, including one of the Mexica's oldest allies, Tezcoco, sided

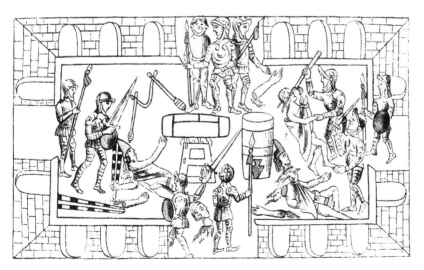

In Cortés's absence, Pedro de Alvarado massacred warriors and priests at the Great Temple during the festival of Toxcatl. (Diego Durán, *Códice Durán.* Mexico City: Arrendadora Internacional 1990 facsimile edition)

with the Spaniards, making the siege as much a native civil war against the Aztecs as anything else. This war is described in dramatic and stirring detail by the Aztecs themselves in the moving recollections given to the Spanish Franciscan friar Bernardino de Sahagún. Consider the following descriptions of how the Aztec warriors defended themselves almost to the last man against the Spanish attacks, beginning with the account of the attack of the Spanish brigantines: "And when they had prepared [each of the guns], thereupon they shot at the wall. And the wall then broke to pieces; it broke through at the back.... It was thrown down in various places.... And the brave warriors who lay by the wall at once dispersed. There was flight, there was escaping in fear."

The breaking of the Aztec walls and the flight of the warriors were followed by the Spanish assault on the Great Temple and the murder of the priests.

Siege of Tenochtitlan. (*Florentine Codex*, from *Historia general de las cosas de Nueva España*, ed. Francisco del Paso y Troncoso. Madrid: Hauser y Menet, 1905)

Then [the Spaniards] carried the gun up; they came to lay it upon the round stone of gladiatorial sacrifice. And at the summit of [the pyramid temple of] Huitzilopochtli [the priests] watched in vain. They struck the two-toned drums: as if excessively they struck the two-toned drums. And then the two Spaniards climbed up. They went striking each one [of the priests]. And when they had gone to strike each of them, they cast them down. They threw them out.[12]

The Aztecs counterattacked and seized the cannon (which had been left on the sacrificial stone) and dumped it into the lake. This resistance to the Spanish penetration of the city intensified to the point where the invaders "had come to arise against a stone" because the Aztec warriors fought back so hard. But people whom the Aztecs thought were their allies turned against them and brought more misery against their own city:

the Xochimilcans thereupon roared, hurled themselves upon the boats. They by no means helped us; they only thereupon robbed the people; they robbed the beloved women and the small children and the beloved old women. Then they slew some there; there they breathed their last.[13]

In desperation, the Mexica began to sacrifice their captives, both Spanish and Indian, to their gods in hopes of drawing down divine power to assist them in their life-and-death struggle. In one skirmish, 15 Spaniards were captured after an Aztec warrior screamed:

"O Mexicans, courage!" Thereupon there was a roar and the blowing of shell trumpets, and the sentinel brandished his shield. Thereupon they pursued the Spaniards. They went upsetting them and taking them. Fifteen of the Spaniards were taken…they thereupon stripped them. They took from them all their battle gear and their quilted cotton armor…they completely disrobed them…they slew them.[14]

We also have a Spanish eyewitness account of this human sacrifice. But nothing the Spaniards wrote can compare to this vivid description:

And thereupon they brought the captives there to Yacacolco. Each was forced to go. They went rounding up their captives. One went weeping; one went singing; one went crying out while striking the mouth with [the] palm of the hand.… They were put in rows. One by one the multitude went to the small pyramid, where they were slain as sacrifices. The Spaniards went first; they went first. But only at the last, following, were all the dwellers of the [allied] cities. And when they had been slain as sacrifices,

Heads of sacrificed Spaniards and horses hang from the Skull Rack. (*Florentine Codex*, from *Historia general de las cosas de Nueva España*, ed. Francisco del Paso y Troncoso. Madrid: Hauser y Menet, 1905)

then they strung each of the Spaniards' heads on the [skull rack] staves. Also they strung up the horses' heads. They placed them below. And the Spaniards' heads were above. As they were strung up, they were facing the sun. But as for all the various allied people, they did not string up the heads of the people of distant places.[15]

In spite of these momentary successes, the Aztecs were continually pushed back and lost control of neighborhoods, walkways, canals, and eventually the walls that were left standing. Catapults, cannon fire, and the relentless slicing of the Spanish swords reduced the Aztec resistance to a small corner of the city where only a few walls remained. Then, in what may be considered one of the most poignant descriptions of male courage overcome by male aggression, the remaining warriors were *turned into walls of resistance*. The Aztecs were surrounded in the place of their last stand, people fled into the water, and a warrior stepped out to confront the end.

And a great brave warrior, a shorn one, called Uitzilhuatzin, placed himself upon the roof terrace above the young men's house. *He yet became as a wall*; the common folk yet followed him a little. But the Spaniards then fell upon them, brought themselves upon them, thereupon they continually struck him, continually cut him, pounded him. Then once again, the brave warrior repulsed the Spaniards and then the brave warriors quickly made them leave him.[16]

But the Spaniards were in pursuit of another great warrior, the Aztec *tlatoani*, Cuauhtemoc (Diving Eagle), who continued to fight until his surviving troops were trapped near the imperial market-place of Tlatelolco. He fled in a boat but was captured by the Spaniards, ending the resistance of the Aztecs and signaling the fall of the capital city to the invaders. The date was August 13, 1521, and the Aztecs remembered it this way: "And when the shields were laid down, when we fell, it was in the year count Three House; and in the day count it was One Serpent."[17] In Mexico City a huge upright stone stands near the spot of this capture, bearing the following words: "On August 13, 1521, heroically defended by Cuauhtemoc, Tlatelolco fell into the hands of Hernán Cortés. It was neither a triumph nor a defeat: it was the painful birth of the *mestizo* nation that is the Mexico of today."

The Spaniards were astonished when they saw how many Aztecs had died of smallpox even before the final battle. Cortés wrote to the king, "Indeed, so great was their suffering that it was beyond our understanding how they could endure it." But the Spaniards increased this suffering many-fold in the immediate aftermath of Cuauhtemoc's surrender. They plundered the city, robbed houses, violated and raped the women, and brutalized the men. "And the Spaniards seized, they selected the women—the pretty ones, those whose bodies were yellow, the yellow ones. And some women, when they were to be taken from the people, muddied their faces, and clothed themselves in old clothing, put rags on themselves as a shift" to disguise their attractiveness.[18] Men were branded, beaten, and forced into servitude.

We began this chapter by asking how this military conquest took place so swiftly and thoroughly against the numerical superiority and hometown advantage in favor of the Aztecs. We can now make the following statements: The Aztec empire fell because of a combination of forces that worked against them. First, the Spaniards arrived at a fateful time in the Aztec calendar. The year 1 Reed (Ce Acatl), or 1519, was associated with the story of the collapse of the Toltec kingdom of Topiltzin Quetzalcoatl, and it is likely that this tradition was in the heads of the Aztec nobles who had been educated so thoroughly in their *calmecac*, as described in chapter 4.

Second, the conquest was more of a massive rebellion of other Indian communities than a conquest by Spanish soldiers acting shrewdly and heroically. The extravagant Aztec empire had been held together by a series of alliances, conquests, intimidations, Flowery Wars, and forced payments of sacrificial captives and wealth. Many rebellions and resistance movements had occurred, both near the capital and in distant regions, especially during the 20 years before the Spaniards arrived. After more than 100 years of Mexica domination, these allies and enemy states were looking for opportunities to break the control the mighty Aztecs held over them. As one writer notes, "The loose structure of the empire was the weapon of its own destruction."[19]

Third, the Aztecs and the Spaniards fought wars on completely different terms, which favored the European invaders. The Aztecs conducted campaigns to capture enemy warriors for humiliation and sacrifice as much as for killing on the battlefield. They entered into conflicts with the Spaniards with those goals in mind. The Spaniards fought to kill on the battlefield with little concern

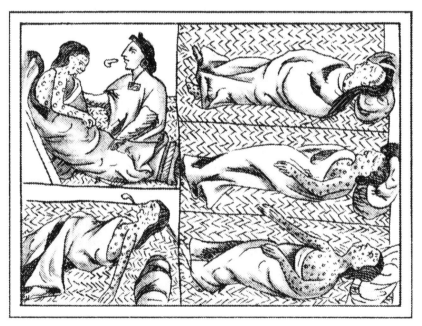

Smallpox and other diseases devastated the native population in the conquest. (*Florentine Codex*, from *Historia general de las cosas de Nueva España*, ed. Francisco del Paso y Troncoso. Madrid: Hauser y Menet, 1905)

for captives except to drag basic information from them through intimidation and torture. The Spaniards also had formidable weapons, including horses, attack dogs, crossbows, cannons, harquebuses, and steel-bladed swords.

Fourth, the impact of European diseases cannot be overestimated in understanding the process of conquest. There was an immediate and profound impact on the health and stability of the population at large and the military units in particular within and beyond the Aztec capital. And throughout the next century there was enormous material destruction in terms of fields, towns, cities, and human beings. When we turn to the statistics of conquest, we learn that the human population in America went from around 80 million people in 1492 to less than 10 million in 1600. In Mesoamerica there were 25 million people in 1519 but only 1 million Indians living in the same territory in 1592. Today there are actually many more indigenous peoples alive and speaking their own languages in Mexico than there were in any century since the 17th.

It seems that all these reasons—religious, military, political, and biological—together give us a fair answer to the question with which this chapter began: "How could the Aztec empire, with its powerful military tradition, complex religious institutions, and long-range trading and spy system in good working order, fall to a conflicted group of Spanish invaders in the short period of two years, and on home ground?" A final observation comes from Bernal Díaz del Castillo, who many years later lamented about the fall of the city: "I say again that I stood looking at it and thought that never in the world would there be discovered other lands such as these, for at that time there was no Peru, nor any thought of it. Of all these wonders that I then beheld today all lies overthrown and lost, nothing left standing."[20]

NOTES

1. Carlos Fuentes, *The Orange Tree,* trans. Alfred MacAdam (New York: Farrar, Straus and Giroux, 1994), 21.

2. Miguel León-Portilla, *Pre-Columbian Literatures of Mexico* (Norman: University of Oklahoma Press, 1969), 83.

3. Miguel León-Portilla, *The Broken Spears: The Aztec Account of the Conquest of Mexico,* trans. Lysander Kemp (Boston: Beacon Press, 1961), 137–38.

4. *The Codex Mendoza,* ed. Frances F. Berdan and Patricia Rieff Anawalt, 4 vols. (Berkeley: University of California Press, 1992), 4: 34.

5. Ibid.

6. Bernal Díaz del Castillo, *The History of the Conquest of New Spain*, ed. Davíd Carrasco (Albuquerque: University of New Mexico Press, 2008), 167.

7. Bernardino de Sahagún, *Florentine Codex: General History of the Things of New Spain*, ed. and trans. Arthur J. O. Anderson and Charles E. Dibble, introductory vol. and 12 books (Santa Fe, NM: School of American Research and University of Utah, 1950–82), 12: 1–3.

8. Ibid., 9.

9. Ibid., 39.

10. For a more detailed discussion of this debate and these various positions, see Davíd Carrasco, "When Strangers Come to Town: The Return of Quetzalcoatl and Millennial Discourse," in *Quetzalcoatl and the Irony of Empire: Myths and Prophecies in the Aztec Tradition*, rev. ed. (Boulder: University Press of Colorado, 2000), 205–40.

11. Quoted in Elizabeth Hill Boone, *The Aztec World* (Montreal and Washington, DC: St. Remy Press and Smithsonian Books, 1994), 149.

12. Sahagún, *Florentine Codex*, 12: 88.

13. Ibid., 95.

14. Ibid.

15. Ibid., 103–4.

16. Ibid., 116; emphasis added.

17. Ibid., 122.

18. Ibid.

19. Boone, *Aztec World*, 151.

20. Díaz del Castillo, *History of the Conquest*, 157.

9

THE LONG EVENT OF
AZTEC CULTURE

In Mexico City there is never tragedy but only outrage…city of
the violated outrage, city witness to all we forget, city of fixed
sun, city ancient in light, old city cradled among birds of omen,
city tempested by domes, city woven by amnesias, bitch city,
hungry city, city in the true image of gigantic heaven. Incandescent prickly pear.

—Carlos Fuentes[1]

These words from Carlos Fuentes's novel *Where the Air Is Clear* prepare us to bring our study of the Aztec world to a close because
they show how modern-day Mexico City is at once an ancient city
("city ancient in light"), a colonial city ("city of the violated outrage"), and a modern center of historical culture ("city witness to
all we forget"). But through it all—the migrations, settlements, cosmologies, families, rebellions, revolutions, earthquakes, invasions,
diseases, muraled walls, and musical inventions—the site of the
Aztec capital is still a "city in the true image of gigantic heaven,"
an "incandescent prickly pear." It and its many millions of people
have been profoundly transformed by the European invasion, by
colonial history with its upheavals and mixtures, and by the revolutions of 1810 and 1910, but there is still a fascinating Aztec presence in the faces, language, food, art, science, dreams, and religions
of Mexican peoples. This chapter will be an all-too-short flyover

of parts of the Mexican cultural terrain that includes important Aztec symbols, ideas, and rituals. In particular we will focus on three religious and cultural practices of contemporary Mexicans in Mexico and the United States that *reflect various degrees of indigenous and Aztec influence*: (1) the modern-day version of the ancient peyote hunt of the Huichols, which, while not Aztec per se, shares many symbols and ritual meanings with the Aztec world we have been reviewing, (2) the ritual celebration of the Día de los Muertos (Day of the Dead), which is both European and Indian, and (3) the profoundly important worship of the Virgin of Guadalupe, the patron saint of Mexico. We will also see some impressive examples of Aztec images and symbols inspiring the Mexican and Chicano mural movements.

In an important way, the cosmology, city, rites of passage, and daily life of the Aztecs constitute something akin to what Fernand Braudel called a "long event" of historical duration. By long event, Braudel meant that some realities, such as geography, language, and biology, impact the daily lives of a society over long, continuous periods of time, as opposed to less influential short or middle-range events. Short events are those that gain immediate notoriety in the newspapers and on television, but pass away after a few years. At the moment of their happening they are all the rage, but they have little long-term significance for the society. A middle-range event is one that influences a society for several decades or a few generations and appears to have contributed significantly to the life of a society. An example of this type of event is the invention of the typewriter, which seemed to revolutionize writing, composing, and the speed at which information could be produced. First invented by Christopher Lathan Sholes in 1867, the typewriter, with its speed and clarity, revolutionized the process of producing and communicating information to large numbers of people. Forty years ago, typewriters were thought to be a permanent, effective way to write out important information. Today, the skill of typing has remained crucial, but personal computers have all but replaced typewriters. And, in the future, who knows what will replace personal computers?

There are also events of long duration. Often events that may appear to us as barely significant in terms of historical influence can in fact be long events—historical events that influence human society for centuries. These long events may be quiet, slow-moving, below the surface. What is being suggested here is that the Aztec world (in fact, all the native cultures of Mexico), in spite of its apparent destruction by the Spanish invasion, is a long event of New World cultures that continues to give meaning, influence, power, and orientation to millions of people in Mexico and beyond. It is remarkable that as Mexico City becomes more and more modern, with subways, skyscrapers, and satellite communications, it also becomes more aware of its ancient Aztec past. New discoveries of ruins, treasures, statues of gods, and temples appear from beneath the streets and buildings of the colonial and modern city. When the subway was cut beneath the colonial part of the city, workers kept uncovering Aztec temples and monuments associated in large part with Aztec noble classes. It must be noted, however, that the world of the noble classes, with their ideas, ritual practices, military ideology, and sacrificial demands, was depleted and largely destroyed by the colonial forces of the 16th century. But the worldviews and practices of the farmers, craftspeople, and other commoners who lived within, on the edges of, and outside the Aztec royal community have continued on in a number of interesting ways, as we shall see. Few know that the Aztec language (Nahuatl) has provided such English words as tomato (*tomatl*), avocado (*ahuacatl*), chocolate (*chocolatl*), coyote (*coyotl*), ocelot (*ocelotl*), and mesquite (*mexquitl*), as well as many Spanish terms for foods and animals used in Mexico. And today in Mexico several million people still speak Nahuatl, to say nothing of the scores of other Indian languages that are spoken, dreamed in, and used for everyday transactions.

TRANSCULTURATION AND THE CONTACT ZONE

In this brief study of the continuities and changes in Aztec symbols, language, ideas, and religious practices, we confront a complex and powerful story of how European meanings and practices became mixed with Aztec meanings and practices. If we had more space, it would be appropriate to explore the African presence in Mexico to try and understand its important contributions as well. The African presence in Mesoamerica has been largely ignored, but recently scholars have begun to uncover the routes of the slaves and the general interactions of African peoples in Mexico. The best way to understand this mixing is in terms of *transculturation*.

There are two parts to the definition of transculturation: the space where the process takes place and the action that takes place. Transculturation takes place in a *contact zone,* which is a social space where different cultures meet, clash, and grapple with one another.

This place of struggle, where the Christian priest meets the Aztec *tlamatimi,* for instance, where Jesus Christ meets Quetzalcoatl, where the Catholic Mass meets practices of collective ecstasy, or where Catholic saints meet native Tlaloque, is a place of unequal social status, psychological domination, and sometimes, but not always, military threat. The action of transculturation includes the work of subordinated or marginal groups who "select and invent from materials transmitted to them by a dominant or metropolitan cultures. While subjugated peoples cannot readily control what emanates from the dominant culture, they do determine to varying extents what they absorb into their own, and what they use it for. Transculturation is a phenomenon of the contact zone."[2]

The terms *contact zone* and *transculturation* are better suited than the more popular term *syncretism* to help us understand how Aztec ideas, meanings, and beliefs continue to have a presence in our modern world. Syncretism refers to the mixing and melding of different beliefs and practices in which some form of resolution or balanced agreement results. There *are* such examples of syncretism, of the seemingly smooth mixing of Aztec and European or African ideas, but the real human story is one of encounter, antagonism, borrowing, rejecting, reinterpreting, renaming, absorbing, stealing, and reinventing. There is no pure Aztec world anymore, nor is there an authentic Spanish or European world in Mexico. Everything that came from Europe or Africa and everything that was originally lodged in the Americas has been changed to some degree, beginning in 1492. In the case of colonial Mesoamerica, Europeans unleashed both powerful fantasies and colonial expeditions, attempting to transform the lands and peoples into extensions of themselves. On the surface, Cemanahuac became Nueva España (New Spain), the Mexica became Indians, and their religions were considered the work of the devil. But beneath the surface, indigenous and European traditions mixed together into a remarkable series of new cultural combinations. The food, languages, ideas, medical practices—even the biological and cultural character of people—were transformed into new social and symbolic forms. As the art historian Elizabeth Weismann writes in her invaluable study of colonial Mexican sculpture, "Two different kinds of life absorbed each other and produced things new and different from anything else in the world."[3]

These new and different things (new for Europeans, new for Africans, and new for native Americans) had to be put into new relationships with one another. Most crucial of all, perhaps, were the efforts to locate where the natives and the mestizos (people of mixed ancestry) were to fit in the new social, legal, and religious schemes. The result has been a complex, varied, and sometimes mysterious social and symbolic landscape mixing Aztec, Mixtec Huichol, K'iche', Tz'utujil, and many other traditions with Catholic, Spanish, Portuguese, French, and other Old World cultural and religious patterns. The student of colonial and modern Mesoamerica is faced, as the Mexican novelist Carlos Fuentes indicates, with a world of outrage, Christian churches, denial of the damage of colonialism, ancient images still visible in daily life, and the persistence of a cosmovision embedded in the largest urban center of the world—Mexico City—"city in the true image of gigantic heaven." Mesoamerica's pre-Hispanic traditions, and especially its Aztec traditions, have continued to play a vital role in the colonial and postcolonial communities of Mexico. Attractive and meaningful traces of these traditions can even be found in Latino communities in the United States, as we shall see.

In this chapter, we will look at a series of creative cultural and religious responses to the crisis of colonialism and modernization that illustrate some of the *continuities and changes* that have taken place in Mesoamerica. To help map out and clarify these changes and continuities, we will use the metaphor of the pilgrimage to

Mexico City. (Courtesy of Scott Sessions)

guide us. Pilgrimages always involve a home base, a journey or ordeal, and the arrival at a valued destination. In each of the following cases, we will see that people, or the souls of people, take special journeys to or through a sacred landscape in order to have a direct experience and gain new knowledge of the sacred.

THE NEW WORLD OF MESOAMERICA

At the end of the previous chapter we surveyed briefly some of the violent, transformative process of colonialism, beginning in the 1520s in Mexico, Guatemala, and other regions of Mesoamerica, which radically altered (to varying degrees) the social and symbolic worlds of the ceremonial centers and communities at large. This process has been consistently referred to as having created a New World with its smaller New Spain, and then eventually New Mexico, and along the north Atlantic coast, New York, New England, New Jersey, Nova Scotia, and so forth. However, the natives of Mesoamerica who underwent the process of colonialism experienced this newness more as forms of dependency, oppression, starvation, disease, death, and dehumanization than as opportunities for salvation and revitalization. It was a newness they could just as well have done without. The formation of new religious movements and cults and mixtures of pre-Hispanic and Catholic religious meanings emerged as strategies to survive and maintain human integrity in relation to their lands and selves.

And it is vital to remember that the colonial process in Mesoamerica began almost 100 years before the English explored the North Atlantic coast and established their settlements in Massachusetts and Virginia. By the early 1600s, when parts of northern Europe were abuzz with rumors, stories, and prejudices about the people and lands of the New World and objects and people from the Americas (these stories and prejudices had largely filtered up from Spain and Portugal), most of the great ceremonial centers and local shrines in the Aztec, Tlaxcalan, Tarascan, and other kingdoms had been dismantled or replaced by Christian churches. Thus, American history did not begin in New England or Virginia, as is still often taught in public schools in the United States. It started in Yucatán, Cempoala, Tlaxcala, Cholula, and Tenochtitlan, and was characterized by misunderstandings, greed, warfare, theft, disease, debate, economic exchange, and a ferocious clash of two types of cosmovisions.

Throughout Mesoamerica today, indigenous and mestizo groups carry out ceremonies combining native and Catholic symbols and beliefs all the time. (Recently, Protestant traditions have been introduced to large numbers of people and are becoming part of the transcultural process.) One of the most powerful Christian images that has been joined to indigenous religious ideas is the image of Jesus Christ as suffering savior. The bleeding, pained image of Jesus on the cross has had special attraction to all social groups and classes in Latin America, including native communities, who in him see a version of their own suffering, struggle, and condition. Upon closer view, it is clear that these images of Christ and the cross reflect a fluid, transculturated image of new power, decoration, and possibility. Often it is the native or mestizo community that takes the initiative in forming these new combinations in the contact zones of Mexico and Mexican communities in the United States.

THE PEYOTE HUNT OF THE HUICHOLS

Not all cultural and religious practices in contemporary Mexico have a mixture of indigenous and imported symbols and beliefs. In some cases Nahuatl- and Mayan-speaking peoples practice pre-Hispanic rituals that have little Catholic, Protestant, or modern secular influence. In some cases there has been limited borrowing by indigenous communities of European or African ideas and symbols. One outstanding example, witnessed by cultural anthropologist Barbara Myerhoff, is the yearly Huichol pilgrimage to Wirikuta, the land of the ancestors, where *hikuri* (peyote) grows. While the Huichol lands and practices are somewhat distant from the areas under direct influence from the ancient Aztecs we can identify similarities to Aztec cosmovision and rites of passage that we studied earlier. Even though the contemporary Huichols are not direct descendants of the Aztecs, a similiar kind of ritual hunting for peyote was carried out by some Aztec communities.

The Huichol people live in the mountainous regions of the Mexican states of Durango, Jalisco, Nayarit, and Zacatecas. The Huichols are famous for their brilliantly colored yarn paintings, which depict myths, images, and fantastic beings from their worldview and environment. Their social and symbolic life is complex and varied, but they are best known for their yearly journey to the ancestral territory of Wirikuta, 200 miles from the city of Guadalajara, in search of peyote and peyote visions. These pilgrimages are always led by a *mara'akame,* or shaman-priest, such as Ramón Medina Silva, who was the chief informant in Barbara Myerhoff's study.[4]

Ramón's role and original decision to become a *mara'akame* reflect the human career as a way of centering the world for a social group. When he was between six and nine years old, Ramón began to have a series of amazing dreams in which the Huichol deity, Tayaupa (Our Father Sun), spoke to him, revealing that he was being chosen to become a spiritual leader of the Huichol people: "Tayaupa spoke to me. He said, 'Look son, do not worry. You must grow a little more so you can go out and become wise, so that you can support yourself.... You will make fine things, things of color. You will understand this and that. It is for this that you were born.' At first, I was frightened. I did not know. I began to reflect."[5]

During this period of reflection Ramón was bitten by a snake and nearly died. His grandfather, who was a *mara'akame,* healed him, and it was slowly revealed to the community that Ramón had been chosen by the Huichol gods to become a shaman-priest. This combination of religious dreams and injury/healing is typical of individuals who become set apart from the community into a status of sacred leader.

Years later Barbara Myerhoff was introduced to the adult artist and shaman Ramón Medina, and became a trusted friend of his family. After two summers of visits, conversations, and taped question-and-answer sessions, Myerhoff was invited to participate, under Ramón's guidance, in the sacred journey to Wirikuta.

The peyote hunt, which is described in some detail by Myerhoff, and which appears in Peter Furst's 1969 film *To Find Our Life,* has many stages and powerful transitions in it. According to Myerhoff, the journey to Wirikuta, 200 miles to the north, is the Huichol version of a universal human quest, namely, the search for Paradise, or the original center of the world, where god, human, animal, and plant were at one with each other during a primordial era. This search for a total unity, or *communitas,* with all of life is reflected in two major themes of the peyote hunt. First, the pilgrims are changed, through ritual, into living images of the first peyote pilgrims, who were gods. The pilgrims are gods in human form. Note the similarity to the *ixiptla* of the Aztecs. Second, the peyote plant is also identified with the deer (animal ancestor). In the Huichol past the deer was a source of food and beauty, a magical animal who is remembered as having given the first peyote to the first peyote hunters. On each subsequent hunt it is believed that the peyote is left by the ancestral deer who comes from the sky. Only the *mara'akame* can see him, while the other pilgrims can see his footprints in the form of peyote plants on the desert floor. This unity of animal and plant is further enriched by the symbolism of maize in Huichol thought. Maize is the source of life today, abundant and all around. In the Huichol cosmovision, the peyote hunt is a time and action of unity, bringing together animal and plant, past and present, and ancestor, spirit, and the human. Therefore, the peyote hunt must be carried out with the utmost care.

This experience of unity is achieved through a series of stages that make up the drama of the hunt. The Huichols sing, dance, play music, and chant during the peyote hunt, which can be said to have nine stages. Stage 1 is preparation and rehearsal. Stage 2 is taking the names of deities. Stage 3 is preparing the fire and confessions. These first three stages take place at a private home before Stage 4, the departure for Wirikuta, which is about a 20-day walk from Huichol communities. Today they drive in cars and trucks. Arrival at Tatei Matinieri (Where Our Mother Dwells), a place of natural springs in the desert, is Stage 5. There the pilgrims witness the sunrise and "help Tayaupa come up."[6]

At each stage there are meaningful and emotional moments of sadness, joy, exuberance, and solemnity, according to the occasion. In Stage 6, *reversals* are established in which the people, now considered living images of the first peyote pilgrims, are designated as the opposite of what they in fact are. For instance, "Merriment and excitement filled the car and animated chatter and laughter. By way of explaining the laughter, Ramón reached over and taking some of his hair in his hand said that now it was cactus fiber. Pointing to himself, he said that he was the Pope, that Lupe was an 'ugly boy,' Victoria a gringa, and Francisco a nunutsi [little child]."[7]

The meaning of these reversals is that the *peyoteros* (peyote hunters) are participating in *another mode of being*, a religious way of being human, and as such change or reverse who they are. This is partly due to the fact that each peyote hunt repeats the first peyote hunt, when the ancestral gods journeyed to Wirikuta.

Stage 7 is the arrival at Wirikuta, which is signified by the *knotting-in*, an act of unification of the pilgrims when they tie knots in a string that links them together at the entrance to the sacred land. Stage 8 includes the actual hunt of peyote, which is considered in Huichol symbolism to be a deer. Myerhoff's description helps us understand this identification of plant and animal:

The hikuritamete [peyote companions] set out across the desert, moving briskly toward the mountains but fanning out instead of following the single file usually observed for ritual processions. Everyone was completely quiet and grave, looking closely at the ground for tracks. As they approached the mountains, the peyoteros' pace slackened, for peyote was more likely to be found here, and tension mounted. Their behavior was precisely that of stalking an animal. There were no sudden movements, no talking. The pilgrims bent over close to the ground, moved in the brush on tiptoe, gingerly raising a branch or poking under a cactus in hopes of catching a sight of the small gray-green peyote plant which is so inconspicuous, growing nearly parallel to the earth's surface and exactly the same color as surrounding vegetation in this region.... Finally Ramón beckoned everyone to his side—he had found peyote, seen the deer. Quickly we all gathered behind him as he drew his arrow and readied the bow. We peered down at the barely noticeable round flat-topped plant, two inches in diameter, segregated into eight sections. Everyone prayed quietly as Ramón began to stalk it, moving ever closer until when he was only a few feet away he aimed and shot one arrow into the base of the plant toward the east and crossed quickly with another arrow pointing north so that the peyote was impaled in the center. The peyote-deer was thus secured and unable to escape.[8]

Following a series of prescribed ritual actions, the *peyoteros* collect, sort, clean, and pack a large number of peyote buttons. During several following nights, peyote is eaten by the group gathered around the fire in order to induce visions. The pilgrims laugh and discuss the beautiful colors and little animals in their visions, finally falling quiet as they stare into the fire. During this entire episode the *mara'akame* gazes quietly into the fire, seeing visions of the ancestral pilgrims, the spirits of the Huichol cosmos. He sees and talks with the main deities, receiving new knowledge about life and the sacred.

Stage 9 is the departure from Wirikuta. This involves the giving of peyote names, the eating of salt, and the untying of the cord that united the group before entering the sacred land.

In this remarkable sacred journey, the Huichols regenerate their sense of identity. In their words, they "find our life," meaning they commune with the beauty and powers of Wirikuta and come to experience what it feels like and what one *sees* when one is a Huichol. All this is a reiteration of how the world of the peyote hunt was first made. As mentioned earlier, the Huichols are not Aztecs, but like the Aztecs of the 14th to the 16th century, their ritual hunt is based on the need to be in contact with the creative origins of the community through storytelling, ritual reenactment, and memory.

Having looked at a pilgrimage in which people travel to a sacred space to find their life, let us now turn to the yearly celebrations called the Day of the Dead, in which the spirits of deceased friends and relatives make the pilgrimage back into the world of the living.

DÍA DE LOS MUERTOS (DAY OF THE DEAD)

One of the most meaningful yearly celebrations in Mexico, in fact throughout Latin America, is the Día de los Muertos (Day of the Dead), celebrated for nearly a week at the end of October and the beginning of November. This elaborate celebration, dedicated to the cult of the dead (also referred to as Todos Santos—All Saints' Day), combines pre-Hispanic rituals and beliefs with Catholic practices and symbols. Although Day of the Dead rituals are complex and difficult to categorize, three outstanding dimensions can be emphasized: (1) the preparations for the ceremonies, (2) the symbolism of the center, embodied in the family altar, and (3) the ceremonial feast of the dead and spiritual union with the dead at the home and cemetery, which give renewal. The central idea is that during this period of public and private (family) rituals, the living and dead family members and friends are joined together in an atmosphere of communion and spiritual regeneration.

Scholars have determined that important elements of Day of the Dead festivities in Central Mexico were practiced by Aztecs and have become integrated into the Catholic traditions of Mexico and other parts of Latin America. Sahagún discovered the following ritual practices associated with the month of Tepeilhuitl in the Aztec capital. In this description we see the importance of the cult of the dead associated with a ceremonial place:

They also used to place the image of the dead on those grass wreaths. Then at dawn they put these images in their shrines, on top of beds of reed, mace, sedge, or rush. Once the images were placed there, they offered them food, tamales, and gruel, or a stew made of chicken [turkey] or dog's meat. Then they offered the images incense from an incense burner, which was a big cup full of coals, and this ceremony they called calonoac. And the rich sang and drank pulque [fermented agave juice] in honor of these gods and their dead, while the poor offered them only food, as has been mentioned.[9]

This same pattern of images of the dead/altar/food offerings/incense/communion is carried out today after elaborate and sometimes economically stressful preparations.

It is important to note that the rituals, symbols, and elaborate decorations of home altars and cemeteries differ somewhat according to region. Some communities emphasize cemetery altars and decorations, whereas others emphasize the processions between home and cemetery. Still others make unusual efforts to decorate their home altars to dead ancestors in baroque, lavish ways. Some communities have open-air competitions of altars and offerings to the dead, ranging from small altars to some that are 10 feet high and 50 feet long. But all Day of the Dead celebrations focus on a spiritual convenant between the human community and supernatural entities of deceased family members, friends, or saints. The following description is taken largely from Day of the Dead celebrations in the Mexican state of Tlaxcala, east of Mexico City, as reported by Hugo Nutini.

In each household, which is the center of the cult of the dead, it is believed that the souls of the dead have taken a journey to the world beyond. The souls of good people travel a straight and narrow path to another world, while the souls of bad people travel a wide and labyrinthine way. All souls arrive at a deep and broad river that can only be crossed with the help of a dog, which lifts the souls on his shoulders and carries them over to the other side. In Tlaxcala, at least, it is believed that the bad souls would be refused transportation across this river, while the good souls could persuade the dog to carry them more easily if they had the coins that were placed in the mouth or hand of the dead at their funerals. In many communities it is believed that dogs must be treated well in this life because they are spirit-helpers in the next.

What is outstanding in all cases (from Aztec times to the present) is the belief that what happens during one's life here on this earth is dependent, in part, on treating the dead well. People believe that if the dead are not worshiped, nurtured, and remembered in the proper manner, their own economic security, family stability, and health will be in jeopardy. Therefore, careful and generous preparations are carried out.

PREPARATIONS

Prominent in the decorations of family altars and cemetery altars are marigold flowers, or *cempoalxochitl* (a Nahuatl word meaning *20-flower*). Many households grow *cempoalxochitl* in their own gardens and plant the seeds in the middle of August so that the flowers will bloom by the last part of October. This sense of preparation for the Día de los Muertos intensifies at the start of October, when the people set out the necessary cash and other goods to be used in the generous decorations of altars and tombs, and at the ceremonial meals for the dead and the living. Also, careful arrangements are made to be free from jobs so that the proper ritual responsibilities can be carried out. In Latin America, where poverty is so widespread, this responsibility entails a sense of sacrifice on behalf of the family. Journeys are made to local and regional markets, sometimes covering several hundred miles, so that the correct foods and decorations can be purchased in time for the sacred week.

Most important are preparations of special foods for the dead. These include baked breads, candied fruit, skulls made of sugar, and human figurines made of pumpkin seeds, as well as apple, pear, and quince preserves. Papier-mâché images of various kinds are purchased or made, to be used in the decorations of the altars and the graves. The last and most crucial items to be picked or purchased are the *cempoalxochitl* flowers. Since these flowers will last only four days, they are placed on altars and tombs and as pathways between the cemeteries and the homes on the day before the Día de los Muertos begins.

THE FAMILY ALTAR

Day of the Dead altars can appear in public plazas, in schools, and even in competitions, but the most important altar appears in the individual household. Within the home it serves as the *axis mundi* of the ritual and ceremonial life of the family. Most homes in the Tlaxcala region have an altar in place all year round, but it is elaborately and colorfully decorated during this ritual period. This altar becomes a sacred precinct or a ceremonial center within the home made up of at least 10 kinds of objects—breads, sweets, cooked dishes, delicacies, fruits and vegetables, liquors and liquids, flowers and plants, clothing, adornments, and (perhaps most important) pictures, images, and statues. These pictures and statues are usually placed in a *retablo* (a structure forming the back of the altar), where images of the Virgin, Christ, the cross, and saints watch over the *ofrenda*, or offering to the dead. This offering takes the shape of a wonderful feast for the spirits of the dead, who will return and be nourished on specific nights during the Día de los Muertos. A typical *ofrenda* in Tlaxcala is shaped like a four-sided pyramid decorated along the edges with *cempoalxochitl* flowers. At each of the four corners are placed mounds of mandarins and oranges on top of sugarcane cuttings. Cooked dishes, liquids, finger foods, loaves of *pan de muertos* (bread of the dead), candied fruits, tamales, bananas, and

Close-up of a Day of the Dead altar. (Courtesy of Scott Sessions)

oranges constitute the bulk of the offering. The most impressive objects of the *ofrenda* are crystallized sugar skulls of different sizes and with various kinds of decorations. These skulls represent the dead infants, children, and adults being honored that year.

Many rich symbolic and social meanings are expressed in this crowded, organic ceremonial center. This cornucopia of goods represents the quest for fertility and the renewal of relations with dead friends and family members. But the overall image is that of a sacred Mountain of Sustenance that orients and nourishes the family community. The Mountain of Sustenance, which we recall was associated with Tlaloc's paradise, is a pre-Catholic, Aztec symbol of rain and fertility, and the container of the most valued supernatural powers. In part, the Día de los Muertos altars and *ofrendas* symbolize the body of the life-giving earth with its forces of regeneration.

COMMUNION WITH THE DEAD

The actual moments of reunion with the dead and the regeneration of family ties are carefully orchestrated. In fact, according to the detailed practices of the Tlaxcala region, there are five categories of dead souls—those who die in accidents, those who die violently, and those who die as infants, as children, and as adults—who return on five consecutive days. On November 2, which is the climax of Todos Santos, all the dead are remembered.

According to Hugo Nutini's research in Tlaxcala, the people believe that the souls of the dead begin to return and hover around their family households beginning at 3:00 P.M. on October 31. In order for the souls of the dead to return to the house where they lived, a trail of *cempoalxochitl* flowers must be laid out for them to find their way. Early in the morning the women in the family prepare a basket of fragrant flower petals, which are sprinkled with holy water from the church. Then the male adults and children lay the petals in a line, marking a trail from the street through the yard or courtyard to the foot of the family altar. This trail is intended to show the spirits of the dead the path home from the cemetery. It is important that the flowers be fragrant, because it is believed that while the souls of the dead are blind, they have acute senses of smell and can find their way home on the path of aroma created by the petals.

By 9:00 P.M. on November 1 it is believed that all the souls of the dead have traveled along the fragrant path of flowers to their old homes. In some homes the room containing the altar/*ofrenda* is closed between 10:00 P.M. and 6:00 A.M. so that the returning souls can enjoy the food and treats and reminisce together about their past lives in the human world. Then it is believed that the souls of the dead return to the cemetery to join the living in a vigil of communion.

This vigil is called Xochatl in Nahuatl, and La Llorada (The Weeping) in Spanish; it is the time when the living and dead join together as a living spiritual community. The souls of the dead reassure the living of their continued protection, and the living assure the dead that they will remember and nurture them in their daily lives.

In the local cemetery a community band with a drum and flute ensemble plays both melancholy and vibrant tunes for eight hours; candles are lit on the graves, and rosaries are said as church bells toll out pleasing music for the souls of the dead, who are about to return to their graves. The living ask the dead souls to protect their families, crops, businesses, health, and property for another year. Part of the ritual speech goes, "Oh, blessed souls who have kindly returned to us . . . to participate with us in this day of remembrance, find it in the goodness of your hearts to protect us and shelter us."[10]

The foregoing description presents one of the many variations of Day of the Dead celebrations that take place throughout Mexico. In fact, there is a resurgence of these practices in Mexico and in Mexican American communities in the United States.

THE VIRGIN OF GUADALUPE

One remarkable example of spiritual protection for all the descendants of the Aztecs, Spaniards, and mestizos is the miracle which legend has it took place on the hill of Tepeyac in 1531, when the Virgin of Guadalupe appeared to Juan Diego, an Indian catechist. This apparition took place in a contact zone, a place where the Aztecs continued to worship their sacred mother, Tonantzin, after the Spanish invasion. According to religious documents in Mexico, the Virgin of Guadalupe appeared as a brown-skinned Mother of God who spoke Nahuatl and announced that she had come in order to shelter the oppressed natives as well as all the other social groups in New Spain. Her story shows that she represents both continuity and change in relation to the Aztecs.

The Virgin of Guadalupe is part of a much larger cult of the Virgin Mary of Immaculate Conception, which permeates religious art, meaning, and practice throughout Latin America. Images of the different sacred Virgins are found on statues, clothes, and jewelry in every conceivable place in Latin American countries, including churches, bars, discos, restaurants, ball fields, hotels, museums, chapels, ice cream shops, parks, and automobiles.

From 1540 to the present, the cult of Mary has dominated churches and even entire villages, which turn to her as the go-between to God the Father and believe that the destiny of the whole community depends on her powers. Powerful cults dedicated to Mary include that of the Virgin of Los Remedios, the Virgin of Candelaria at San Juan de los Lagos, and the Virgin of Zapopan. It is obvious that the Virgin Mary is a European importation into Mesoamerica. Each Iberian colonial incursion into Mesoamerica was accompanied, if not led, by the standard of one of the Virgins, who protected, inspired, and comforted the invaders as they claimed new territories and peoples for the Spanish empire. But in each case new meanings were given to the Spanish cult of the Virgin by mestizos, Indians, and *criollos* (Spaniards born in the New World). This remarkable creativity shows that many native peoples and mestizos, in varying degrees, *did* embrace elements of Christianity, *did* come to regard themselves as Christians, and *did* develop *new forms* of Christian stories, art, and ritual expression that included native and European elements. But this process of becoming Christian and *transforming* Christian meanings and practices was wonderfully complex and is difficult to describe adequately.

The cult of the Virgin of Guadalupe contains many rich patterns of religious life, including pilgrimage, *axis mundi,* world renewal, ecstasy, and transculturation. According to the official tradition in Mexico, a dark-skinned Virgin of Guadalupe appeared to a lowly Indian who was passing by the hill of Tepeyac on his way to receive Catholic training in 1531, just 10 years after the capital of Tenochtitlan fell to the forces of Hernán Cortés and his native allies. The Virgin appeared and spoke to Juan Diego in Nahuatl and used phrases to describe herself that were similar to those used to describe gods prior to the coming of the Spaniards. She said that she was In Tloque Nahuaque, the Lord of What Is Around Us and Touching Us, the title used by the Aztecs to describe their pervasive god. Guadalupe told him to announce to the bishop of Mexico that she wanted him to build her "a sacred little house" from which she could express her compassionate gaze. She told him that she had come to love "all the people who live in this land…all the people of different ancestries…those who cry to me, those who seek me, those who trust in me…I will nurse all their troubles, all their different miseries."

When Juan Diego reported the apparition to church authorities, they immediately scoffed at the idea that the Mother of Jesus
would reveal herself to an Indian. When Juan Diego returned to
the site to ask for the apparition's assistance, he lamented, "I am
a poor Indian, a porter's rope, I am a backframe, a tail, a wing
of a man of no importance." These phrases are very similar to
the way the more humble Aztec workers described themselves
to Sahagún when he was doing his research with native peoples.
The Virgin told him in Nahuatl that he was "in the hollow of my
mantle, in the crossing of my arms," and to take roses from a
nearby bush that was blooming out of season and roll them up
in his cloak. He did as he was told, and when he unrolled the
cloak in front of the bishop, the roses fell out and a magnificent
color image of the Virgin of Guadalupe, surrounded by a blazing
solar corona, was imprinted upon it. The astonishing miracle was
accepted, and the scene of the revelation was chosen as the site
of the new church she had commanded. Today, Mexico's greatest
basilica stands at the bottom of the hill and is visited every day by
thousands of the faithful, who gaze upward at the glass-encased
cloak with the miraculously painted image of the Virgin. Some
come in pilgrimages from hundreds of miles away and walk the
last part on their knees, praying along the way.

Even in the middle of the 16th century, priests complained that
there were pre-Hispanic pagan statues, or memories of statues,
behind the Catholic altars at places like Tepeyac. On the one hand,
however, the apparition of Guadalupe was familiar and even
affirmed by the Spaniards, who brought a tradition of apparitions
and shrines to the New World. Mexico was a training ground for
priests who expected apparitions to be part of their ministry. On
the other hand, the Franciscan and Dominican priests, who spoke
Nahuatl and observed the indigenous peoples adjusting painfully to
the colonial order, realized that the Indians were not merely adopt-
ing Spanish Catholic practices. Rather, they were mixing native and
European beliefs together and sometimes disguising their continued worship of their spirits, deities, and ancestors in their devotion
to Mary and other saints. They were reinventing both religious traditions in a new form.

It was known that the site of Juan Diego's experience was the
sacred hill dedicated to the Aztec mother goddess Tonantzin,
who was worshiped throughout the history of the Aztec empire.
Recently historians of religion have shown how Tepeyac was associated with important pre-Hispanic ceremonial routes traveled to

stimulate the rain-giving mountains to release their vital waters. It appears that Aztec ceremonial life involved ceremonial pilgrimages and processions to many of the sacred mountains around the Basin of Mexico and that Tepeyac and its nearby hills were shrines of high importance to the rain god cults of Tenochtitlan. The point is that the cult of Guadalupe, while strongly Catholic in meaning, also expresses a Mesoamerican sense of sacred space and worship of a goddess and her cults.

One of the most difficult realizations for students of culture is that religious images or symbols may have multiple, sometimes contradictory meanings. In a religious cosmovision, whether in Mesoamerica, Europe, or China, a single symbol will have multiple meanings. An obvious example of this multivalence is the Christian cross. On the one hand, it represents the betrayal, suffering, sacrifice, and death of Jesus Christ. On the other hand, it represents the beginning of resurrection, life, victory over death, and faith in God. When the Christian cross was brought by the Spaniards to Mexico, the Aztecs saw other meanings in its design. Some recognized it as a variation of the cosmic tree, or tree of life, which stood at the corners and center of the Aztec cosmos, holding it up and giving it order and renewal. Christ on the cross is transculturated and becomes the cosmic tree that not only resurrects life but also holds up the sky, giving the world stability. The multiplicity of meanings is also stimulated by the variations a symbol or deity may take according to local history, geography, politics, and ecology. There are many local meanings and stories associated with the different holy Virgins in Mexico. At the same time, Guadalupe is special because she integrates the tensions between Indian and Spaniard, mestizo and Indian, and Spaniard and mestizo into *one* community of faith and devotion.

We can see very different images and meanings associated with Guadalupe during her career in Mexico. She is certainly a long event with many middle-range events included. First, since the 16th century she has been considered the nourishing Mother who embraces, protects, and loves the people and nation of Mexico. She is kind, loving, forgiving, and accessible in all the shrines and images dedicated to her. Second, when theologians and priests began to observe her spreading popularity in the 17th century, she was the wonderful intercessor, the go-between to whom humans turn in order to reach the miraculous power of God the Father. Third, in the 18th and 19th centuries she became the female warrior of the revolution. During different, violent upheavals in Mexican history, priests and rebels have turned to her power and authority to inspire them to overthrow oppressive governments. She becomes the natural ally of the common people, often Indians and mestizos, in their spirit of rebellion. She is approached for aid in the resistance against hated taxes. For example, in the Indian town of Tulancingo in 1769, rebel leaders called for the death of Spanish officials and the creation of an Indian priesthood. "They dreamed of the day when bishops and *alcaldes mayores* would kneel and kiss the rings of Indian priests. The leader of their theocratic utopia called himself the New Savior, and his consort was known as the Virgin of Guadalupe."[11]

To summarize, in Guadalupe we see a curious and even furious transculturation. She is Indian and Spaniard. She is an Earth Mother and a Holy Mother. She is a comforter and a revolutionary. She is the magnet for pilgrimages and a pilgrim herself, traveling in front of the rebel soldiers and entering into every heart who needs her protection and comfort, as did the poor Indian, Juan Diego, in 1531. She appeared in the contact zone where Christian priests were seeking to establish new converts in the shadow of the Aztec goddess's sacred hill. And she chose to appear to the down-and-out, the laborer, the backframe Indian, Juan Diego, who became her partner in the conversion of both the bishop and the masses of Indians, mestizos, and Spaniards who came to worship her.

GUADALUPE

The Virgin of Guadalupe has become extremely popular among people all over the world, even beyond the Roman Catholic community. Her story, symbols, and beauty have attracted artists, storytellers, and pilgrims as she continues to grow in influence and popularity.

MEXICAN MURALISTS, CHICANO WALLS

One of the most creative social and artistic movements in 20th-century Latin America was the Mexican muralist movement led by Diego Rivera, José Clemente Orozco, David Alfaro Siqueiros, and Rufino Tamayo. Along with scores of other painters, including the extraordinary Frida Kahlo, these artists revived a national interest in the Aztec past that continues to thrive in Mexican and Mexican American communities. The Mexican muralists, in different ways, attempted to uncover and illuminate the rich, contradictory, painful, and beautiful physical, spiritual, and political history of the Mexican nation. This included, in the case of Diego Rivera for instance, a celebration of the indigenous Mexican past in his home, paintings, and philosophy. This celebration of the Aztecs, Maya, Totonacs, and Huaxtecs was sometimes intended as a criticism of the cultural fashion of celebrating European trends and influences from Spain and France in Mexican society, which had become prevalent in the latter part of the 19th century. Rivera painted a number of spectacular murals on the walls of public and government buildings that highlighted or included the cosmovision, royalty, dignity, agricultural achievements, and spiritual power of the Aztecs and their neighbors. A visitor to Mexico City today can see Aztec symbols, faces, and scenes on many important government and educational buildings.

When the descendants of Mexican peoples who settled (beginning in the 16th century) in what is today the southwestern United States seek to understand their identity, culture, and responsibility, they inevitably include references and images of the indigenous cultures of Mexico. While dozens of indigenous communities contributed to the colonial and modern formation of Mexican and Chicano identity, it is impressive how the Aztecs and the Maya have come to be the dominant, overall symbols of indigenous Mexico. This is especially true in the Chicano movement, which has spread to every community where U.S. citizens of Mexican descent live. Chicanos are people of Mexican descent who have formed a movement to liberate themselves from Anglo stereotypes, political oppression, poverty, unequal opportunity, and spiritual doubt. This movement was most vocally represented by the Farmworkers' Union led by César Chávez, the Crusade for Justice led by Corky González in Denver, and by social movements for equal education and the recovery of ancestral lands in New Mexico. It receives its most vivid expression and energy in the music, mural artwork, and community service programs found in every Mexican American community from El Paso, Texas, to Boston, Massachusetts. A visitor to any of these communities will find beautiful and inspiring murals depicting Quetzalcoatl, Huitzilopochtli, Malinche, Nezahualcoyotl, *tlamatinime*, merchants, warriors, rulers, farmers, and other vital dimensions of Aztec, Maya, Olmec, Toltec, and Teotihuacan society. Of the scores of Chicano muralists who have nurtured the neighborhoods of Mexican American communities around the United States, let us mention briefly three: Ray Patlan, José Antonio Burciaga, and George Yepes.

In Chicago's Pilsen community, where Chicanos have gained important political power, stands Casa Aztlan, an all-purpose community center housing colorful murals painted by Ray Patlan that depict Mexican history from the time of the Toltecs to the present. Casa Aztlan is named after the mythical homeland north of the Aztec capital that the Mexica ancestors left in order to build their great center, Tenochtitlan. Chicanos in Chicago claim that that original homeland is in their *barrio,* where struggle and celebration are joined in a movement to ease the pain of urban living. They know in their minds that, geographically speaking, Aztlan is much further south. But in the creative imagination of the Mexican American people, a sacred place can be anywhere there is a revelation of the spiritual and artistic resources that nurture the destiny of a people. Ray Patlan (his last name comes from Nahuatl), like the Aztec *tlacuilo,* discovered in his art a message for the heart of the people. His murals cover the walls of Casa Aztlan with images that seem to vibrate, come alive, and move around the visitors who come to the community center seeking educational, legal, or family assistance. Patlan's dynamic art develops the styles of Orozco and Rivera as he uses fiery reds, rich earth browns, and sunrise colors, which animate the figures of the Toltecs, the Mexican revolutionaries, the farmworkers from Delano, California, and the everyday struggles of the Chicanos in Chicago. Because of Patlan's artistic genius in depicting the hope and history of Mexican peoples, Casa Aztlan is a modern-day ceremonial center for Chicanos to recall the pre-Hispanic past, colonial struggles for dignity, and revolutionary spirit to strengthen themselves.

Stanford University is another center where Aztec symbols inspire, criticize, and educate the viewer. In 1972 (responding, in part, to the pressures of the Chicano movement), Stanford University set up Casa Zapata, a theme house to support U.S. Mexican students. There José Antonio Burciaga painted three large murals in the 1980s depicting various aspects of Mexican history and culture. Each one carries important symbols of the Aztec and Maya worldview. One mural, called the *Mythology of Maize,* depicts the creation of the human race, which came about in part through the creative work of Quetzalcoatl, the Toltec/Aztec god discussed in previous chapters. Among the people Burciaga creates are modern-day *pachucos, cholos,* and *cholas*—the young representatives of working-class people whose struggles against racism, violence, and poverty often involve them in some of the destructive forces of U.S. culture. Another mural at Casa Zapata, entitled *Last Supper of Chicano Heroes,* also includes Aztec imagery. Flanking the crowd of heroes who sit and stand at the Last Supper (including Che Guevara, Benito Juárez,

Members of the community gather for the unveiling of *Tepeyac de Los Angeles*, painted by Los Angeles muralist, George Yepes, at St. Lucy's Church. (George Rodríguez photo, courtesy of George Yepes Studio)

Martin Luther King, Sor Juana de la Cruz, Carlos Santana, César Chávez, and Dolores Huerta), Burciaga painted two Toltec statues that are still standing today at the archaeological site of Tula, the great Tollan of Quetzalcoatl's kingdom. Hovering above the entire scene is the Virgin of Guadalupe, the brown-skinned messenger of God who came to embrace all of the peoples of Mexico in her compassionate arms.

Finally, one of the most powerful, cutting-edge painters in the United States today is George Yepes, whose paintings appear on community centers, universities, churches, and schools in Los Angeles, California. Yepes is perhaps best known for his painting *La Pistola y el Corazón*, which appeared on the Los Lobos album of the same name. His works have been purchased by Madonna and Sean Penn and other actors and artists drawn to the themes of passion and healing in his art. One of Yepes's most powerful works covers the façade of St. Lucy's Church in one of the roughest *barrios* of Los Angeles. In this mural, entitled *Tepeyac de Los Angeles*, Yepes relocates the Guadalupe miracle from the Aztec hill of Tepeyac to the Los Angeles hillside where the church sits and serves people caught up in the agony of the city. The image of the apparition of the Virgin to Juan Diego is transformed, through Yepes's genius, into a tableau of the birth of a child guarded by the angels of hope and love, all of whom sit on her lap, cradled in the compassion of her arms. Below the Virgin, Yepes painted the image of a young Juan Diego as a symbol of the city of Los Angeles; in his lap is another youth, about to be stabbed to death by a personification of street violence, who is miraculously pulled out of harm's way by an angel.

Among Yepes's powerful paintings is a shimmering triptych (series of three paintings) of the Aztec gods Huitzilopochtli, Coatlicue, and Coyolxauhqui (discussed in chapters 2 and 3), but reimagined in terms of the daily struggle of Mexican people in East Los Angeles. Yepes has taken the furious Aztec gods who created the cosmos and the Great Aztec Temple and turned them into muscular, erotic, and vulnerable teenagers and young adults struggling mightily to overcome violence, sexual exploitation, and the degradation of women. Yepes's thick, pulsating, red-hot imagery uses Aztec symbols to unmask the oppressive attitudes of modern-day males and institutions whose quest for total power has resulted in *barrio* violence, the humiliation of young women, and the hopelessness of the newborn. But his murals also reveal the long event of creative struggle and the wellsprings of the healing human imagination that started back before the Chichimec warrior, Xolotl, came to shoot his arrows into the four quarters of the blue-green bowl. Yepes's extraordinary paintings show that this imagination dwells today in the hearts and minds of Mexican American people who seek a community safe for families, the humane education of teenagers, and the nurturing of children.

NOTES

1. Carlos Fuentes, *Where the Air Is Clear,* trans. Sam Hileman (New York: Farrar, Straus and Giroux, 1971), 5.

2. Mary Louise Pratt, *Imperial Eyes: Travel Writing and Transculturation* (New York: Routledge, 1992), 6.

3. Elizabeth Wilder Weismann, *Mexico in Sculpture, 1521–1821* (Cambridge, MA: Harvard University Press, 1950), 2.

4. Barbara Myerhoff, *Peyote Hunt: The Sacred Journey of the Huichol Indians* (Ithaca, NY: Cornell University Press, 1974).

5. Ibid., 33.

6. Ibid., 142.

7. Ibid., 147.

8. Ibid., 153.

9. Quoted in Hugo Nutini, *Todos Santos in Rural Tlaxcala: A Syncretic, Expressive, and Symbolic Analysis of the Cult of the Dead* (Princeton, NJ: Princeton University Press, 1988), 56.

10. Ibid., 152.

11. William B. Taylor, "The Virgin of Guadalupe in New Spain: An Inquiry into the Social History of Marian Devotion," *American Ethnologist* 14, no. 1 (February 1987): 9–33, passage quoted from 21.

GLOSSARY

PRONUNCIATION GUIDE FOR NAHUATL TERMS

The Nahuatl language was phonetically transcribed using the Roman alphabet and Spanish pronunciation during the 16th century. Vowels and consonants are pronounced as in the following English examples:

Vowels:	Consonants:
a as in f**a**ther	**c** (followed by **a**, **o**, or consonant) as "c" in **c**at
e as in b**e**d	**c** (followed by **e** or **i**) as "c" in **c**ite
i as "ee" in d**ee**p	**c** (followed by **ua**, **ue**, or **ui**) as "qu" in **qu**it
o as in t**o**te	**c** (followed by **u** and consonant) as "c" in **c**ool
u as in r**u**le	**g** (followed by **a**, **o**, or consonant) as "g" in **g**o
	g (followed by **e** or **i**)as "h" in **h**ouse
	g (followed by **ua**, **ue**, or **ui**) as "Gu" in **Gu**atemala
	g (followed by **ue** or **ui**) as "gu" in **gu**est
	h (followed by **u**) as "wh" in **wh**eat
	h (before other vowels) as in **h**at
	h (before consonant) is almost silent

Consonants (cont.):

q (followed by **ua**) as "qu" in s*qu*ash

q (followed by **ue** or **ui**) as "k" in *k*it

ll as in fu*ll*y

tl pronounced together as in lit*tl*e

tz pronounced together as "ts" in ha*ts*

x as "sh" in *sh*out

y as in *y*oke

z as in "s" in *s*it

Glossary terms are broken down into syllables in parentheses immediately following the glossary entry. Capitalized syllables indicate where the accent or stress should be placed. Consonants other than those indicated above are pronounced as in English.

altepetl—(al-TE-petl) "Mountain filled with water," meaning "village" or "community," formed from the Nahuatl words for water (*atl*) and mountain (*tepetl*).

altepeyollotl—(al-te-pe-YOL-lotl) "Heart of the town" or "heart of the community," formed from the Nahuatl words for water (*atl*), mountain (*tepetl*), and heart (*yollotl*).

Atl—(atl) "Water."

Atlcahualo—(atl-ca-HUA-lo) "Detention of Water" or "Shortage of Water," a month in the annual festival cycle.

Aztlan—(AZ-tlan) "Place of the White Heron," the mythical homeland, north of the Basin of Mexico, where the Mexica ancestors began their migration.

cacique—(*Arawak*: ca-CI-que) A native leader or chieftain.

calli—(CAL-li) "House."

calmecac—(cal-ME-cac) "File of houses," temple schools where young men and women were trained to become priests.

calpolli—(cal-POL-li) Kin-based social groups or clans in Tenochtitlan that had their own temples and schools, organized community labor, and provided warriors in times of war.

Cemanahuac—(cem-a-NA-huac) "Land Surrounded by Water," the terrestrial level of the cosmos in which the Aztecs lived.

cempoalxochitl—(cem-poal-XO-chitl) "Twenty flower," orange and yellow marigolds used to adorn home altars and cemeteries in rituals related to the Day of the Dead.

Centzon Huitznahua—(CEN-tzon huitz-NA-hua) The "Four Hundred Southerners," siblings of Coyolxauhqui and Huitzilopochtli in the Myth of Coatepec.

Chalchiuhtlicue—(chal-chiuh-TLI-cue) "Precious Jade Skirt," water goddess of lakes, rivers, and streams.

Chalco—(CHAL-co) 1. A community located on the lakeshore southeast of Tenochtitlan. 2. one of the lakes in the Basin of Mexico.

Chichihualcuauhco—(chi-chi-hual-CUAUH-co) A place where infants who died while still nursing from their mothers went after death.

Chichimec/s or Chichimeca—(chi-chi-ME-ca) "Lineage [or] rope of the dogs," peoples from north of the Basin of Mexico from whom the Mexica or Aztecs descended.

Chicomoztoc—(chi-co-MOZ-toc) "Place of Seven Caves," mythical place of origin of the Mexica and other Mesoamerican groups.

chimalli—(chi-MAL-li) A shield used by warriors.

chinampa—(chi-NAM-pa) A highly productive agricultural system developed in the lake region based on intensive cultivation of long, rectangular gardens made from reclaimed swampland.

Cihuacoatl—(ci-hua-CO-atl) "Serpent Woman," earth and mother goddess; also the title of the political and military leader second to the *tlatoani*.

cihuatlamacazqui—(ci-hua-tla-ma-CAZ-qui) A woman priest.

Coatecoalli—(co-a-te-co-AL-li) "House of Foreign Gods," temple that housed the gods of communities conquered by the Aztecs.

Coatepec—(co-a-TE-pec) "Serpent Mountain," birthplace of Huitzilopochtli.

Coatlicue—(co-a-TLI-cue) "Serpent Skirt," earth goddess and mother of Huitzilopochtli in the Myth of Coatepec.

copaltemaliztli—(co-pal-te-ma-LIZ-tli) The act of smudging or incensing a ceremonial or ritual space.

Coyolxauhqui—(co-yol-XAUH-qui) "Painted Bells," moon goddess and warrior daughter of Coatlicue and sister of Huitzilopochtli, who killed and dismembered her in the Myth of Coatepec.

criollos—(*Spanish*: cri-O-llos): People of Spanish or European parentage born in the New World.

Cuahuitlicac—(cua-hui-TLI-cac) The son of the mother goddess, Coatlicue, who warned her of the impending attack from Coyolxauhqui and her 400 siblings in the Myth of Coatepec.

Cuauhtemoc—(cuauh-TE-moc) "Diving Eagle," the last Aztec *tlatoani*, who surrendered Tlatelolco to Cortés in 1521.

cuauhxicalli—(cuauh-xi-CAL-li) "Eagle vessel," a stone receptacle for sacrificial offerings, especially human hearts and blood for the gods.

cuicacalli—(cui-ca-CAL-li) "House of songs," a preparatory school where children were taught sacred songs, ritual dances, and important mythological and historical information.

cuztic teocuitlapitzqui—(CUZ-tic te-o-cui-tla-PITZ-qui) Goldworkers.

difrasismo—(*Spanish*: di-fra-SIS-mo) A linguistic device common in Nahuatl that combines two or more words or phrases to form a different concept or metaphor incorporating the meanings of the original words or phrases.

Ehecatl—(e-HE-catl) Lord of the Wind, an apparition of Quetzalcoatl, the Feathered Serpent.

haab—(*Mayan*: haab) A 365-day count related to the solar cycle in the Maya calendar.

hikuri—(*Huichol*: hi-KU-ri) Peyote.

huactli—(HUAC-tli) "Laughing falcon" whose cry served as an omen determining the success or failure of merchant-warriors.

huehuetl—(HUE-huetl) A large vertical wooden drum.

huehuetlatolli—(hue-hue-tla-TOL-li) The "ancient words" or "sayings of the elders," elegant orations representing the traditional teachings of the ancestors.

Huey tecuilhuitl—(huey te-CUIL-huitl) "Great Feast of the Lords," a month in the annual festival cycle.

Huey tocoztli—(huey to-COZ-tli) "Great Vigil," a month in the annual festival cycle.

huipilli—(hui-PIL-li) A blouse-like garment worn by women.

Huitzilopochtli—(hui-tzi-lo-POCH-tli) "Hummingbird on the Left" or "Southern Hummingbird," god of the sun and of war and patron deity of the Mexica.

ihiyotl—(i-HI-yotl) A spiritual force residing in one's liver that could attract and cast spells over other humans, plants, animals, and events.

in xochitl in cuicatl—(in XO-chitl in CUI-catl) "Flowers and songs," metaphor for artistic expression in the forms of words, songs, and paintings that connected the human personality with the divine.

ixiptla—(i-XIP-tla) *See* **teotl ixiptla**.

Izcalli—(iz-CAL-li) "Growth," a month in the annual festival cycle.

Iztaccihuatl—(iz-tac-CI-hua-tl) "White Woman." 1. A high, snow-capped volcano on the eastern rim of the Basin of Mexico. 2. A priestess's female assistant responsible for preparing the ritual area and lighting and extinguishing the ritual fires during the Ochpaniztli festival.

Iztli—(IZ-tli) The knife god.

macehualli (ma-ce-HUAL-li), *pl.* **macehualtin** (ma-ce-HUAL-tin) Commoner, the class of commoners.

maguey—(ma-GUEY) An important plant of the genus *Agave* from which paper, needles, and a ritual drink called *pulque* (or *octli*) are made.

malinalli—(ma-li-NAL-li) Two pairs of intertwined bands flowing in constant motion that helped the forces of the underworld rise to the surface and the forces of the celestial world descend to the earth.

manta—(MAN-ta) A colorful cloak worn by warriors.

maquahuitl—(ma-QUA-hui-tl) A wooden club used by warriors.

mara'akame—(*Huichol*: ma-ra-a-KA-me) A shaman-priest among the Huichol Indians.

Mayahuel—(ma-YA-huel) "Circle of Arms," goddess of the *maguey* plant, *pulque*, and ritual drinking.

mayeque—(ma-YE-que) A social group of agricultural workers who worked other people's land and paid taxes to the owner.

mestizo—(*Spanish*: mes-TI-zo) A person of mixed Indian and European ancestry.

metate—(me-TA-te) A grinding stone for processing corn into tortillas.

Mexica—(me-XI-ca) An ethnic group who, after a great migration from the north, settled in the lake region at Tenochtitlan and Tlatelolco and came to dominate the Triple Alliance, or Aztec empire.

Mictecacihuatl—(mic-te-ca-CI-huatl) "Lady of the Underworld," goddess of death.

mictlampa—(mic-TLAM-pa) "Region of the dead," the underworld.

Mictlan—(MIC-tlan) The ninth level of the underworld where the souls of people who died ordinary deaths resided.

Mictlantecuhtli—(mic-tlan-te-CUH-tli) "Lord of the Underworld," god of death.

mitl chimalli—(mitl chi-MAL-li) "Shield and arrows," an Aztec metaphor meaning "war."

Motecuhzoma Ilhuicamina—(mo-te-cuh-ZO-ma il-hui-ca-MI-na) The fifth *tlatoani* who ruled from 1440 to 1469.

Motecuhzoma Xocoyotzin—(mo-te-cuh-ZO-ma xo-co-YO-tzin) The ninth *tlatoani* of Tenochtitlan who reigned from 1502 to 1520; he was the great-grandson of Motecuhzoma Ilhuicamina.

Nahuatl—(NA-huatl) The language spoken by the Nahua peoples of the Basin of Mexico.

nemontemi—(ne-mon-TE-mi) "Empty days," five consecutive unlucky days situated at the end of the 365-day solar cycle.

Neteotoquiliztli—(ne-te-o-to-qui-LIZ-tli) "Impersonation of a God," a ritual in which men, wearing the skins of sacrificed warriors, went throughout the city engaging in mock battles and begging for food and other items.

Netzahualcoyotl—(ne-tza-hual-CO-yotl) "Fasting Coyote," philosopher-poet-ruler of Tezcoco.

Netzahualpilli—(ne-tza-hual-PIL-li) "Fasting Prince," astrologer-ruler of Tezcoco.

nextlaoalli—(nex-tla-o-AL-li) "Debt payment," a sacrifice to the gods.

nezahualiztli—(ne-za-hua-LIZ-tli) A preparatory period of four (or a multiple of four) days of "priestly fasting" before a sacrificial ritual.

Ochpaniztli—(och-pa-NIZ-tli) "Sweeping of the Way," a month in the annual festival cycle.

octli—(OC-tli) A ritual drink, also known as *pulque*, made of the fermented juice of the *maguey* plant.

ofrenda—(*Spanish*: o-FREN-da) "Offering."

ollamaliztli—(ol-la-ma-LIZ-tli) The Mesoamerican ballgame, played with a large rubber ball in an I-shaped court.

Olmec—(OL-mec) "People from the Land of the Rubber Trees," the first major Mesoamerican civilization, which emerged along the Gulf Coast around 1800 B.C.E.

Ometeotl—(o-me-TE-otl) "Giver of Life" or "Master of Duality," a celestial and dual male/female deity, represented in the pair Ometecuhtli and Omecihuatl; primordial creator of the universe.

Omeyocan—(o-me-YO-can) "Place of Duality" or "Dual Heaven," the 12th and 13th celestial levels of the cosmos.

pan de muertos—(*Spanish*: pan de MUER-tos) "Bread of the dead," a special sweetbread made for Day of the Dead rituals.

patolli—(pa-TOL-li) A board game similar to Parcheesi or backgammon.

peyoteros—(*Spanish*: pey-o-TE-ros) Peyote hunters.

pilli—(PIL-li), *pl.* **pipiltin** (pi-PIL-tin) A noble; the nobility or ruling class.

pochteca—(poch-TE-ca) Merchant-warriors.

Popocatepetl—(po-po-ca-TE-petl) "Smoking Mountain," a high, snow-capped volcano on the eastern rim of the Basin of Mexico.

pulque—(PUL-que) A ritual drink, also known as *octli*, made of the fermented juice of the *maguey* plant.

Quecholli—(que-CHOL-li) A month in the annual festival cycle.

Quetzalcoatl—(que-tzal-CO-atl) "Feathered Serpent" or "Precious Serpent," important pan-Mesoamerican deity with complex symbolism.

Quinquechanaya—(quin-que-cha-NA-ya) "They Stretch Their Necks," a growth ritual performed every four years in the month of Izcalli, when children of both sexes were purified by fire, had their earlobes pierced and earrings inserted, and were lifted by their foreheads and had their limbs stretched.

retablo—(*Spanish*: re-TA-blo) A structure forming the back of an altar where images are placed.

Tamoanchan—(ta-mo-AN-chan) The paradise in which the gods created humans.

techcatl—(TECH-catl) A sacrificial stone.

tecpatl—(TEC-patl) A sacrificial flint knife.

telpochcalli—(tel-poch-CAL-li) "Young men's house," a school where young men were taught to be warriors.

temalacatl—(te-ma-LA-catl) A circular stone used for gladiatorial sacrifices.

Templo Mayor—(*Spanish*: TEM-plo ma-YOR) The Great Temple of Tenochtitlan, symbolic center and physical replica of the Aztec cosmos.

Tenochtitlan—(te-noch-TI-tlan) The capital city of the Triple Alliance, founded by the Mexica around 1325, located on an island in the lake system of the Basin of Mexico.

teoatltlachinolli—(te-o-atl-tla-chi-NOL-li) "Divine liquid and burnt things," a metaphor meaning "war."

teocalli—(te-o-CAL-li) "Deity house," a temple.

teocuaque—(te-o-CUA-que) "God-eaters," certain priests and priestesses who fasted more than a year before a specific sacrificial ritual.

Teotihuacan—(te-o-ti-HUA-can) "The City of the Gods" or "The Place Where One Becomes Deified," an important archaeological site and ceremonial center northeast of Tenochtitlan that flourished from 1 to 550 c.e.

teotl—(TE-otl), *pl.* **teteo** (te-TE-o) A deity or sacred power manifested in natural forms, in persons of high distinction, or in mysterious and chaotic places.

teotl ixiptla—(TE-otl i-XIP-tla), *pl.* **teteo ixiptla** (te-TE-o i-XIP-tla) A human being, animal, plant, or object ritually transformed to become an image or impersonator of a god.

Tepanec—(TE-pa-nec) A powerful alliance of communities that dominated the lake region when the Mexica first settled in the Basin of Mexico.

Tepeilhuitl—(te-PEIL-huitl) "Feast of the Mountain," a month in the annual festival cycle.

tepetl—(TE-petl) "Mountain" or "hill."

teponaztli—(te-po-NAZ-tli) A small horizontal drum.

tetecuhtin—(te-te-CUH-tin) Members of the nobility who achieved their status by excelling in war.

tetzahuitl—(te-TZA-huitl) A person who sent out harmful forces and created fear, scandal, and danger.

teyolia—(te-YO-lia) The spiritual force residing in the human heart, providing one with intelligence and sensibilities.

Tezcatlipoca—(tez-ca-tli-PO-ca) "Smoking Mirror," an important deity related to warfare, rulership, magic, and the night.

Tezcoco—(tez-CO-co) 1. A city and member of the Triple Alliance located on the western shore across the lake from Tenochtitlan. 2. The large central lake in the Basin of Mexico.

tianquiztli—(ti-an-QUIZ-tli) "Marketplace."

Tianquiztli—(ti-an-QUIZ-tli) The star cluster or constellation known to us as the Pleiades.

tlacahuapahua—(tla-ca-hua-PA-hua), **tlacazcaltia** (tla-caz-CAL-tia) "To strengthen persons" or "to make persons grow," to educate.

tlacatecuhtli—(tla-ca-te-CUH-tli) A great lord and military leader.

tlacateteuhti—(tla-ca-te-te-UH-ti) "Human paper streamers," children with certain attributes chosen to be sacrificed during the festival of Atlcahualo.

tlacatlaolli—(tla-ca-tla-OL-li) A stew made of dried maize in which nobles would eat small portions of the flesh of sacrificed warrior captives.

Tlacaxipehualiztli—(tla-ca-xi-pe-hua-LIZ-tli) "The Feast of the Flaying of Men," a month in the annual festival cycle.

tlachtli—(TLACH-tli) The I-shaped court in which the ballgame was played.

Tlacopan—(tla-CO-pan) The city allied with Tenochtitlan and Tezcoco in the Triple Alliance.

tlacuilo—(tla-CUI-lo), *pl.* **tlacuiloque** (tla-cui-LO-que) Artist-scribes who painted books or manuscripts.

Tlahuizcalpantecuhtli—(tla-huiz-cal-pan-te-CUH-tli) "Lord of the House of Dawn," deity representing the planet Venus as the Morning Star and related to Quetzalcoatl.

Tlaloc—(TLA-loc), *pl.* **Tlaloque** (tla-LO-que) "He Who Makes the Plants Spring Up," important rain and fertility deity or deities.

Tlalocan—(tla-LO-can) Tlaloc's mountain paradise, where individuals who died from water-related causes would reside after death.

Tlaltecuhtli—(tlal-te-CUH-tli) "Lord of the Earth," the earth monster.

tlamacazqui—(tla-ma-CAZ-qui) The head priest.

tlamatini—(tla-ma-TI-ni), *pl.* **tlamatinime** (tla-ma-ti-NI-me) "Knower of things," wise man, sage, or scholar.

Tlatelolco—(tla-te-LOL-co) A sister city of Tenochtitlan, on the north side of the island, site of the great marketplace.

tlatoani—(tla-to-AN-i), *pl.* **tlatoque** (tla-TO-que) "Chief speaker," the supreme ruler.

tlatocayotl—(tla-to-CA-yotl) Small local states or city-states.

Tlaxcala—(tlax-CA-la) The polity that resisted conquest by the Aztecs and allied with the Spaniards to conquer Tenochtitlan and Tlatelolco in 1521.

Tlazolteotl—(tla-zol-TE-otl) "Goddess of Filth," goddess of sexual sin and patron deity of weavers and midwives.

tochyacatl—(toch-YA-catl) The special hairstyle of a seasoned warrior, with only a forked heron feather ornament with a quetzal feather spray attached to the head.

Toci—(TO-ci) "Our Grandmother," a mother goddess.

Tollan—(TOL-lan) "Place of Reeds," archetype city in Aztec mythology.

Toltec—(TOL-tec) A civilization that flourished in Central Mexico from 950 to 1150 from whom the Mexica claimed legitimacy and ancestral ties.

toltecatl—(tol-TE-catl) "Keepers of the great Toltec artistic tradition of excellence," craftsmen and artisans.

Tonacacihuatl—(to-na-ca-CI-huatl) "Lady of Sustenance," a creator deity.

Tonacatecuhtli—(to-na-ca-te-CUH-tli) "Lord of Sustenance," a creator deity.

tonalamatl—(to-na-LA-matl) "Book of days," painted manuscript depicting the ritual calendar used for divination.

tonalli—(to-NAL-li) The spiritual force collected and nurtured in the human skull, determining one's temperament and destiny.

tonalpohualli—(to-nal-po-HUAL-li) "Count of days," the 260-day ritual cycle in the calendar.

Tonantzin—(to-NAN-tzin) "Our Venerable Mother," a mother goddess.

Tonatiuh—(to-NA-tiuh) A solar deity who presided over the age known as the "Fifth Sun," in which the Aztecs lived.

Topiltzin Quetzalcoatl—(to-PIL-tzin que-tzal-CO-atl) "Our Young Prince the Feathered Serpent," the priest-ruler of Tollan in Aztec myths, who was banished from that city but vowed to return.

Toxcatl—(TOX-catl) "Dry Season," a month in the annual festival cycle.

Toxiuhmolpilia—(to-xiuh-mol-PIL-ia) "Binding of Years," the New Fire Ceremony, a ritual of renewal that took place once every 52 years at the end and beginning of the calendar round.

tozohualiztli—(to-zo-hua-LIZ-tli) Nocturnal vigils performed before certain sacrificial rituals.

Tula—(TU-la) A ceremonial center north of Tenochtitlan that flourished from 950 to 1150 C.E.

tzolkin—(*Mayan*: tzol-KIN) The 260-day ritual cycle in the Maya calendar.

tzompantli—(tzom-PAN-tli) "Skull rack," where the severed heads of sacrificial victims were hung on poles at the Great Temple of Tenochtitlan.

Xaltocan—(xal-TO-can) 1. A community located on an island north of Tenochtitlan. 2. One of the lakes in the Basin of Mexico.

Xipe Totec—(XI-pe TO-tec) "Our Lord the Flayed One," a deity closely related to human sacrifice.

xipeme—(xi-PE-me) The warriors sacrificed during the festival of Tlacaxipehualiztli and their captors, who wore the victims' skins in emulation of Xipe Totec.

xiuhpohualli—(xiuh-po-HUAL-li) The 365-day calendar cycle corresponding to the solar year.

Xiuhtecuhtli—(xiuh-te-CUH-tli) A fire deity, lord of the hearth.

xiuhtototl—(xiuh-TO-totl) "Turquoise bird."

xochicalli—(xo-chi-CAL-li) "House of flowers," a sweat bath prepared by a midwife for an expectant mother.

Xochimilco—(xo-chi-MIL-co) 1. Community located on the lakeshore to the south of Tenochtitlan where *chinampa* agricultural production took place. 2. One of the lakes in the Basin of Mexico.

xochimiquiztli—(xo-chi-mi-QUIZ-tli) "Flowery death," death on the battlefield.

Xochiquetzal—(xo-chi-QUE-tzal) "Precious Flowery Feather," goddess of love and romance, associated with flowers, feasting, and pleasure.

Xochiyaoyotl—(xo-chi-ya-O-yotl) "Flowery Wars," scheduled battlefield confrontations between warriors from various kingdoms.

Xolotl—(XO-lotl) "Divine Dog."

Xumpango—(xum-PAN-go) One of the lakes in the Basin of Mexico.

Yacatecuhtli—(ya-ca-te-CUH-tli) A patron deity of merchants.

yollopiltic—(yol-lo-PIL-tic) "One who has an ennobled heart," a noble who attained remarkable success in leadership or artistic expression.

yollotl—(YOL-lotl) "Heart."

yolteotl—(yol-TE-otl) "A heart rooted in god," an exceptional painter able to capture divine reality in painted manuscripts and murals.

SELECTED BIBLIOGRAPHY

Armillas, Pedro. "Gardens on Swamps." *Science* 174 (1976): 653–61.

Arnold, Philip. *Eating Landscape: Aztec and European Occupation of Tlalocan.* Boulder: University Press of Colorado, 2001.

Aveni, Anthony F. *Empires of Time: Calendars, Clocks, and Cultures.* New York: Basic Books, 1989.

Aveni, Anthony F. *The End of Time: The Maya Mystery of 2012.* Boulder: University Press of Colorado, 2009.

Aveni, Anthony F. *Skywatchers: A Revised and Updated Version of Skywatchers of Ancient Mexico.* Austin: University of Texas Press, 2001.

Bakewell, Liz, and Byron Hamann. *Mesolore: Exploring Mesoamerican Culture.* Providence, RI: Brown University; Wilmington, DE: Scholarly Resources, 2001.

Bernal-García, María Elena. "Carving Mountains in a Blue-Green Bowl: Mythological Urban Planning in Mesoamerica." PhD dissertation, University of Texas at Austin, 1993.

Bierhorst, John. *Four Masterworks of American Indian Literature.* New York: Farrar, Straus and Giroux, 1974.

Boone, Elizabeth Hill. *The Aztec World.* Montreal and Washington, DC: St. Remy Press and Smithsonian Books, 1994.

Boone, Elizabeth Hill. *Stories in Red and Black: Pictorial Histories of the Aztecs and Mixtecs.* Austin: University of Texas Press, 2008.

Bray, Warwick. *Everyday Life of the Aztecs.* London: B. T. Batsford, 1968.

Broda, Johanna. "Tlacaxipeualiztli: A Reconstruction of an Aztec Calendar Festival from the Sixteenth-Century Sources." *Revista española de antropología americana* 5 (1970): 197–279.

Broda, Johanna, Davíd Carrasco, and Eduardo Matos Moctezuma. *The Great Temple of Tenochtitlan: Center and Periphery in the Aztec World.* Berkeley: University of California Press, 1987.

Brumfiel, Elizabeth M., and Gary M. Feinman, eds. *The Aztec World.* New York: Abrams, 2008.

Brundage, Burr. *The Fifth Sun: Aztec Gods, Aztec World.* Austin: University of Texas Press, 1979.

Carmichael, Elizabeth, and Chloë Sayer. *The Skeleton at the Feast: The Day of the Dead in Mexico.* Austin: University of Texas Press, 1992.

Carrasco, Davíd. *City of Sacrifice: The Aztec Empire and the Role of Violence in Civilization.* Boston: Beacon Press, 1999.

Carrasco, Davíd. *Quetzalcoatl and the Irony of Empire: Myths and Prophecies in the Aztec Tradition.* Rev. ed. Boulder: University Press of Colorado, 2000.

Carrasco, Davíd. *Religions of Mesoamerica: Cosmovision and Ceremonial Centers.* San Francisco: Harper and Row, 1990.

Carrasco, Davíd, ed. *To Change Place: Aztec Ceremonial Landscapes.* Niwot: University Press of Colorado, 1999.

Carrasco, Davíd, ed. *The Oxford Encyclopedia of Mesoamerican Cultures.* 3 vols. New York: Oxford University Press, 2001.

Carrasco, Davíd, Lindsay Jones, and Scott Sessions, eds. *Mesoamerica's Classic Heritage: From Teotihuacan to the Aztecs.* Boulder: University Press of Colorado, 2000.

Carrasco, Davíd, and Scott Sessions, eds. *Cave, City, and Eagle's Nest: An Interpretive Journey through the Mapa de Cuauhtinchan No. 2.* Albuquerque: University of New Mexico Press, 2007.

Clendinnen, Inga. *Aztecs: An Interpretation.* Cambridge: Cambridge University Press, 1991.

Codex Borbonicus. *Códice borbónico.* Introduction and commentary by Ferdinand Anders, Maarten Jansen, and Luis Reyes García. Mexico City and Graz: Fondo de Cultura Económica and Akademische Druck- und Verlagsanstalt, 1991.

Codex Borgia. *Los tiempos del cielo y de la oscuridad: oráculos y liturgia, libro explicativo del llamado Códice Borgia.* Introduction and commentary by Ferdinand Anders, Maarten Jansen, and Luis Reyes García. Mexico City and Graz: Fondo de Cultura Económica and Akademische Druck- und Verlagsanstalt, 1993.

Codex Fejérváry-Mayer. *El libro de Tezcatlipoca, señor del tiempo: libro explicativo del llamado Códice Fejérváry-Mayer, M/12014, Free Public Museum, Liverpool, Inglaterra.* Introduction and commentary by Ferdinand Anders, Maarten Jansen, Luis Reyes García, and Gabina Aurora Pérez Jiménez. Mexico City and Graz: Fondo de Cultura Económica and Akademische Druck- und Verlagsanstalt, 1994.

Codex Magliabechiano. *The Book and Life of the Ancient Mexicans.* Introduction, translation, and commentary by Zelia Nuttall. Berkeley: University of California Press, 1903.

Codex Mendoza. *The Codex Mendoza.* Edited by Frances Berdan and Patricia Anawalt. 4 vols. Berkeley: University of California Press, 1992.

Cortés, Hernán. *Letters from Mexico.* Translated and edited by Anthony Pagden. New Haven, CT: Yale University Press, 1986.

Davies, Nigel. *The Aztec Empire: The Toltec Resurgence.* Norman: University of Oklahoma Press, 1987.

Davies, Nigel. *The Aztecs: A History.* London: Macmillan, 1973.

Davies, Nigel. *Human Sacrifice: In History and Today.* New York: William Morrow, 1981.

Davies, Nigel. *The Toltec Heritage: From the Fall of Tula to the Rise of Tenochtitlan.* Norman: University of Oklahoma Press, 1980.

Davies, Nigel. *The Toltecs: Until the Fall of Tula.* Norman: University of Oklahoma Press, 1977.

Díaz del Castillo, Bernal. *The History of the Conquest of New Spain.* Edited by Davíd Carrasco. Albuquerque: University of New Mexico Press, 2008.

Durán, Diego. *Book of the Gods and Rites and The Ancient Calendar.* Translated and edited by Fernando Horcasitas and Doris Heyden. Norman: University of Oklahoma Press, 1971.

Durán, Diego. *Códice Durán.* Mexico City: Arrendadora Internacional, 1990.

Durán, Diego. *The History of the Indies of New Spain.* Translated by Doris Heyden. Norman: University of Oklahoma Press, 1995.

Edmonson, Monro S., ed. *Sixteenth-Century Mexico: The Work of Sahagún.* Albuquerque: University of New Mexico Press, 1974.

Eliade, Mircea. *The Myth of the Eternal Return, or Cosmos and History.* Translated by Willard R. Trask. Princeton, NJ: Princeton University Press, 1954.

Fuentes, Carlos. *The Orange Tree.* Translated by Alfred MacAdam. New York: Farrar, Straus and Giroux, 1994.

Fuentes, Carlos. *Where the Air Is Clear.* Translated by Sam Hileman. New York: Farrar, Straus and Giroux, 1971.

González Torres, Yólotl. *El sacrificio humano entre los mexicas.* Mexico City: Fondo de Cultura Económica, 2006.

Gruzinski, Serge. *Aztecs: Rise and Fall of an Empire.* New York: Abrams; London: Thames and Hudson, 1992.

Hanke, Lewis. *Aristotle and the American Indians: A Study in Race Prejudice in the Modern World.* Chicago: Henry Regnery, 1959.

Harner, Michael. "The Ecological Basis for Aztec Sacrifice." *American Ethnologist* 4 (1977): 117–35.

Harris, Marvin. *Cannibals and Kings: The Origins of Culture.* New York: Random House, 1977.

Hassig, Ross. *Aztec Warfare: Imperial Expansion and Political Control.* Norman: University of Oklahoma Press, 1988.

Hassig, Ross. *Mexico and the Spanish Conquest.* Norman: University of Oklahoma Press, 2006.

Heyden, Doris. *Mitología y simbolismo de la flora en el México prehispánico.* Mexico City: Instituto de Investigaciones Antropológicas, Universidad Nacional Autónoma de México, 1983.

Jansen, Maarten, and Gabina Aurora Pérez Jiménez. *Encounter with the Plumed Serpent: Drama and Power in the Heart of Mesoamerica.* Boulder: University Press of Colorado, 2007.

Jones, Lindsay. *Twin City Tales: A Hermeneutical Reassessment of Tula and Chichén Itzá.* Niwot: University Press of Colorado, 1995.

Jones, Lindsay, ed. *Encyclopedia of Religion.* 2nd ed. 15 vols. Detroit, MI: Macmillan, 2005.

Katz, Friedrich. *Ancient American Civilizations.* New York: Praeger, 1972.

Keen, Benjamin. *The Aztec Image in Western Thought.* New Brunswick, NJ: Rutgers University Press, 1971.

Klor de Alva, J. Jorge, H. B. Nicholson, and Eloise Quiñones Keber, eds. *The Work of Bernardino de Sahagún, Pioneer Ethnographer of Sixteenth-Century Aztec Mexico.* Albany: Institute for Mesoamerican Studies, State University of New York, 1988.

Knab, Tim. "Geografía del Inframundo." *Estudios de cultura náhuatl* 21 (1991): 31–57.

Knab, Tim. "Tlalocan Talmanic: Supernatural Beings of the Sierra de Puebla." In *Actes du XLIIe Congrès International des Américanistes, Congrès du Centenaire: Paris, 2–9 Septembre 1976,* 6: 127–36. Paris: Société des Américanistes, 1979.

Laso de la Vega, Luis. *The Story of Guadalupe: Luis Laso de la Vega's Huei tlamahuiçoltica of 1649.* Edited by Lisa Sousa, Stafford Poole, and James Lockhart. Stanford, CA: Stanford University Press; Los Angeles: UCLA Latin American Center Publications, 1998.

Lee, Jongsoo. *The Allure of Nezahualcoyotl: Pre-Hispanic History, Religion, and Nahua Poetics.* Albuquerque: University of New Mexico Press, 2008.

León-Portilla, Miguel. *Aztec Thought and Culture.* Norman: University of Oklahoma Press, 1963.

León-Portilla, Miguel. *Pre-Columbian Literatures of Mexico.* Norman: University of Oklahoma Press, 1969.

León-Portilla, Miguel, ed. *The Broken Spears: The Aztec Account of the Conquest of Mexico.* Translated by Lysander Kemp. Boston: Beacon Press, 1961.

León-Portilla, Miguel, ed. and trans. *Native Mesoamerican Spirituality: Ancient Myths, Discourses, Stories, Doctrines, Hymns, Poems from the Aztec, Yucatec, Quiche-Maya and Other Sacred Traditions.* New York: Paulist Press, 1980.

Lienzo de Tlaxcala. *El Lienzo de Tlaxcala: explicación de las láminas.* Edited by Alfredo Chavero. Mexico: Editorial Cosmos, 1979.

Lockhart, James. *Nahuas after the Conquest: A Social and Cultural History of the Indians of Central Mexico, Sixteenth through Eighteenth Centuries.* Stanford, CA: Stanford University Press, 1992.

Lockhart, James. *We People Here: Nahuatl Accounts of the Conquest of Mexico.* Berkeley: University of California Press, 1993.

Long, Charles H. *Alpha: The Myths of Creation.* New York: G. Braziller, 1963.

López Austin, Alfredo. *Educación mexica: antología de documentos sahaguntinos.* Mexico City: Universidad Nacional Autónoma de México, 1985.

López Austin, Alfredo. *Hombre-dios: religión y política en el mundo náhuatl.* Mexico City: Universidad Nacional Autónoma de México, 1973.

López Austin, Alfredo. *The Human Body and Ideology: Concepts of the Ancient Nahuas.* Translated by Thelma Ortiz de Montellano and Bernard Ortiz de Montellano. 2 vols. Salt Lake City: University of Utah Press, 1988.

López Austin, Alfredo. *Tamoanchan, Tlalocan: Places of Mist.* Translated by Bernard R. Ortiz de Montellano and Thelma Ortiz de Montellano. Niwot: University Press of Colorado, 1997.

López Luján, Leonardo. *The Offerings of the Templo Mayor.* Translated by Bernard R. Ortiz de Montellano and Thelma Ortiz de Montellano. Rev. ed. Albuquerque: University of New Mexico Press, 2005.

López Lujan, Leonardo, and Guilhem Olivier, eds. *El sacrificio humano en la tradición religiosa mesoamericana.* Mexico City: Instituto Nacional de Antropología e Historia and Universidad Nacional Autónoma de México, 2010.

Matos Moctezuma, Eduardo. *The Great Temple of the Aztecs: Treasures of Tenochtitlan.* New York: Thames and Hudson, 1988.

Matos Moctezuma, Eduardo. *Life and Death in the Templo Mayor.* Translated by Bernard R. Ortiz de Montellano and Thelma Ortiz de Montellano. Niwot: University Press of Colorado, 1995.

Myerhoff, Barbara. *Peyote Hunt: The Sacred Journey of the Huichol Indians.* Ithaca, NY: Cornell University Press, 1974.

Nicholson, H. B. "The Problem of the Identification of the Central Image of the 'Aztec Calendar Stone.'" In *Current Topics in Aztec Studies: Essays in Honor of H. B. Nicholson.* Edited by Alana Cordy-Collins and Douglas Sharon. San Diego, CA: San Diego Museum of Man, 1993.

Nicholson, H. B. "Religion in Pre-Hispanic Central Mexico." In *The Handbook of Middle American Indians,* 10: *Archaeology of Northern Mesoamerica,* Part One: 395–446. Austin: University of Texas Press, 1976.

Nicholson, H. B. *Topiltzin Quetzalcoatl: The Once and Future Lord of the Toltecs.* Boulder: University Press of Colorado, 2001.

Nutini, Hugo. *Todos Santos in Rural Tlaxcala: A Syncretic, Expressive, and Symbolic Analysis of the Cult of the Dead.* Princeton, NJ: Princeton University Press, 1988.

Olivier, Guilhem. *Mockeries and Metamorphoses of an Aztec God: Tezcatlipoca, Lord of the Smoking Mirror.* Translated by Michel Besson. Boulder: University Press of Colorado, 2003.

Ortiz de Montellano, Bernard R. "Counting Skulls: Comment on the Cannibalism Theory of Harner-Harris." *American Anthropologist* 85 (1983): 403–6.

Pasztory, Esther. *Aztec Art*. New York: Henry N. Abrams, 1983.

Pratt, Mary Louise. *Imperial Eyes: Travel Writing and Transculturation*. New York: Routledge, 1992.

Quiñones Keber, Eloise, ed. *Representing Aztec Ritual: Performance, Text, and Image in the Work of Sahagún*. Boulder: University Press of Colorado, 2004.

Read, Kay A. "Human Sacrifice: An Overview." In *Encyclopedia of Religion*. 2nd ed. Edited by Lindsay Jones. 15 vols. Detroit, MI: Macmillan, 2005. 6: 4182–85.

Restall, Matthew. *Seven Myths of the Spanish Conquest*. Oxford: Oxford University Press, 2004.

Restall, Matthew, and Amara Solari. *2012 and the End of the World: The Western Roots of the Maya Apocalypse*. Lanham, MD: Rowman and Littlefield, 2011.

Sahagún, Bernardino de. *El códice florentino*. Mexico City: Archivo General de la Nación, 1979.

Sahagún, Bernardino de. *Florentine Codex: General History of the Things of New Spain*. Translated and edited by Arthur J. O. Anderson and Charles E. Dibble. Introductory vol. and 12 books. Santa Fe, NM: School of American Research, and University of Utah, 1950–82.

Sanday, Peggy Reeves. *Divine Hunger: Cannibalism as a Cultural System*. New York: Cambridge University Press, 1986.

Sanders, William T., Jeffrey R. Parsons, and Robert S. Santley. *The Basin of Mexico: Ecological Processes in the Evolution of a Civilization*. New York: Academic Press, 1979.

Scarborough, Vernon L., and David R. Wilcox, eds. *The Mesoamerican Ballgame*. Tucson: University of Arizona Press, 1991.

Schele, Linda, and Mary Ellen Miller. *The Blood of Kings: Dynasty and Ritual in Maya Art*. Fort Worth, TX: Kimball Art Museum, 1986.

Smith, Jonathan Z. *Imagining Religion: From Babylon to Jonestown*. Chicago: University of Chicago Press, 1982.

Smith, Michael. *The Aztecs*. 2nd ed. Malden, MA: Blackwell, 2003.

Soustelle, Jacques. *Daily Life of the Aztecs: On the Eve of the Spanish Conquest*. Translated by Patrick O'Brien. Stanford, CA: Stanford University Press, 1970.

Sugiyama, Saburo. *Human Sacrifice, Militarism, and Rulership: Materialization of State Ideology at the Feathered Serpent Pyramid, Teotihuacan*. New York: Cambridge University Press, 2005.

Taylor, William B. "The Virgin of Guadalupe in New Spain: An Inquiry into the Social History of Marian Devotion." *American Ethnologist* 14 (1987): 9–33.

Todorov, Tzvetan. *The Conquest of America: The Question of the Other*. Translated by Richard Howard. New York: Harper and Row, 1984.

Townsend, Richard. *The Aztecs*. London: Thames and Hudson, 2009.

Townsend, Richard. *State and Cosmos in the Art of Tenochtitlan*. Washington, DC: Dumbarton Oaks, 1979.

van der Loo, Peter L. *Códices, costumbres, continuidad: un estudio de la religión mesoamericana*. Leiden: Archeologisch Centrum Rijksuniversiteit, 1987.

van Zantwijk, Rudolph A. M. *The Aztec Arrangement: The Social History of Pre-Spanish Mexico*. Norman: University of Oklahoma Press, 1985.

Weismann, Elizabeth Wilder. *Mexico in Sculpture, 1521–1821*. Cambridge, MA: Harvard University Press, 1950.

Wheatley, Paul. *The Pivot of the Four Quarters: A Preliminary Enquiry into the Origins and Character of the Ancient Chinese City*. Chicago: Aldine, 1971.

Whittington, E. Michael, ed. *The Sport of Life and Death: The Mesoamerican Ballgame*. New York: Thames and Hudson, 2001.

Wolf, Eric R. *Sons of the Shaking Earth*. Chicago: University of Chicago Press, 1959.

INDEX

About the Authors

DAVÍD CARRASCO is the Neil L. Rudenstine Professor of the Study of Latin America and the director of the Moses Mesoamerican Archive at Harvard University. His previous works include *Moctezuma's Mexico: Visions of the Aztec World* (with Eduardo Matos Moctezuma, 1992 and 2003), *Quetzalcoatl and the Irony of Empire: Myths and Prophecies in the Aztec Tradition* (1982, 1992, and 2000), *To Change Place: Aztec Ceremonial Landscapes* (1991 and 1999), *Religions of Mesoamerica: Cosmovision and Ceremonial Centers* (1990), *City of Sacrifice: The Aztec Empire and the Role of Violence in Civilization* (1999), *Mesoamerica's Classic Heritage: From Teotihuacan to the Aztecs* (co-edited with Lindsay Jones and Scott Sessions, 2000), and *Cave, City, and Eagle's Nest: An Interpretive Journey through the Mapa de Cuauhtinchan No. 2* (co-edited with Scott Sessions, 2007).

SCOTT SESSIONS is a lecturer in the Department of Religion at Amherst College and managing editor of the African-American Religion Documentary History Project. He has served as development editor for the *Oxford Encyclopedia of Mesoamerican Cultures* (2001), and co-edited *Mesoamerica's Classic Heritage: From Teotihuacan to the Aztecs* (with Davíd Carrasco and Lindsay Jones, 2000) and *Cave, City, and Eagle's Nest: An Interpretive Journey through the Mapa de Cuauhtinchan No. 2* (with Davíd Carrasco, 2007).